Undermining Risk and Technical Communication

A volume in the SUNY series, Studies in Technical Communication

---

Miles A. Kimball, Derek G. Ross, and Hilary A. Sarat-St. Peter, editors

Undermining Risk and Technical Communication

Extractive Industry, Cascading Disaster, and the Global Climate Crisis

Timothy R. Amidon,
Ehren Helmut Pflugfelder,
Daniel P. Richards, and
Donnie Johnson Sackey

Cover credit: Unsplash.

Published by State University of New York Press, Albany

Printed in the United States of America

EU GPSR Authorised Representative:
Logos Europe, 9 rue Nicolas Poussin, 17000, La Rochelle, France
contact@logoseurope.eu

For information, contact State University of New York Press, Albany, NY
www.sunypress.edu

Library of Congress Cataloging-in-Publication Data

Names: Amidon, Timothy R., author. | Pflugfelder, Ehren Helmut, author. | Richards, Daniel P., author. | Sackey, Donnie Johnson, author.
Title: Undermining risk and technical communication : extractive industry, cascading disaster, and the global climate crisis / Timothy R. Amidon, Ehren Helmut Pflugfelder, Daniel P. Richards, and Donnie Johnson Sackey.
Description: Albany : State University of New York Press, [2026]. | SUNY series in Technical Communication | Includes bibliographical references and index.
Identifiers: ISBN 9798855807417 (hardcover : alk. paper) | ISBN 9798855807431 (epub) | ISBN 9798855807448 (PDF)
Further information is available at the Library of Congress.

Contents

Illustrations

Figures

Tables

Boxes

Abbreviations

AMD	acid mine drainage
BPMD	Bonita Peak Mining District
CDC	California Development Company
CRB	Colorado River Basin
CRC	Colorado River Compact
CRD	Colorado River Delta
EIS	environmental impact statement
EDB	ethylene dibromide
GKMS	Gold King Mine Spill
LoR	Law of the River
MAF	million acre-feet
NAIDOC	National Aborigines and Islanders Day Observance Committee
NASW	North American South West
PKKP	Puutu Kunti Kurrama and Pinikura people
RS	Reclamation Service
SWE	Standardized Written English
STB	Surface Transportation Board
TPC	technical and professional communication

Acknowledgments

Timothy R. Amidon

Foremost, I am grateful for my wife, Erin, with whom I am lucky to share laughter, conversation, and life. You are an incredibly supportive and loving spouse, and I am thankful that you're always willing to pick up the slack when my plate gets too full. Cole, thank you for the joy you bring to our life and for inspiring me to care about the legacy that surrounds risk. I am thankful, too, for Colorado, which has materially, intellectually, and spiritually sustained me during the past decade. Special recognition must be bestowed to the Arapaho, Cheynne, and Ute Nations and Peoples, who have long served as stewards of the lands and watersheds comprising the headwaters of the Colorado River. I am also thankful for Colorado State University, which provided financial support necessary for hosting the writers' retreat, and to colleagues Sue Doe, Tiffany Lipsey, Megan Suter, and Dinaida Egan, who have been supportive thought partners. Last, it's been immensely gratifying to have the privilege to work and write alongside of y'all, Ehren, Dan, and Donnie: I look forward to whatever comes next.

Ehren Helmut Pflugfelder

I'd first like to thank my partner in all things, Kristin Griffin. Your love, support, and thoughtfulness are what really matters most in this world—especially when we're wrangling our feisty malshipoo, Penny, whose demands for pets and treats take a committed team effort. My thanks also go to my parents Helmut and Elissa and Kristin's parents Tom and Lynne. You're always encouraging and willing to listen, and there's no way we can see you often enough. Thanks, too, to Heidi, my sister, who is always helpful, and to Matthew, Kim, Luke, and Chase, who bring the joy. My colleagues at Oregon State University also deserve thanks, especially those in rhetoric and writing studies, Tim Jensen, Ana Milena Ribero, Sarah Perrault, Dennis Bennett, and Kristy Kelly, and countless other colleagues who support environmental communication and education throughout the university. Maybe most significantly to this project, though, I should thank Tim, Dan, and Donnie—I can't imagine a better group of rhetoricians, scholars, teachers, and friends to work with. Here's to more collaborations.

Daniel P. Richards

First: to the infinitely patient Jes, always—and our two bespectacled rapscallions, Emery and Jack. Your unending grace and background noise, respectively, fueled my work on this project. Second: to Tim, Ehren, and Donnie, who I am humbled to work with on meaningful projects. I'd be hard-pressed to find a more discerning, rigorous, and amusing group of collaborators.

Donnie Johnson Sackey

I am deeply grateful to my husband, Paul LaBrant, for his unwavering love and encouragement throughout this project and many other projects. My heartfelt thanks also go to my friends and coauthors—Dan, Ehren, and Tim—for their insight, collaboration, generosity, and patience in our shared work. I especially wish to honor the memory of my dissertation advisor, Bill Hart-Davidson, whose guidance and belief in my research and scholarship shaped me in ways beyond measure; his passing, just months before my first book was published in August 2024, meant he never had the chance to read it. His influence is felt in this book and beyond.

All

We'd all like to thank the editors at State University of New York Press, including Richard Carlin, who has carefully steered this project from the very beginning, and series editors Derek Ross, Miles Kimball, and Hilary

Sarat-St. Peter, who have offered exceptional advice and encouragement. We'd also like to thank our four anonymous peer reviewers for their labor, thoughtful feedback, and generosity, which contributed meaningfully to the final version of this work.

Chapter One

Under*mining* Institutions of Risk

> We need, I believe, to engage a different kind of violence, a violence that is neither spectacular nor instantaneous, but rather incremental and accretive, its calamitous repercussions playing out across a range of temporal scales. In so doing, we also need to engage the representational, narrative, and strategic challenges posed by the relative invisibility of slow violence.
>
> —Rob Nixon, *Slow Violence and the Environmentalism of the Poor*

In this book, we argue that technical and professional communication (TPC) stands to gain much by defining the spatial scales and temporal scopes through which risk has been engaged within the field. Specifically, we consider the theoretical and methodological affordances and limitations associated with existing approaches to risk in TPC, arguing that a more expansive approach to the spatial and temporal complexity that surrounds risk might open up possibilities for more sustainable justice-oriented risk work. While existing approaches to risk in TPC have offered valuable and groundbreaking considerations of rhetorical and social factors that shape risk and risk communication, this project is necessary because issues like global energy, food, and water inequality, cascading climate disaster, per- and polyfluoroalkyl substances, and colonial genocide pose risks that span the temporal and spatial frames traditionally used within our studies. TPC has provided useful, historically situated studies of risk (for instance, working within regional or local communities to support change within those locales). Indeed, TPC has commonly used case studies of risk to elucidate power structures, identify ineffective communication systems, critique public-facing risk messages, promote inclusive processes for civic participation, and proactively intervene within disasters. Yet, despite these advances, TPC has struggled to grapple with how harm flows or might flow beyond the tidy spatial and temporal frames that we've employed to bound our studies of risk. Therefore, we posit that TPC must first turn toward a concerted and cohesive ethical reckoning with our field's historical relationship to risk—its legacy with the material effects and consequences of risks—before it can meaningfully realize its visions, ethics, and ideals of justice-oriented work.

Indeed, much of TPC's theoretical and methodological framing toward risk has been rooted in what might be understood as an institutionalist orientation to rhetorical activity and agency. Put simply, the scale and scope at which our field has structured studies on risk have involved working with and through institutions to identify strategies for reducing and mitigating risk at specific levels of spatial and temporal resolution, while overlooking other closely related considerations. For instance, Sauer's (1993) study of the mining industry demonstrated that "feminist interpretation strategies can save lives in the nation's mines" (63). Yet these studies also laid aside consideration of risks that operated on other levels of temporal or spatial scope, such as the risk that future shifts in the US energy economy would precipitate economic instability for communities that had been sustained through their participation in the coal mining industry or the long-term risk of developing coal-workers' pneumoconiosis, or black lung disease, that coal miners shouldered as a result of repeated exposure to respirable dust.

A more holistic envisioning of risk is now appropriate. The changing dynamics of climate and the interconnectedness of the planet necessitates that we revisit assumptions about risk in the past, present, and future. The fact that we are enmeshed in complex and competing interconnected systems requires that we think and act differently about risk. There is no doubt that appealing to and acting at an institutional level of scope will continue to be important, but we also need to envision how research and practice within TPC might intervene to mitigate harm at other levels of scope and scale. Risk is increasingly interconnected and thus requires more complex thinking and action. This book, then, seeks to "under*mine*" how TPC works with risk by inviting the field to imagine how risk operates across temporal scale and geographic scope.

This chapter offers a brief introduction to the study of risk and risk communication within TPC, including closely related fields of disaster and crisis communication, arguing that the practice of risk communication in the field of TPC has been complicit in the unequal distribution of harm, often for the sake of field building. Put bluntly, *many people have died so that technical communication could live*. To move toward an ethical reckoning of this disciplinary history, we begin this chapter by sketching some of the methodological limitations associated with TPC's approach to risk, including an urgency that demonstrates the importance and timeliness of this project. Thereafter, the book unfolds in the following progression. In chapter 2, we construct a deep historiography of risk and risk communication within TPC spanning roughly the last thousand years. In chapter 3, we trace the contours of a spatiotemporal methodology that productively complicates risk-based ontology and could be applied to critically consider industrial, civic, and social practices for managing and communicating risks and the material environmental conditions wrought by them. Chapters 4, 5, and 6 apply the methodology with case studies that accentuate the importance of tracing risks across the boundaries of geographic scope and temporal scale. The conclusion offers a brief dialogic discussion of the implications of this project for future work in risk within TPC.

The Scope and Scalability of Risk

In 2020, during the height of the COVID-19 pandemic, the multinational mining corporation Rio Tinto expanded their "Brockman 4" iron ore mine in Western Australia by exploding a large portion of the Juukan Gorge, a geographic feature of the remote Hammersley Ranges in the Pilbara region. In literally blowing up the gorge, Rio Tinto wanted to expand their mine system in the area (this particular gorge was linked to their other "Brockman" mines) and uncover an additional $135 million USD worth of iron ore (Saldanha 2020). While exposing these ore reserves, however, Rio Tinto destroyed an Australian Aboriginal sacred site that had been the only inland location to show signs of continual human occupation since the last ice age. By some estimates, Australian Aboriginal peoples had been inhabiting the location for at least thirty-two thousand years and for as many as forty-six thousand years (Slack et al. 2009). While archeological research has only been recently completed (in response to the threat of impending mining activity), some seven thousand artifacts have been recovered from the gorge, including a twenty-eight-thousand-year-old bone tool and a four-thousand-year-old plait of human hair. Within the gorge are several natural caves that served as shelter for tens of thousands of people across tens of thousands of years. Despite the rich cultural and historical significance of the gorge, Rio Tinto, as the modern-day occupant and owner of the land, controlled access to these sites and largely operated without appreciable regulatory oversight. In fact, under an agreement with the mining corporation, Aboriginal groups had to apply for visitation. These visits were allowed until the National Aborigines and Islanders Day Observance Committee (NAIDOC) applied to visit during NAIDOC week in 2020, when they were told that by the time of their planned annual pilgrimage, the land, the site, the artifacts, and the direct connection to thousands of years of land-based practices would no longer exist.

The Juukan Gorge holds invaluable significance to the Puutu Kunti Kurrama and Pinikura (PKKP) people, who are the current custodians of the land. Burchell Hayes, director of the PKKP Aboriginal Corporation and head of Kurruma Land Committee, specified that any evaluation as to how much the gorge meant to Aboriginal Australians would simply be an exercise in abstraction. "Speculating on what could have been will never replace the emptiness we feel over what was lost by our people at Juukan Gorge," he explained (Young and Ingram 2021). An interim report conducted by the Australian Parliament argued that "for the PKKP the destruction was personal and visceral—and a sharp reminder of how vulnerable their culture and heritage are to the imperatives of governments and corporations" (Parliament 2020, 4). Further, the report explained that Rio Tinto employed a mining campaign based upon a strict legal defense of its rights, unfair agreements containing gag clauses, a lack of transparency, and a corporate culture that prioritized commercial gain over meaningful engagement with Traditional Owners (7). Some of this strategy included basing their legal rights in an original mining grant given to Rio Tinto in 2013, under the conditions of the Aboriginal Heritage Act of 1972, a contentious law that, until recently, governed Indigenous Australian cultural sites (Government of Western Australia 1972). Specifically, section 18 of that 1972 act was applied in the Juukan Gorge case, which offers leeway to "land owners" who claim that damage to a site is unavoidable. The 1972 act had been under review since 2018—as Rio Tinto was well aware—and has now been superseded by the Aboriginal Cultural Heritage Act of 2021, which imposed stronger governance over culturally significant land by present-day landowners. (The 2021 act has since been repealed, and a revised 1972 Act reinstated.)

This brief example sets the scene for how TPC might study the destruction of a cultural site through a lens of risk communication. One approach that TPC researchers might take would be to examine the events leading up to the blasting by analyzing the legal, regulatory, and legislative documents that unfairly benefited present-day landowners and ongoing extractive activities. Researchers employing this approach might also confront documents that were produced by Rio Tinto and the PKKP and NAIDOC (among others) and interrogate how risk to the site was defined in relation to the way Rio Tinto's ambitions had been concealed behind legalese. Indeed, textual analysis of regulatory, legal, technical, and legislative documents has been and continues to be an incredibly rich research method for illustrating how veiled power is exercised through the practice of TPC (e.g., Dombrowski 1991; Jones and Williams 2022; Richards 2017, 2025; Sauer 1994, 2002; Simmons 2007; Williams 2006, 2010; Winsor 1998, 2001). Alternatively, TPC scholars interested in studying risk at this site might leverage qualitative approaches (Richards and Stephens 2022) or community-engaged research (Olman and DeVasto 2020) to frame an investigation through the voices of the individuals, groups, and communities impacted by the destruction of the gorge. For example, a community-engaged researcher in TPC might partner with Australian Aboriginal advocacy groups to articulate the situation to federal powers or media groups who could have assisted in the confrontation (Crabtree and Sapp 2005). Or it's possible that TPC researchers could have studied how recent archeological studies paid for by Rio Tinto could have occluded the current significance of the sites, portrayed the Juukan Gorge as culturally important only in terms of archeological interest, and presented the archeological work at the site as largely complete. These would all be insightful and useful investigations to develop, in line with best practices in risk communication research within TPC.

Yet we posit that these possible approaches to the study of risk in the Juukan Gorge reveal methodological limitations—most notably in terms of the geographic scope and temporal scale—through which TPC, as a field, epistemologically and ontologically orients to risk. These sample approaches described above *are valuable* and help extend TPC's relationship to risk-based work. *There is no denying that.* Analyses of accident reports and other risk-based technical documents have allowed TPC to foreground the human impact of disasters and attend to the realities associated with loss of life. Moreover, gathering on-the-ground stories allows us to connect back to the centuries-long narrative of climate change. Disaster or risk-based case studies allow us to account for or link the isolated situation to forces of a larger geological age. Yet there are broader frameworks that might provide opportunities for us to attend to such variables before deciding if and how to approach a case (see box 1.1).

Box 1.1
Further Considering the Temporal and Spatial Complexity of Risk in Rio Tinto

Methodological choices impose limitations that encircle but can also productively extend the parameters by which the field of TPC might understand risk. A significant implication of the boundaries of methodological choices is that they, in turn, limit or facilitate the kind of work in TPC that might extend social justice through policy formation, institutional critique, activism, and advocacy campaigns.

The following questions provide entry points for further discussion about possible methodological choices associated with the Rio Tinto case:

- How might the Puutu Kunti Kurrama and Pinikura peoples' epistemological and ontological orientations to place and time influence how they understand and relate to risk?
- How might, in turn, their orientations align with and deviate from Western epistemologies and ontologies of risk?
- How have legacies and economies surrounding mining and industrial manufacturing contributed to the decision by Rio Tinto to blast the Juukan Gorge?
- How should or could the deep cultural, archeological, and historical value of the Juukan Gorge be understood in relation to and distinct from the economic and material value that motivated Rio Tinto executives to blow up the Juukan Gorge to access iron ore?
- How does the circulation of extracted minerals move within the global economy and how does that circulation further expand the possibilities of risk?

We contend, consequently, that the field of TPC stands to gain much by considering when and where opportunities exist for a methodological expansion that extends beyond engaging the in-the-moment practice of risk communication that has implications for situated constituencies, user experience, and participatory democracy/design and those retrospective, after-the-fact analyses of risk following disasters, crises, and failures. That is, we believe that expanding the temporal scale and spatial scope through which we consider risk within the field could offer productive avenues for sketching a contingent yet comprehensive paradigm of risk that defines a sense of how risk manifests at a particular level. Here, we neither suggest a one-size-fits-all approach to risk, nor do we argue that TPC has inadequately considered how to make sense of risk. We, ourselves, are humbled and indebted to the consequential and critical studies of risk that exist in TPC. As such, we hope to continue that tradition by asking questions that might lead TPC to critically interrogate the methodologies that we have used over the last several decades to approach risk and risk communication as objects of study, as well as question the influence these inquiries have had in contributing to the legitimization of TPC as a field.

Through our collaborations and discussions as risk communication researchers, we have come to believe that TPC has yet to consider the spatial and temporal complexity that encircles risk, broadly understood. Our own initial critique of our field's approach to risk reveals the inconsistency of approaches, or perhaps the inconsistent ways in which we have discussed risk. From our perspective, TPC would benefit from a coherent and cohesive paradigm or paradigms that might help "locate" studies within a better-defined sense of what risk *is* or *means*. While we are not arguing for a monolithic structure, we do want to move toward a paradigm or paradigms that might provide entry points for building connectivity between the layers of archaeological scope and scale through which we have been working. Put simply, now is an important moment to take stock of the spatial and temporal frames that have been privileged within the field. Moreover, we're less interested in critiquing what individual case studies have and have not accomplished and more interested in constructing a sense of how the critical mass of studies within the field might contribute to a revised, "global" redux of existing frameworks, like Grabill and Simmons's (1998) foundational work on the critical rhetorics of risk.

To be sure, questions of scale have been forwarded across numerous disciplines over the last few years. For Joshua DiCaglio, whose recent book *Scale Theory: Nondisciplinary Inquiry* (2021) provided a foundational theory of scale, scale is best defined not as a "level of observation, but a tool for establishing a reference point for domains of experience and interaction. Scale enters in the relation between two very different modes of experience. It shows how an entity not apparent in our perceptual field—for example, a carbon atom—fits within one's normal experience" (4). Scale can be understood as more than a kind of framing, rather as a schema for perception, which then changes the relations, forces, hierarchies, and processes that are made to matter. Considerations of scale also help us recognize that, methodologically, we often attend to only some levels of scale at any given time—for good reason, too. Historical, social, economic, and political pressures can influence which scales are available to those investigating a phenomenon. Most frustrating, though, is the sneaking suspicion that the scale of inquiry that we're undertaking is being constrained by forces that we can't quite grasp. From the perspective of the philosophy of science, DiCaglio claimed: "We find ourselves sequencing, replicating, and even copyrighting genes, making statements about the possible toxicity of molecular components, and know that, somehow, the collective actions of *Homo sapiens* scratching, hacking, and fracking at the Earth are manifesting as ecological effects, but find ourselves struggling to describe how such scale domains work. We want to think globally and act locally but don't consider how we made that distinction in the first place" (2). We contend that TPC approaches to risk would benefit from a scalar reconfiguring, one that moves toward accounting for global, cultural, and historical forces even in the most traditional approaches to analyzing technical writing documents. This might require us to put scale in a more central location in our positioning and interpretation of risk. We'll need, as a field, to come to a sense of what the scale of risk is and can be—and *should* be—in our TPC-specific projects. We'll also need to come toward some sense about how the existing studies of risk in TPC offer a useful coverage of how risk might operate within a particular scale, while also leaving considerable opportunities and questions about the ways those risks might work at other levels of scale. *Scale first, then methods*. Decisions about scale, after all, reflect the fundamental ideologies and values that drive our methodologies in the first place.

Indeed, a central methodological challenge that surrounds the study of risk has been that it can be a tricky thing to define. We appreciate the applicability of Leiss and Powells's (2004) definition, where risk is "the probability of harm in any given situation . . . determined by two factors: (a) the nature of a hazard and (b) the extent of anyone's exposure to that hazard" (33). While this definition might seem conventional, they articulated a sense of risk in broad and expansive terms:

> For each person the risk of being injured or killed in a traffic accident, for example, is first a function of the various hazards

> inherent in using powered vehicles—mechanical failure, driver's level of skill and care, actions of other drivers, state of mind, road conditions, and so forth. The other factor is exposure, that is, the amount of time any person spends on the road in the midst of the above-mentioned hazards. The product of the two factors (hazards and exposures) adds up to the overall risk. (33)

Adding to this vehicular example, we would seek to question the risks that come from an expanded sense of scope and scale: the geologic and economic conditions that present fossil fuels as exploitable commodities; the history of imperial conquest and slave labor for energy extraction; the neocolonial, capitalist forces that drive the creation of cheap fuels and generate polluting transportation networks; the feedback mechanisms from increased pollution and atmospheric carbon; the historical economic inequalities that push people's homes further from their jobs; the structures of race, power, and privilege that influence which bodies encounter dangerous intersections, at more dangerous times of day, in less safe vehicles; and the same inequalities that result in various localities receiving differential funding levels to equip and prepare front-line responders to mitigate emergencies when risks manifest in disasters, crises, and accidents. Extractive industries operate within ancient exposure timelines and affect communities exposed to hazards unwillingly.

Moreover, the time frames through which extractive industries have approached and considered risk within projects illustrates that those exposures can not only fail to consider the cascading effects that various known and unknown risks may have but also fail to recognize the ways in which specific locations are always already historically situated and laden with cultural and social significance. While Rio Tinto might be seen as a stand-alone case study, a researcher simply cannot cordon off time by framing exposure as merely the time an individual spends in proximity to a mine, as the consequences and impacts of mining extend beyond the job. We wonder, consequently: How might Leiss and Powell's definition of risk accommodate, if at all, ancient hazards and millennia-long exposures? Can we "scope out" their definition? How could "risk" be stretched, horizontally along time and vertically along space? Or would it cease to be considered a "risk" in a meaningful sense of the word? This book is concerned with these questions, and attempts to devise a methodological framework for understanding how TPC might engage risk in the future. We'll be reconfiguring the concept of risk as used in the field and reorienting some long-standing assumptions about risk. First, though, we need to contend with how TPC has been working with risk.

TPC and Risk

Since the late 1990s, risk has been a sustained area of inquiry within TPC. For example, several groundbreaking studies have been conducted via precise and thoughtful case studies, including Katz and Miller's (1996) research on North Carolina nuclear waste and Sauer's (2002) study of mining industry safety and embodied communication. Further, articles on the *Challenger* disaster, perhaps the most studied example in all of TPC, have revealed the advantages of focusing a case study methodology for a specific disaster and investigating how risk was articulated leading up to an accident. Visible and heartbreaking events have been ripe areas for researching connections between risk communication, ethics, and rhetoric (Stratman et al. 1995; Zoetewey and Staggers 2004), as have the occluded risk communication logics of safety regulation (Miller 2003; Mirel 1994; Reamer 2015). TPC scholars have considered risk in the context of how technical communicators can become advocates for the public (Grabill and Simmons 1998; Herndl 1996; Simmons 2007); advocates for documentation, design, interfaces, and policy (Evia and Patriarca 2012; Ohman and DeVasto 2020; Potts 2013; Richards 2019; Sackey 2020); advocates within the much-wider realm of medical rhetorics (Ding 2009; Giles 2010; Scott 2003); and contributors to sense-making during disasters (Ding 2014; Frost 2013; Lee 2021), emergencies (Amidon et al. 2018; Angeli 2019), and crises (Pflugfelder 2019; Potts 2013). More recently, TPC has considered risk at international, transcultural, and transnational levels (e.g., Chen 2022; Ding 2009; Frost 2013; Lee 2022). However, despite the expanding breadth and depth of research, TPC's conceptions and subsequent definitions of risk have infrequently been shaped by the fields of risk communication (e.g., Fischhoff 1995), risk analysis (e.g., Slovic 2010), or sociology (e.g., Beck 1992) and rarely tackle definitions of risk head-on.

We believe that there are several reasons for this inattention to risk work in other arenas—reasons beyond the natural attraction of communication scholars to the symbolic, representative, or communicative aspects of a topic. That is, we contend that one of the reasons that TPC has perhaps less frequently addressed or specifically defined risk is because of a long-standing history of uncomfortable connections with risk. To put it plainly, we argue that the historical practice of TPC has experienced fraught relationships to risk throughout time; in some cases, TPC has been deeply embedded within larger power dynamics that have constituted unequal distributions of risk for people and ecosystems. For instance, TPC has been used to reduce the rights of workers, dismiss the conditions of safety, and emphasize profit over ecological flourishing. Examples of this unequal power dynamic abound, but let's pause for some notable ones. Georgius Agricola, in the oft-esteemed technical communication text *De re Metallica* (1556/1950), explained at length the dangers of mining as an occupation and the destruction it brings to ecosystems, yet also dismissed these concerns as minor hiccups on the road to achieving greater profit. Similarly, the first TPC textbook, *A Guide to Technical Writing*, written in 1908 by mining engineer T. A. Rickard, emphasized assimilation to Western culture and control over nature as a necessary condition for the increase of capital. Even today, TPC practices concerning risk are often made complicit with injustice; in the Juukan Gorge example explained above, industry-aligned technical risk communication practitioners focused on the immediate dangers to mining engineers working on-site, but not the cultural harm done to the Puutu Kunti Kurrama and Pinikura people. Risk communication, in many cases, is a practice aligned with an industry, constrained by time, and ambivalent about injustice. To some extent, this is a problem of Western colonial capitalism, and technical communication practitioners, like many other professions, have been unwillingly enrolled in much broader economic, political, and social actions. Understanding how to redress this history entails recognizing that injustice has occurred, how it has occurred, and how it is still occurring, in places like the Juukan Gorge and inside our technical writing classrooms as well.

TPC has, for much of its history, been a practice, profession, and pedagogy complicit in multiple ways in causing harm. Evidence for this relationship, which we will strive to make clear throughout the following chapters, builds upon existing articulations between TPC and structural inequality. In describing this connection, we rely on the work of Rebecca Walton, Kristen Moore, and Natasha Jones (2019) and their framing of why the social justice turn is continually meaningful for TPC. Specifically, we believe their explanation as to why the social justice turn is necessary also speaks to our focus on risk, "because our field is complicit in injustice" (8). As they explained, "Because technical communication often appears to be removed (sometimes twice removed) from the atrocities of domination, the field can maintain (and has maintained) its distance from the violence, oppression, and injustices it perpetuates" (17–18). Further, while individual technical communicators have been—and continue to be—victims of oppression in systems of inequality, TPC has not been blameless in continuing the unequal distribution of the likelihood of harm. The study of risk in TPC should be able to address the greater harms to which it has been complicit and the harms that it has not yet explored.

TPC research has grown and benefited from the rhetorical analysis of situations where people have been harmed, hurt, or killed—yet the field has not fully investigated its own role in perpetuating the historical inequities of risk. In particular, the kinds of methodological decisions that researchers have tended to employ when carefully bounding a study, in turn, pose epistemic limitations to the ways in which risk might be understood within the field and beyond. While we, of course, do not want to define all forms of TPC as exploitative, TPC's history has been dominated by bureaucratic representational techniques that have intentionally and unintentionally assisted with foisting the burden of risk onto communities of people and communities of nonhumans who were never invited to help perform this representation in the first place. For example, consider Williams's (2010) research on the aggressive legalese used in the Texas Black Codes of 1866, or the plain language used in Texas farming manuals, which often included old or inaccurate information—details that would harm Black sharecroppers for years to come. Or consider the infamous management treatise that led to the development of assembly line production; *The Principles of Scientific Management,* written in 1911 by Frederick Winslow Taylor, emphasized efficiency and profit while failing to consider how the division of labor would isolate workers from their craft. The impact of "scientific management" on TPC in the workplace was—and continues to be—significant, to the detriment of workers everywhere. While our field has previously produced accounts of its origins, some of which have explored unique constellations of harm, it has yet to reckon with these relationships. Chapter 2 will explore this ground in more detail, but before we attend to the interrelated histories of risk and TPC, we'll consider how risk has been shaped in modern TPC.

To more fully understand what it means to subsume the logics of risk communication into the gestalt of TPC, we should consider just how this has occurred. The most often cited TPC article concerning rhetoric and risk is Jeffrey T. Grabill and W. Michele Simmons's 1998 article, "Toward a Critical Rhetoric of Risk Communication: Producing Citizens and the Role of Technical Communicators." Grabill and Simmons argued that then-current risk communication failed to tackle rhetorical issues, identified what a social construction of risk might mean for TPC, sketched a critical rhetoric of risk, and located what that critical perspective offers for usability methods in general and TPC more specifically. Their article has also been rightly heralded as bringing ethical and rhetorical significance to risk within TPC. Crucially, Grabill and Simmons advanced a critical rhetoric of risk communication that (1) questioned the perceived separation of risk assessment from risk communication, underscoring the fact that processes for assessing risk are inherently rhetorical in the first place; (2) foregrounded the role of power dynamics in risk communication, spotlighting how different agents have differential access to participating in the rhetorical activities through which risk is constructed and known; and (3) argued for technical communicators as key personnel in understanding and communicating risk, particularly in their local contexts. These contributions articulated risk as rhetorical, considered audiences and cultural formations of risk with great intensity, and applied the tenets of usability studies to help give voice to those with less power.

Grabill and Simmons made their argument quite clear: "Risk is socially constructed, and the failure to see risk as socially constructed leads to an artificial separation of risk assessment from risk communication" (416). "When there are disputes and communication 'problems' in a risk situation," they explained, "these problems are a public contestation over the meaning of risk—the 'truth' about risk is actually a product of such disputes" (423). The inherent dangers stemming from a lack of awareness about the social construction of risk involve placing people in line for harm, not only by excluding at-risk residents in decision-making structures but also in the reinforcement of hierarchical information structures that are part and parcel of the information deficit model of risk communication. The discussion over risk, for Grabill and Simmons, and for many other TPC researchers, was not about the contributions of quantitative risk assessment, but instead about considering the value of risk perception from the publics whose lives are constrained and impacted by risks—risks largely generated by institutions (see box 1.2). As they noted, "Conceptualizing risk as socially constructed is important because (1) it locates knowledge-making within communication processes, and (2) it considers how power is differentially exercised in such processes" (423–24). As such, their work reflected the broader trends in government and industry of including the public as part of the risk communication process (Davies et al. 1987; NRC 1989; Plough and Krimsky 1987).

Following Grabill and Simmons's work, TPC concentrated the study of risk in two ways. First, researchers localized the impacts of risk within specific risk analyses. Risk was connected to specific publics, users, and those disempowered in response to institutions of power—the field focused on the local sites of risk perception and communication, in part because those concerns were seen as central. As Haas and Frost (2017) explained, this commitment was "situated in local community settings where economic,

Box 1.2
Positivist and Social Constructionist Approaches to Risk

Risk methodologies can take many forms—some quantitative, some qualitative, and some mixed methods—but there's been a long-standing tension about social constructivist approaches.

Let's take a moment to consider methodological tensions toward risk between positivism and constructivism. Whereas positivist approaches draw from objective approaches toward reality, most notably in the use of empirical scientific methods for assessing and quantifying risk, constructionist approaches relate to a range of perspectives that account for social processes, behaviors, and practices for perceiving, understanding, and communicating risk. Here we suggest that there are methodological dangers of pushing either perspective too far. Too-positivist approaches can lead toward the kinds of Western and technocratic (e.g., information deficit model) approaches that tend toward domination/oppression with respect to risk. For Grabill and Simmons, a hallmark of this approach is that experts assess risk using positivist methods and then communicate that objective reality to audiences. Conversely, a too-constructionist approach tends toward relativism where all accounts of risk must be treated as equally valid and viable. Risk communication researchers in TPC have well documented the tensions between these camps, including the implications various approaches have for the processes by which audiences, publics, citizens, and various stakeholders might interface with risk.

Here we argue for a third space toward social constructionism where risks can be understood as objectively real, and where those realities also grow from and contribute to shared and ongoing negotiations of risk rooted in socio-collective orientations, behaviors, and practices such as the social validation and acceptance of scientific knowledge. For example, during the COVID-19 pandemic public health officials worked to communicate known dangers of the virus, though the objective knowledge about virology will always fail to encompass the entirety of what constitutes "risk." Without a doubt, the risk of COVID-19 had, and continues to have, material consequences for humans and societies, as nearly seven million people have now died as a result of this pandemic. Yet risk as a concept is composed of a wide array of relations, from the agreed-upon outcomes from experts' best knowledge practices, to ways that knowledge maps onto communities, geographies, and situations, to non-Western models of knowledge making, to how any and all knowledge about risk is put into practice and connected to lived experience. In this view, the objective reality (COVID-19 poses mortality risks for human populations) also must circulate in conjunction with and garner assent from publics in terms of a social reality (risk assessment and risk communication work in conjunction). For the latter, examples of positions include the framing that while COVID-19 poses a mortality risk, the risk is not so great that we should mandate the wearing of masks.

environmental, geopolitical, and technological risks are understood as inextricably tied" (169). Second, researchers came to study risk largely *within* the disciplinary world of TPC, but rarely connected TPC research to the existing questions and considerations in risk communication as a broader field of study (and, albeit with lesser relevance, to risk analysis and risk management). While work articulating the rhetorical construction of risk was both deeply influential and extremely helpful for the field of TPC—in conceptualizing risk, in broadening the definition of what TPC could address, and in encouraging researchers to work with local communities unjustly impacted by risk—this approach was also bound in some ways by the era in which it was achieved. Here, we mean that the research about risk in TPC that emerged from the 1990s and 2000s was in part a reaction to several factors: (1) the field's previous inattention to risk and frustration with instrumental approaches to risk in other, related fields; (2) the emergence of TPC into/as a humanities discipline throughout the twentieth century, but most acutely in the 1980s and 1990s; (3) a recognition of neoliberal rollbacks of governmental and institutional risk protection throughout the 1980s combined with the subsequent reevaluation of how institutional power was constructed and an increased interest in organizational communication that focused on how risk is understood and communicated between an organization and both internal and external audiences. These responses were an inherent part of the development of TPC into a humanities discipline. While we explore this historical depth in more detail in the following chapters, here we need to highlight the framework through which TPC's main forays into risk were accomplished.

Throughout the 1990s, the academic discipline of TPC responded to several complex historical issues, from the pedagogical to the governmental.

For much of the twentieth century, TPC could be described as a teaching practice that taught Standard Written English via industry-aligned current-traditional approaches. By the 1990s, the field had become much more aware of this legacy and was busy rearticulating its pedagogical approach against this history, as was rhetoric and composition. The history of TPC as an academic teaching field can also be defined by a century-long identity crisis between its status as a technical/practical skill-based field and a marginalized humanities field. By the 1980s, this controversy had moved front-and-center. Here, we can point to the visible debates between Carolyn R. Miller and Elizabeth Tebeaux (Miller 1979; 1980; Tebeaux 1980), but also to dozens of articles that defined TPC, argued for its boundaries, and focused on what an appropriate ethics could be for the field. Finally, TPC researchers would have certainly been aware of the impact of Reagan- and Bush-era neoliberal state deregulation of environmental protections and acknowledged environmental problems. This included the defunding of a range of important agencies, the increased prominence of evidence for long-standing environmental racism, and several substantial environmental disasters. These three historical factors—a current-traditional approach to teaching writing, a largely practical orientation, and a frustration with reactionary government deregulation—led TPC to engage risk through institutionally focused case studies. While we deal more with these historical nuances in the following chapters, here we focus on the construction of risk as an institutional issue. Given the context of the 1990s, it made perfect sense for TPC to focus on risk as a result of industry and governmental failings and consider what the field could do to disrupt these manifestations of risk. How TPC responded to these historical pressures, then, shaped how the field would engage with risk.

Institutional Risk

TPC's approach to risk in this era is perhaps best represented by its focus on the 1986 Space Shuttle *Challenger* disaster, wherein the shuttle broke up seventy-three seconds into the flight, killing all seven crew members. The mechanical failure of an O-ring was meticulously documented, as was the discussion over the decision to launch on a cold morning. The Rogers Commission, the official body investigating the disaster, identified the failure as largely communication-related and blamed the decision to launch on interactions between Morton Thiokol engineers and NASA management, focusing on a particularly fraught conference call the night before the decision to launch. Represented by at least fifteen articles throughout the 1980s, 1990s, and 2000s, the *Challenger* disaster is the most discussed case study in TPC (Pflugfelder 2018). Most scholars in TPC looked to understand how risk was communicated within the meetings and documents that passed between managers and engineers—a ripe and bountiful harvest for TPC researchers trying to make sense of the complex situations in which risk was being articulated and decisions were made. Many of these studies focused on the discursive and rhetorical factors in communicating risk, and how a more completely considered representation of risk, perhaps performed by rhetorically savvy TPC professionals, could have averted the communication failure and thus the disaster. Such an articulation fits within TPC's larger efforts in discipline-building in this era. How does a newly emergent academic field prove the viability of their methods and the validity of the field? Well, one approach is to argue for how professionals from that field could be of use to the institutions that played a large role in producing situations in which risk became manifest, but that had also failed to fully understand that risk. TPC researchers, in these articles, are often situated as professionals who understand the rhetorical complexities of risk and who could be helpful—not only to the institutions but also to the people who experience the material risks that these institutions conjure.

For these reasons, and others, TPC came to understand risk as an impact of institutional power and studied how that power manifested in people's lives—an inherently Foucauldian framework. But let's pause a second before we dive into the approach TPC used to engage risk from the 1990s through the 2000s and talk a bit about our approach to historiography. While the following chapters will consider a long and broad history of TPC's relationship with risk in more detail, we want to make our stance on our rereading of TPC clear. Broadly, our conceptions of a history of risk within TPC have been influenced by work in rhetorical historiography. Most notably, scholars advancing cultural rhetorics (Mailloux 1998; Cobos et al. 2018), revisionist (Vitanza 1987, 1996; Shelton and Riley 2022), pan-historiographic (Hawhee and Olson 2013), and other technology oriented (Kimball 2017) approaches have led us toward an approach that is cultural, revisionist, and pan-historiographic.

By "cultural," we mean that TPC has historically defined culture in relation to theories of risk and how those theories have occluded opportunities to understand risk in competing or intersectional ways that foreground how a white supremacist, heterosexist, colonialist, capitalist patriarchy has normalized inequitable exposures to risk within our world. By "revisionist," we mean to emphasize a distinction that Vitanza (1996) drew between revisionist approaches that simply "reclaim . . . what has been excluded, and usually along the lines of race, class and sex" and those that work to "critique traditional, historical discourse to discover how it is coded to prevent members of a field of study from seeing how they are thinking and acting against their own best ethical-political interests" (324–25). Additionally, we are interested in Shelton and Riley's (2022) recent call for members of our field to "turn their attention back onto the field itself as a condition of inquiring into its ability to contribute to social justice in society" (313). Finally, by "pan-historiographic," we mean to emphasize an approach that Hawhee and Olson (2013) have theorized that offers a wide scope that is especially helpful for projects that engage "questions not yet broached by scholars in our discipline" (92). In particular, their approach to history values diachronicity "to attend to a long-view of history" in contrast to Foucault, who examined specific moments in time, often via kairotic moments within a larger, assumed framework (92–93). Hawhee and Olson (2013) argued for a diachronic approach that "responds to the aspects of rhetorical history or theory that the study hopes to illuminate and the contributions a rhetorical perspective might make to clarifying the broad theme" (92). In the case of Hawhee and Olson, the study of human-animal relations and national formation, respectively; in our case, the relationships between risk, harm, and TPC.

Our approach to a cultural, revisionist, and pan-historiographic history of TPC's engagement of risk seeks to dwell between synchronic and diachronic approaches, both deeply engaging the diachronic as we historicize TPC. This approach affords us opportunities to stop and look at specific moments within a larger history, while also synchronically critically attending and reorienting to the power differentials that surround risk as historically situated and emplaced in ways that have led toward inequitable material and symbolic distributions of risk throughout three case studies. We seek to embrace the productive tensions between synchronic and diachronic approaches. Rather than adopting pan-historiographic or revisionist approaches wholesale that might simply recover a sliver of what's absent, we reorient and reconsider what we can recover from those glimpses and what it might mean with and for the "ethical-political" quality of the methodologies, theories, and practice of risk within TPC at this moment.

Grabill and Simmons (1998) noted that their understanding of risk was built upon Foucault's framing of institutional and disciplinary power relations, and examined how disciplines of risk assessment, cognitive psychology, and communication have shaped the conversation around risk. They treated these disciplines, and other forces too, as institutions, "as rhetorical systems of decision making formed by the discourses that make them possible (e.g., legislation, business plans, policies, procedures, research protocols)" (436). Grabill and Simmons defined institutions "as a discipline [or regular, shared ways of producing and distributing knowledge] and as an organization [or bureaucracies with policy and decision-making power]" and explained that their focus was on "the interrelationships between disciplines and organizations that mark the institutionalization of knowledge production and policy making about risk" (417). "In many ways," Grabill and Simmons suggested, "most people are dominated in some aspect of their lives, usually at work or school—institutional systems that often do not allow people fundamental access to decision making. . . . This is precisely what happens when experts, committees, or closed agencies control the decision-making processes involved with risk assessment/communication" (427).

Foucault described how power becomes manifest in the institutions that govern our lives; he framed the discursive construction of institutional power as the consolidation of "micro-practices" that crystallize into institutions and their governing rules and norms. For Foucault, institutions are not universals, but sites of congealed practices, ideas, and representations that can be disrupted. Because Foucault described institutional power as constructed, we are therefore encouraged "to study the state and other political institutions not, as we typically do, from the top down, but rather from the bottom up. We should examine how numerous techniques of discipline and technologies of the self operate throughout society to fix the ways in which people construct themselves, their conduct, and their relations to others" (Bevir 1999, 353). TPC scholars might have seen this articulation of institutional power as an invitation to study the constructed situations where the interrogation of risk communication could expose, and possibly rectify, ongoing power imbalances. However, while this institutional understanding of risk can help TPC researchers contribute to local formations of risk, it also has restricted the scope of studies of risk to the *industrial present.*

In TPC, risk communication was (and is) seen as a practice engaged by people, through texts that construct power within institutions, where, crucially, communication is also an inherent element of the process of creating and reproducing power. Institutions are seen as being made up of a vast network of decisions, and those decisions coalesce into the conditions in which risk is articulated and then perceived. Regardless of whether that institution is the Environmental Protection Agency, the Occupational Health and Safety Administration, or the National Aeronautics and Space Administration, TPC has recognized this Foucauldian foundation for the rhetorical production of risk and sought to intervene on behalf of those most impacted. Grabill and Simmons's insight was exceptional because it highlighted TPC's point of entry into this formation of meaning-making: usability studies and community-engaged research. Further, even though Grabill and Simmons only briefly referenced Foucault's conception of institutions in their landmark risk communication article, we know that this formation of institutional power was at play. In a 2000 article, Grabill, along with other Purdue researchers, explicitly argued that institutional power is a rhetorically constructed human design—one that is changeable (Porter et al., 611). They argued that they "aim to change the practices of institutional representatives and to improve the conditions of those affected and served by institutions . . . (e.g., the economically disadvantaged)" (611). Key to this position is their understanding of Foucault's belief that institutions are not "innately oppressive or as necessarily unchangeable" (637). Simmons would also later draw on this work to support the idea that Foucault's claims about institutions fit squarely into the world of TPC. If Foucault's ideas about institutional power were "extended to risk communication," Simmons (2007) claimed, "we would expect that changing current risk communication practices requires change at the level of the institutions involved in risk communication. Institutions regulate and constrain knowledge making, production, distribution, and consumption through a system of rules and practices" (10). In order to address this institutional formation of risk communication, we should focus on "practices, micropolitics, and local arrangements, using discourse to examine historically and socially situated relationships in the production of knowledge, power, and ethics" and showcase how "institutions work to make certain types of participation possible and others impossible" (Porter et al. 2000, 10).

Collectively, this work would change how TPC studied risk communication; the only limitation is that it framed risk almost entirely as the negotiation of meaning between institutions and people, possibly limiting further analysis, and therefore definitions of risk, to the industrial/historical past or present and to mesoscopic regional or local impacts. To connect back to the Rio Tinto example from the start of this chapter, most TPC approaches would consider the production of institutional texts that allowed for the destruction of an Australian Aboriginal site that is effectively beyond value. Yet could this same conception of risk consider the geologic conditions that created the gorge, the forty-thousand-year-long habits of Aboriginal people at the site, or the long-term impacts on the Puutu Kunti Kurrama and Pinikura people? Are these impacts not also inherently connected to risk?

A second complication, aside from the temporal and spatial limitations, is that TPC's approach to risk became caught in a larger emergence of field-building. In much of the scholarship of this era, TPC was concerned with incorporating elements of risk communication *into* TPC and less concerned with engaging *the nuances of* risk communication. In 1994, while studying nuclear energy debates, Mirel (1994) argued that TPC scholars engaged in risk communication research had not yet framed "their analysis in a theoretical understanding of the overall purpose of risk communications" (42). Mirel pointed out that studies of Three Mile Island and the *Challenger* were problematic in this manner. Specifically, she argued that TPC researchers have performed "retrospective examinations of the communications," addressed "what caused ineffectual and even disastrous communications and what choices writers might have made instead," and assumed "that the purpose [of communication] is to resolve debate and arrive at a right decision" (42). Such examinations are perhaps best represented by the article-length, rhetorically focused analyses of the *Challenger* disaster. Mirel explained that to gain a better sense of how persuasion occurs in risk communication, "rhetoricians need the insights offered by studies in the social science subdisciplines of risk perception and communication. These theories explain the persuasive aim of such texts and the psychological and cultural issues that writers must address to achieve these aims" (42). (Perhaps chapter 3 of this book, which focuses on an expansive approach to risk, can fulfill Mirel's wishes, albeit belatedly.)

From Mirel's perspective, TPC researchers of the era did not fully engage risk communication practices, but instead performed short, often rhetorical, analyses of complex communication situations in notable disasters—which undoubtedly helped justify our presence and the need for more critical attention to TPC as an academic and professional practice. But the context for engaging risk in TPC had not changed much two decades later. In 2015, David Reamer likewise lamented that "within the field of technical communication, scholarship [on risk] is limited. Those scholars of TPC and rhetoric who have addressed risk communication tend to focus on time-bound case studies of risk communication in specific times of crisis . . . or deconstructing the risk-communication context" (Reamer 2015, 350). In contrast, Reamer tackled a longitudinal history of the Nuclear Regulatory Commission and their approach to risk communication over time, noting that tracking one industry's risk communication strategies over time could offer a useful approach to risk (350). Reamer's critique largely matched the pattern established in studies of the *Challenger* disaster, and we would argue that, with few exceptions, most TPC work has repeated this pattern until very recently.

Reconfiguring Risk

Recent TPC scholarship on risk has extended our field's scope beyond the historically and geographically framed examples described above. For example, J. Blake Scott's work (2003) focused on how people are implicated in embodied ways in risk discourse, prompting additional medical- and health-related rhetorical approaches to risk (e.g., Welhausen 2017; Arduser 2017; and Pender 2018). Likewise, other scholars have emphasized the importance of transcultural and intercultural approaches to TPC and risk, including Ding (2014), Olman and DeVasto (2020), and Baniya (2024). Cagle and Tillery (2015) model the type of historical work that is necessary for extending the role of TPC in risk communication, as they performed an interdisciplinary literature review of research at the intersection of climate change and communication. Their work has filled gaps in TPC's conceptualization of STEM (science, technology, engineering, and mathematics) and social science research on communicating climate change and ensured our field is up to date on qualitative and quantitative work that many other scholars may not have the resources to conduct. Itchuqiyaq et al. (2022) also expanded the scope of risk communication by being more inclusive of marginalized and minoritized communities that do not follow the typical institutionally sponsored risk communication initiatives from experts to a public audience. Further, Stinson and Le Rouge (2022) provided a platform for TPC scholars to diversify our methodological approaches to risk, with particular attention to materiality and embodiment. Understanding risk, for Stinson and Le Rouge, is a situated process that attends to one's locality, sense of place, and immediate decision-making, and they defined the scope of risk via the human body, the earth, and the interrelations of human and earth bodies together. These moves to extend the scope of risk by way of interdisciplinarity, inclusion, and nontraditional methodologies are vital as TPC progresses to being a field that participates meaningfully in larger conversations around risk and that consists of scholars doing real, difficult work in their communities.

Yet, despite these recent efforts, TPC has not fully reckoned with our past relationships with extractive industries or how the field has benefited through its connection with its massive carbon footprint, ecological devastation, or the affect on human and nonhuman life. Throughout much of its history, TPC had been complicit with regimes, practices, professions, industries, and, yes, institutions that have placed the burden of risk onto people and systems possessing less cultural, economic, and material power. Because of our field's close connection to these extractive and exploitative forces, we have also been partially complicit with what Rob Nixon (2013) described as "slow violence." Nixon has called this form of environmental harm "a violence of delayed destruction that is dispersed across time and space, an attritional violence that is typically not viewed as violence at all" (2). Such violence manifests in centuries of colonialism, slavery, and worker exploitation and results in what Lauren Berlant has called "slow death," "the physical wearing out of a population and the deterioration of people in that population that is very nearly a defining condition of their experience and historical existence" (2007, 754). The causes of this harm are Western regimes of capitalism and the economic formations of what David Harvey (1999) has previously framed as the "standard view" of interaction between economies and environments. "In the standard view," Harvey explained, "the general approach to environmental problems is to intervene only 'after the event.' . . . This 'after-the-event' emphasis means that environmental issues are essentially regarded as 'incidents'—the result of 'errors' and 'mistakes' (often based on ignorance)—that should be dealt with on a case-by-case (and often place-by-place) basis" (161). We argue that TPC has often been focused on responding to the "standard view," reacting to the local impacts of industrial-era events after they have occurred, and has been therefore less likely to associate risk with the expansive geographic scope and temporal scale of slow violence and death.

What would it mean to reconsider the blowing up of the Juukan Gorge by Rio Tinto from a methodological approach that includes the potential for an expansive sense of scope and scale? Well, to encounter such an incident, TPC researchers could certainly take a document-centric after-the-fact analysis, or engage in empirical research via community-engaged research that emphasizes the voices of the individuals impacted by the destruction. These are still *very valid* TPC methodologies, so they are still warranted in the circumstances in which they would be beneficial. However, they are only some of the many approaches to investigating risk that can be accomplished. Risk exists in much more than the industrial present; risk has millennia old foundations, so TPC researchers could catalog the interrelationships between geology and climate for the Pilbara region, and establish the foundation for the emergence of more recent ecosystems, including the region's unique subterranean species, their capacity to survive despite ongoing mining activities, increased noise, dust, and industrial equipment, and the future harms they could incur. When the Aboriginal groups who have inhabited the gorge, including the Puutu Kunti Kurrama and Pinikura, established Indigenous knowledge about the area, including the significance of the cave systems, they also established a history of relationships that were disrupted when colonial gold mining arrived in the nineteenth century, and later when asbestos and iron ore were extracted in the twentieth and twenty-first centuries. These relationships encompass tangible knowledge of the flora and fauna, certainly, but also less tangible historical, social, cosmological, and spiritual dimensions. When Indigenous land is so heavily mined (the Pilbara has twenty-five industrial-scale iron ore mines), the cultural and physical integrity of "dreaming tracks" and "songlines" are irrevocably harmed (Holcombe and Fredericks 2021); similarly harmed is access, because mining operations have carved up, restricted, and destroyed so much irreplaceable Indigenous land. TPC researchers can assess how harm has been unequally distributed in these deep histories and investigate the future dimensions of harm.

Slow violence and slow death can occur in numerous other ways, too. For the slow violence of climate change that results in the intensification of slow death for people and ecosystems, the harms have been predominantly caused by white, Western, capitalist Minority World (corrective of Global South) nations. Roughly 10 percent of humans have generated 50 percent of all carbon emissions from consumption; for example, "the emissions of the richest 1 percent of Americans, Luxembourgers, and Saudi Arabians are 2,000 times greater than those of the poorest Hondurans, Mozambicans, or Rwandans [those who are] infinitely more vulnerable to the consequences of the very same emissions" (Malm 2016, 245). A conception of risk in TPC that is unable to account for these historically deep and geographically dispersed harms—as well as more immediate and local ones—is also ill-equipped to address the future of risk. This formation of risk contains both the slow violence Nixon described as "violence that occurs gradually and out of sight, a violence of delayed destruction that is dispersed across time and space," and how that violence empirically manifests in ecosystems, communities, immediately dangerous situations, and bodies (2). Such an understanding of risk must also confront the limitations of the concept of slow violence. While "slow violence" is useful in thinking across scales of time and space—"unchaining our geographical imaginations from the shackles of the present [and provoking us] to delve into the past to unearth the violent structures of inequality that saturate contemporary life"—it is less appropriate in recognizing the burdens of risk that are more immediate (Davies 2022, 410). That is, a slow violence framework can too often assume a violence of extended temporality, where harm is invisible. An understanding of risk that can also represent the "relationships between the complex interleaving of everyday lived experiences with broader structures" of violence is likewise necessary (Pain and Cahill 2021, 364).

Only recently has TPC research (Ding 2009; Frost 2013; Haas and Frost 2017) advanced foregrounding the relations that eclipse the temporal and geographically bounded focus of the industrial/historical past or present and to (mesoscopic) regional or (microscopic) local impacts. In particular, Haas and Frost have articulated an *apparent decolonial feminist* framework for examining "localized global risk" (171)—to anticipate DiCaglio's thinking on scale—that calls on TPC "to extend our commitments . . . to international communities as well as underrepresented and disenfranchised communities disproportionately affected by risk" (169). Our approach in this book, and more specifically detailed in chapter 3, is indebted to Haas and Frost's apparent decolonial feminist risk framework, and we wish to continue their methodology by digging further into the temporal and spatial dimensions of risk and offering a detailed critique of our "indebtedness" to modern industrial practices and approaches to risk communication. Our goal is to broaden the geographic scale and temporal scope from which TPC scholars engage in work that concerns risk. We want to showcase how TPC has functioned via a constrained understanding of risk communication (and risk) in the past and then outline how this framework can be broadened by a more explicit articulation of how risk operates throughout time and across geographies. In order to do this work of expansion, and see the benefits for addressing ecological risk, environmental harm, political rights, and human sovereignty, however, we need to first under*mine* TPC.

Under*mining* Technical Communication

As part of their education, many students of technical and professional communication—ourselves included—are introduced to a brief history of the field. Often, this history explores where and how technical writing emerged and which industries supported that development. Some students will read Tebeaux's research on the history of technical writing or more likely Bernadette Longo's *Spurious Coin* (2000), perhaps the most influential history written to date, and learn how technical writing was first taught at schools of mines, using a textbook created by mining engineer T. A. Rickard (1908). These same students might also learn of (what is often represented as) the first technical writing manual, Georgius Agricola's *De re Metallica* ([1556] 1950), which demonstrated how to blend empirical knowledge with more occluded forms of alchemical lore, representing both in precise technical language. They might also read workplace studies, like Paradis, Dobrin, and Miller's (1985) overview of their experience observing the writing activities of thirty-three engineers and scientists in research and development at the Exxon Corporation's intermediate technology division, in which the authors sought to uncover the unexplored and untheorized practices of editing and writing at a large petrochemical organization. The "main concern of the [Exxon] ITD R&D division was the production of phthalate esters," which are widely used as plasticizers in the manufacture of polyvinyl chloride (PVC) (Paradis et al. 1985, 282). (Vinyl chloride is the toxic chemical spilled in the East Palestine, Ohio, derailment in 2024—one of the subjects of our case study in chapter 6.) Too often, these historical details are treated as somehow natural, in part because it made sense for the important industries of the day—mining, metallurgy, and related extractive industries—to be represented in precise, technical language. Mining is one of the world's oldest organized professions, dating back tens of thousands of years; the practice of extracting coal, copper, or cobalt is dangerous, and human lives often depend upon the precise transmission of knowledge about how to follow a seam or how to avoid mine collapse. For many of us who study TPC, this story frequently begins here, with our reflection upon the shared history of mining and TPC prompting only a few questions about the field's oddly close relationship with the practice of mining.

Yet this relationship warrants further questioning. Why, for example, does this particular industry have such a tight relationship with the development of TPC—both in practice and in pedagogy? Considering the vast scale of human exploitation involved in the history of mining, mineral extraction, and petrochemical industries over time, many involving enslaved peoples, land dispossession, and genocide, how do we feel about this origin story? Do we feel similarly about the widespread environmental damage done by these same industries as hilltops are stripped, rivers are diverted, and tailings and slag piles pollute ecosystems? Why, in this story about the origins of technical writing, do we not consider the relationship between our chosen field of study and the risks inherent to the practices that fostered the development of the field? Why is risk often seen as a special form of communication, analysis, or management, and why don't we also see risk in the bigger (colonial) picture—where choices have been made as to which peoples and which environments are made to bear the burden of risk? If TPC can be strongly linked to mining and other extractive industries throughout history—and we argue that it can—why are we not both more aware of the relationships between these fields and the *application of* the burden of risk onto certain people and ecosystems? Why are we not more outraged by these actions, both past and present? The answer is that, with some exceptions, the field has yet to fully come to terms with this history and its long-standing relationship with risk.

Our questions derive in part from Cecilia D. Shelton and Sarah Warren-Riley's position: "The long quest for power and legitimacy, we argue, has served to fuel narcissistic tendencies and positioned technical communicators to reproduce harmful systemic oppression both inside and outside our field. It is important to historicize the legacy of these concepts to determine what power and legitimacy means in light of the social justice turn's shift toward equity and inclusion" (2022, 317). They further explained that "TPC's existence as a discipline is legitimized by its *relationships* rather than its content and therefore its power is arguably contingent on forces beyond the reach of its scholars and practitioners" (318). Our legitimacy has been inextricably tied to risk and disaster, and attending to more than disaster might become one way to frame a reconciliation between social justice and power and legitimacy. Like Shelton and Warren-Riley suggested, our relationships with risk must be fully and explicitly unpacked before moving forward.

There are (at least) three reasons for the lack of attention to the scalar complexities of risk in TPC—two of which we have already explored. One reason is TPC's focus on doing research in risk communication through the lens of its existing areas of interest; as we noted above, TPC has only been in the process of academic field-building since the early 1980s. A second explanation comes from understanding the significant influence of Foucauldian and rhetorical assumptions about how institutions are built, how they work, and how they wield power. TPC found its voice in part through the analysis of modern-day institutional power and how TPC practitioners could confront and potentially resist that power on behalf of users and their needs. A final reason for our lack of attention to historical risk is that TPC, as an academic field, can be described as a broadly horizontalist discipline, a claim that requires some additional explanation. TPC has been a humanities field (Miller 1979), or at least one that has been arguing for its inclusion into the humanities, on and off, for roughly 120 years (see chapter 2). The focus on asserting TPC's positionality within the humanities has created an attention to the spaces where people work and dwell—an attention to life within the earthly zones of human habitation.

What does it mean to work within a "horizontalist" discipline? By and large, it means that a field attends to landscape, to the cartographic, featureless, geographic "lived-in landscapes of the surface" (Scott 2008, 1866). Humanities fields, almost by definition, have focused on a limited sense of the human sphere, where we have, as Clark (2011) explained, adhered to Immanuel Kant's injunction to "steer clear of what the turbulent forces of the universe could do on their own account, and fix our attention on our own interface with the world around us" (Clark 2011, xii–xiii). Since the emergence of TPC as an academic discipline in the 1980s, we have quite closely attended to the relations we have with others in our horizontalist positionality, partially as a result of our own complex process of discipline-building (see box 1.3). However, caught in the throes of becoming a humanities discipline, or at least in arguments for its legitimacy as a humanities discipline, TPC has become overly attuned to short-term institutional actions within the immediate zones of human habitation and less focused on how other vertical actors (across geological space and throughout deep historical time) have produced the conditions for risk.

Box 1.3
Technical and Professional Communication as a Humanities Discipline

Is technical and professional communication in the humanities? Possibly. Why does it not often feel that way?

It's difficult to represent technical and professional communication as a straightforwardly "humanities" discipline—and to consider most humanities disciplines as broadly "horizontalist." As we have learned from Teresa Kynell-Hunt's *Writing in a Milieu of Utility* (1996), technical writing programs have been wrestling with their identity for quite a long time, with control over the technical writing course fluctuating between engineering faculty, English faculty, and writing faculty. This argument landed more substantially in the discussions between Carolyn Miller and Elizabeth Tebeaux in the early 1980s, especially as who teaches technical writing became a larger conversation about what should be taught in technical writing courses. The conversation continued in TPC journals and conferences for another couple decades. As the field expanded, instrumental ways of thinking about language, positivist representations of truth, and current-traditional forms of teaching fell by the wayside, as the field considered—and taught—the ethical complications related to technical writing, valued theoretical traditions aside from empiricism or positivism, and opened up what audiences a broader range of technical communicators were writing (or could write) for.

We think that many early arguments for TPC as a humanities discipline attuned the field to the scope and scale of its institutional boundaries. With our current emphasis on social justice—along with a range of other approaches that borrow from critical theory, ecological thinking, and human geography—we feel comfortable arguing that modern TPC in university settings has a place in the humanities writ large—a setting that can also help us think beyond our modern institutions. Of course, this framing does not mean that all TPC scholars exclusively make use of humanities methodologies—far from it. Many researchers of technical, professional, and scientific writing and communication happily use quantitative methodologies that some humanities scholars would find uncomfortable or unapproachable. The point is not to limit our ways of understanding TPC, but engage with multiple methods of understanding a vastly complex research area.

Attention to the vertical by TPC is essential, especially if we are to confront how those in power have exploited land (and water and atmosphere) over hundreds of years; these powers have consistently devoured the resources available to their extractive way of thinking, often veiling such an awareness of verticality through horizontalist framing. This narrative has occurred time and time again throughout history, as imperial, colonial, and capitalist powers have sought to extract as much energy as possible from the people, systems, and geographies they have sought to dominate. Andrew Nikiforuk (2012) detailed the vast scale of energy extraction by such systems, detailing how from the Roman Empire to medieval Britain, and from the Atlantic slave trade to the Spanish colonies, the extraction of fuel from all available resources, human and geologic, was intrinsically vertical. The intensity of this perspective on energy extraction, as Macarena Gómez-Barris explained in *The Extractive Zone* (2017), was a kind of "vertical seeing" that "rendered Native populations invisible, . . . legally rendered the settlement of foreign populations onto communal properties, and facilitated the taking of those territories' resources. European colonization throughout the world cast nature as the other and, through the gaze of *terra nullius*, represented Indigenous peoples as nonexistent" (6). Verticality is more than a latent awareness that our lives are supported by actions above our heads and below our feet, but also a recognition that historical power imbalances have been supported through the domination of these spaces as resources that fuel inequality, figuratively and literally.

Critical and human geography studies, perhaps most notably, have been interrogating what a robust incorporation of verticality into historicization and theoretical framing might mean. Paul Carter (1996) has argued that Western coloniality can be explained via "scenographic conception of space" that imagined the world as a "continuous planar surface," regardless of Western powers' ambitions and abilities to mine, destroy, and devour their colonized landscapes (1996, 116). In order to bring such actions to the surface, Heidi Scott (2008) has argued that we need to begin constructing an alternate politics of the subterranean, in part because the "undeniable 'horizontality' of colonial and imperial expansion should not be allowed to overshadow the dimension of verticality that, in many times and places, was equally central to colonial and imperial ventures and was manifest in practices concerned with the subterranean such as mining and the mapping of geological formations" (1853). Scott focused on Spanish and Portuguese colonial mining enterprises in America to trouble horizontalist-oriented politics, and to explain how these colonial projects "were also quite literally grounded by means of material practices such as mining and treasure hunting that extended below the surface of the earth" (1864). For both, the claims made by Eyal Weizman were central to their considerations of vertical politics. Weizman's critical work on the West Bank emphasized how this specific territory is made up of much more than contested surface-level land, but tunnels, bridges, and airspace too (Segal and Weizman 2003; Weizman 2007). These evaluations of what exists both beneath and above the spaces in which humans most often dwell emphasized the lack of critical attention paid to verticality and, crucially, highlighted how these spaces are deeply important in our understanding of who or what is put at risk.

By arguing that TPC needs to attend to both the subterranean and the atmospheric, we do not mean to suggest that the field has completely ignored risk in these spaces. After all, some of the most influential accounts of risk include Sauer's study of embodied risk communication among mine workers and the numerous articles written about the NASA *Challenger* disaster. No, TPC has investigated these spaces before, but this research has proven to be as similarly constrained as those studies noted above. By focusing on human institutions and institutional power, TPC has addressed the communication that mediates people and the structures that pay (or coerce, force, or enslave) them to work in dangerous situations. For example, Sauer's (2002) work has strived to "investigate the full range of genres and communication practices that arose in response to particular problems of work, risk, authority, uncertainty, and disaster" and make those forms of representation more visible to those that can act upon them (6). Beverly Sauer further traced this approach as "Six Critical Moments of Rhetorical Transformation in large regulatory industries," where "writers must extract information that is presented in one rhetorical modality (oral testimony, for example) and literally change the form so that the information can be re-represented for a different audience" (17). Our argument here is not that Sauer's work has not been extraordinarily insightful and useful, *which it has*, but instead that in this approach there has been less capacity to explore, for example, the impact of the steam engine and its initial design for raising the water level of mines and its role in the expansion of CO_2 pollution since the seventeenth century. There is less capacity to consider a more expansive history of the Earth from above and below, including more human and nonhuman agencies and actions into a more comprehensive understanding of risk.

In order to pay closer attention to verticality in TPC, the field needs to be under*mined*. Here, we mean "undermine" in more than one sense. On one hand, we hope to "burrow under" or "make insecure" the existing history of the field through a new examination of TPC's relationship with risk. But, in order to do so, we must also consider the subterranean passages where risk has often been articulated, and where the field has often gone to ground its origins. That is, we also need to "dig or excavate beneath" the horizontalist norms for the field. In practice, what we'll do in chapter 2 is locate events throughout history where TPC and risk have intersected with each other, and we'll articulate several major shifts in the past. This history is not meant to stand as a new "grand narrative" of TPC, but instead to undermine existing histories and ask modern-day researchers to confront some of these episodes in the long relationship between technical writing and risk. Our purpose is not to overshadow the many counterhistories of the field, or disregard how specific communities have been able to take agency in accounting for their exposure to risk, but instead to showcase some of the ways that risk has been disproportionately imposed upon people and ecosystems with less power, and describe how TPC has functioned alongside these injustices over time.

Chapter Descriptions

This chapter has introduced some of the core ideas that the rest of the book will explore in more detail. In order to truly undermine TPC, however, we need to first reconsider and reframe TPC's interactions with risk—which is where chapter 2 comes in.

In order to explain the many moments and locations throughout history where risk and TPC have come into contact, chapter 2 reads these interactions across historical time and geographic space. This chapter seeks to reframe the history of TPC as one where the practice, and eventually the academic field, has been complicit in the unequal distribution of harm on people, land, and ecosystems. We focus on the substantial and persistent connections between mining, metallurgy, and extractive industries throughout time and reevaluate the commonly held, but often unexamined, assumptions about how TPC formed alongside mining activities. Technical writing in these industrial locations was often secretive and the workers were often treated as expendable, as were the natural environments that held those energy resources. To be clear, we are not arguing that TPC *has only existed* in relation to extractive industries throughout history, nor are we selectively identifying the worst practices in human history and aligning some subset of TPC to them. However, in considering TPC's relationship with risk, extractive industries become a major locus for the emergence and justification of TPC—as a practice, as a language for empirical thought, as a teaching subject, and as an academic field. Looking at this long history, we identify three general eras: (1) Western colonization, the scientific revolution, and industrialization, (2) the emergence of TPC as a teaching field within higher education, and (3) the development of the modern research field of TPC, which transitions into our recent focus on theorizing and researching risk.

Consolidating the lessons from the historiography offered in chapter 2, chapter 3 considers how the industrial practice of risk communication grew and evolved into a more substantive practice and academic discipline following the National Environmental Policy Act (1969) and the Occupational Safety and Health Act (1970). This chapter interrogates past relationships between TPC and industrial models of risk communication and articulates a methodology for reconsidering risk within the field. To connect with industrial approaches to risk communication, we survey major approaches within the field. While methods used within industry and government have been critiqued for being overfocused on quantitative measures like validity, risk researchers in TPC dismissing these approaches have struggled to see beyond the industrial present—as TPC emerged from, and reacted to, the same historical, cultural, and theoretical conditions. This chapter seeks to conceptually expand risk by historicizing risk via Ulrich Beck's formulation of a risk society (1992). Specifically, we act upon Beck's claim that risk can be fluid and expansive in temporal scale and geographic scope—scale because he reads risk across time and scope because he sees newer human-instigated risks able to escape the locations where risk is generated. We build from work that critiques Western, expansionist, exploitative approaches toward people and land, and use the concept of cultural, structural, and slow violence to expand how risk is defined. Fanon ([1961] 2004), Galtung (1969), Farmer (2006), Berlant (2007), Nixon (2013), and others help establish the foundations of structural violence and allow us to argue that any conception of risk that does not take into account both the history of inequality and the scope of injustice—for both people and ecosystems—understands only a portion of what counts as risk. In order to challenge this structuring of risk throughout TPC, we turn to scale theory (e.g., DiCaglio 2021; Levin 1992) and identify how risk in TPC can build from ecological science and reorient against the spatiotemporal slice that has confined risk analysis to the industrial present. We define risk as the unequal distribution of harm—harm that should be articulated from different perspectives that include those most impacted, but also that values evidence-based experts. The methodological approach we derive from this consolidating gesture presents TPC practitioners—and risk researchers—with a heuristic framework that allows researchers to identify how they are engaging risk, which methods would be most appropriate to capture detail at that level of engagement, and, perhaps most importantly, recognize other scales at which they might make sense of how risk is manifest in any given situation. In considering time, we articulate five topoi that reflect variance in temporal scale (deep time; industrial/historical past; present; immediate future; long-term futures), and regarding geographic space, we name three points that reflect variance in scope (macroscopic/global, mesoscopic/regional, and microscopic/local). These points allow us, and others, to move across global, regional, and local scales in terms of understanding the development of risk.

Thereafter, we offer three case studies of risk within the Colorado River Basin that develop and apply the methodological framing we created in chapter 3. Each chapter considers a distinct risk event, highlighting the methodological opportunities to rethink how spatial scope and temporal scale operates, while also illuminating the interconnected and cascading dimensions of risk encircling the watershed. Chapter 4 foregrounds the social and material spatial complexity of risk as it relates to thousands of abandoned mines in the American West. Introducing the concept of *riskscapes* (Müller-Mahn and Everts 2012), we trace the spatial distribution of risk associated with mining from the industrial/historical past to the present. Specifically, the chapter offers a case study of the collapse of the abandoned Gold King Mine, which resulted in the release of three million gallons of toxic wastewater and mine tailings into the Colorado River watershed (Anderson 1983; Appadurai 1990). The chapter considers the riskscape across local, regional, and global scales, attending to the (de)territorialization of risk as it is geographically and politically bounded in relation to the Gold King Mine disaster. The case study demonstrates how risk, as it is rhetorically bound within one space or context, spills into other locations and contexts. Consequently, we argue that the spatial boundaries through which risk is perceived and communicated can work to conceal risks operating at larger and smaller scales. In this case, the Gold King Mine spill has been framed as an isolated disaster, but also functions as an example of the larger, more systemic, and persistent risks associated with abandoned mines.

Chapter 5 foregrounds the social and material temporal complexity of risk as it relates to the ongoing megadrought and water crisis affecting the Colorado River Basin. Introducing the concepts of *timescape* (Barbara Adam) and *kinship time* (Kyle Whyte), we trace the temporal distribution of risk associated with water diversion and management practices from the present back toward the industrial/historical past. Specifically, the chapter offers a case study of climate risk through the lens of the Law of the River (Bureau 2008), a corpus of technical and legal documents that not only created the material infrastructure to divert and store large quantities of water from the Colorado River but also promulgated a seniority system to distribute water rights within the watershed. This chapter considers the messy temporal interconnections between the industrial/historical past, present, and immediate future, sketching the risk relationally across global, transnational, and ecological nexuses. More simply, the case study highlights how global warming trends associated with anthropogenic climate change have exacerbated water insecurity within the region that is directly associated with the industrial timescape that the Law of the River instantiated. Here we highlight the connections between Western colonialist expansion through aggressive agricultural development and the disproportionate levels of harm Native Americans indigenous to the Colorado River Basin and key ecosystems and species within the region have shouldered through the promulgation of this water management system. Ultimately, the chapter spotlights a deeply interconnected risk horizon, impacting actors as varied as farmers and ranchers in Mexicali, homeowners in the Front Range Urban Corridor (east of the Rocky Mountains), the greenback cutthroat trout, and the yellow-billed cuckoo, and recognizes how climate risk and water scarcity is impacting migratory patterns and amplifying extant social and economic inequities.

Chapter 6 merges the spatial and temporal complexity of risk in the immediate future in relation to the proposed Uinta Basin Railway, which, if approved, will be used to transport waxy crude oil from extraction fields in Utah's Uinta Basin across the Colorado River Basin to connect to the national rail network and facilitate energy production. Introducing a concept that we refer to as *contradictory risk flows,* we trace the temporal and spatial distribution of risk associated with the railway—as infrastructure that scaffolds the extraction, transportation, and refinement of energy—from the present forward toward the immediate future. Specifically, the case study accounts for how these contradictory flows, manifest as energy, are extracted from the earth and moved, redistributing the benefits and risks to people and ecosystems located distal and proximal to these sites of energy extraction, transportation, and refinement of that energy. This chapter highlights Western orientations to energy, including an underlying technological determinism that more energy is better and that energy should be made available on demand. Moreover, we sketch how this logic perpetuates petrochemical and hydrocarbon industry rationales for continued extraction, despite the long-standing material and historical inequity that has followed the contradictory flow of risk within extractive industries. Temporarily approved, the environmental impact statement for the project was found to be severely lacking, specifically because it did not account for the causal impacts beyond those that are within shouting distance of the proposed railway. These "downstream impacts" are precisely the causal relations that an expanded sense of scope and scale can bring to light. Within the case study, we discuss more recent energy transportation disasters, such as the 2013 Lac-Mégantic rail disaster and the 2023 East Palestine derailment, as these events demonstrate the importance of attending to the immediate and long-term future and structural violence associated with the proposed railway. In emphasizing these disasters, we're not suggesting that a TPC scholar, armed with the right level of rhetorical knowledge and foresight, could have avoided these accidents, but that case studies, while also accounting for an expansion in scope and scale, can be situated toward future-oriented deliberative action.

In accepting the Robert H. MacArthur Award in 1989, ecological and evolutionary biologist Simon Levin explained his concern and fascination with scale. He argued that scale, the different levels at which patterns manifest, was "the fundamental conceptual problem in ecology, if not in all of science" (1992, 1944). In our conclusion, we collectively reflect on how scale might be the fundamental conceptual problem of risk, not only philosophically but in how the field of TPC has decided to carve out its case studies and artifacts. This conversational chapter takes advantage of the polyvocality of authorship to explore questions about how TPC has approached risk historically, the ethical reckoning that we believe is required to happen before we move forward, and subsequent alterations to risk researchers' approaches to risk, disaster, and crisis.

As a whole, this book calls on TPC to employ methods and methodologies that resist framing risk as "an environmental phenomenon [that] appear[s] suddenly as an event, because as a structural or predictable condition it has not engendered the kinds of historic action we associate with the heroic agency a crisis implicitly calls for" (Berlant 2011, 101). We employ scale theory in conversation with Hass and Frost's (2017) apparent decolonial feminist rhetoric of risk in order to establish a larger conception of risk that can include risk analysis, less granular conceptions of risk communication, and formations of risk that encompass a deep sense of time and an expansive sense of space. This book is a conversation about the future of the field, including questions about what unique contribution TPC can have with risk and risk communication.

Chapter Two

Many People Have Died So That Technical Communication Can Live

An Alternate History of Risk and Technical and Professional Communication

> As soon as you identify a situation as a problem you have endorsed the perspective from which it is problematic.
>
> —Richard Ohmann, *English in America: A Radical View of the Profession*

This chapter offers a history of technical and professional communication (TPC), one that deals with some of the harms that have been present throughout time. It is *not* a history that seeks to excoriate the individual technical writers involved. Instead, it highlights technical and professional communication's historical proximity to risk, and emphasizes that while this relationship has evolved over time, technical communicators have held an indentured relationship to power, and therefore risk, at times working amid horrifying conditions or at others transferring the conditions of risk onto others. We will only be able to capture some of this long narrative of interactions between TPC and risk, so while we endeavor to describe the many power relationships present, we paint with a fairly broad brush.

In considering TPC's long historical relationship with risk, we want to make clear our stance on rereading TPC. Broadly, our conceptions of a history of risk within TPC have been influenced by work in rhetorical historiography. Most notably, scholars advancing cultural rhetorics (Mailloux

1998; Cobos et al. 2018), revisionist (Vitanza 1987, 1996; Shelton and Warren-Riley 2022), pan-historiographic (Hawhee and Olson 2013), and technological (Kimball 2017) approaches have led us toward a cultural, revisionist, and pan-historiographic approach. Specifically, this is a kind of field history. Madison Jones (2021) explained how field histories are "intellectual counterhistories that use historiographic methods to place moments of disciplinary change within the context of their paradigms in order to understand how place-times rhetorically shape and influence our contemporary practices and lived experiences within the field" (347). "Field histories," according to Jones, "help rhetoricians to situate relationality in terms of geological (or 'deep') time, revealing important ways of understanding rhetoric as well as the fields that shape it as relations" (348). To pursue the history of technical and professional communication, this chapter illustrates historical moments in which technical communication emerges as a human activity, but an activity that also emerges alongside structures that place people into the unequal likelihood of harm. We reveal these historical, often place-specific, moments to complicate our more recent disciplinary approaches to risk. Jones also noted that "working within a framework of deep time can be difficult, requiring research that crosses numerous disciplinary boundaries and within a sometimes overwhelming spatiotemporal scope," and we find this to be all too accurate (348). The history that is presented in this chapter engages archaeology, geology, the history of labor and industry, and political science, among other disciplines. Because this chapter explores such an extensive period of time, it examines locations and instances where the definition of technical writing and communication is challenging to understand. That is, the definition of TPC is relative to the time periods and cultures in which it has been embedded—modern definitions, and certainly the ones that we've continuously worried about since the 1970s, are less applicable to instances distant to us currently.

In his counterhistory of rhetorical ecologies, Jones (2021) explained that some approaches, while emphasizing experienced time and physical embodiment, can also serve to mask longer histories and past violences. A particular synchronic spatiotemporal cut brings certain events, actors, and relationships to the fore, but can also function to mask past histories only discoverable via diachronic approaches to time and scale. Our approach to the history of TPC is accomplished through what Debra Hawhee and Christa Olson (2013) have called a "pan-historiographical" approach. A pan-historiography takes a big-picture look that is especially helpful for projects that engage "questions not yet broached by scholars in our discipline" (92).

It values a diachronic approach "to attend to a long-view of history"—in distinction to a Foucauldian approach, which examines specific moments in time, often via kairotic moments within a larger, assumed framework. Hawhee and Olson also noted that Foucault's histories are often synchronic histories that give off a diachronic effect, though his approach is ultimately synchronic. "A diachronic approach," in contrast, is an "expansive, thematic approach [that] responds to the aspects of rhetorical history or theory that the study hopes to illuminate and the contributions a rhetorical perspective might make to clarifying the broad theme" (92; see box 2.1). We recognize the value in both diachronic and synchronic histories. Diachronic approaches can emphasize specific instances of a critical theme, bringing some stories and relationships to light, while synchronic approaches can generate alternative narratives by providing a coherent trajectory. As such, our approach here is to present largely synchronic histories—both in this chapter and in the case studies that follow in chapters 4, 5, and 6—but ones that allow for diachronic effects that emphasize the many relationships between risk, harm, and TPC.

Box 2.1
Out of Africa? Martin Bernal and the Black Athena Debates

The construction of any history requires writerly choices that encourage readers to understand the past through the historian's worldview. The function and order of how history is written depends upon the time, space, and motivation for writing history.

In 1987, Martin Bernal published *Black Athena: The Afroasiatic Roots of Classical Civilization*—the first of a three-volume series. Bernal, a historian, asked: What if we entertained the idea that ancient Greek civilization was significantly influenced by Egyptian and Phoenician (or broader Afroasiatic) cultures? At the time, Bernal's idea challenged long-standing Eurocentric beliefs that Greek civilization had arisen through influences from Indo-European cultures. *Black Athena*'s publication and the responses—or the *Black Athena* Debates—addressed fundamental questions about historical interpretation, cultural appropriation, and the biases underlying Western historiography. Bernal argued that from the eighteenth century onward, European historians either downplayed or erased evidence of Afroasiatic influences on Greece. Perhaps, this is why scholars of Afrocentrism, postcolonial studies, and some classics scholars were largely supportive of his argument, especially during the culture wars of the 1980s and 1990s. The idea that Greek thought is not exclusively Greek deconstructed Eurocentric ideas of Western civilization. For Bernal, this erasure of contributions from North Africa and the Near East was a practice of racism resulting from scholars embracing a "pure" view of the origins of Greek thought to justify Enlightenment and imperial intellectual development. The *Black Athena* Debates largely divided scholars as to whether Bernal's argument was based on evidence or speculation. The larger takeaway is that his decision to undertake a diachronic rather than a synchronic approach to history by rhetorically rereading and expanding the relation of time and space revealed how much scholars in classics, Egyptology, ancient Near Eastern history studies, archaeology, and European intellectual history were indebted to whiteness. *Black Athena* demonstrates how interpretations of history (much like risk) are influenced by ideological commitments over time and our willingness to realize them.

Because this history is largely synchronic, with diachronic effects, that is, a history that illustrates only one idea throughout a much richer span of time while emphasizing specific relationships, it will only be able to highlight so much; a wealth of information remains beyond the scope of our discussion. This story includes many instances in which people have been able to fight against unjust systems of harm. The missing elements to this chapter's version of TPC history include many examples of key women's roles in technical and professional communication, empowering tactical communication strategies used by communities of color, and the non-Western, Indigenous ecological knowledges that are also very much part of the history of TPC. These stories are central to a larger history, but not all of these counterstories can be included here. The reason for omitting some of the more empowering histories of technical communication is that our particular retelling of TPC history seeks to highlight injustices associated with bearing an unequal burden of risk. To be clear: there are many TPC practices, pedagogies, and theories throughout history that have been employed to fight injustice and harm; we have included situations that exemplify *how inequitable distributions of power have resulted in disproportionate levels of harm*. We exemplify the bleaker side of the historical relationship between technical communication and risk. This history dwells within this bleakness. Additionally, while this chapter examines a broader expression of technical communication throughout history, it also narrows its historical scope starting in the late nineteenth century to focus on US contexts for teaching and research. In sum, we aim to under*mine* technical and professional communication.

In chapter 1, we explained what it means to under*mine* the field of TPC; in this chapter we destabilize the history of TPC by metaphorically "digging under." Specifically, we follow how extractive industries have contributed to the history of the field and contributed to the ongoing destruction of the environment, while exploiting people through unsafe working conditions and degraded living conditions. To connect the history of TPC and risk, we need to examine the spaces the field has overlooked due to its horizontalist worldview. In practice, this means identifying the connections between mining, drilling, excavating, extracting, and TPC—and highlighting where risk has manifested in harm through these practices and industries. Along with agriculture, these extractive activities have been the defining form of human labor for the last few thousand years, what we call the industrial/historical past; the products of mining, including building materials, semiconductors, metals, and the vast majority of energy technologies created by humans throughout history shape the impacts humans have had upon the earth. This chapter will specifically target mining and other extractive activities for its sources of evidence, in part to identify where and how risk is present in these extraordinary systems of injustice.

Simply, our approach resonates with Cecilia D. Shelton and Sarah Warren-Riley (2022), who argued that TPC is unlikely to advance social justice without first confronting its long-standing struggles with power and legitimacy. However, Shelton and Warren-Riley argued that the obstacle to achieving social justice in the field is not power and legitimacy itself, but rather "our field's relationship—both historical and contemporary—to power and legitimacy that impedes progress" (322). Furthermore, a reframing of power and legitimacy in TPC scholarship is necessary, and our historical approach here supports this aim. That is, while we are aware that a synchronic history may not explicitly emphasize alternate power dynamics within this history, our goal is to highlight the relationships between TPC and risk in dramatic, diachronic ways. Like Shelton and Warren-Riley, we hope that this retelling of TPC's history will contribute to a critical interrogation of "our allegiances to power and to reevaluate our institutional relationships" (322). Certainly, this history is incomplete, and this chapter invites future researchers to continue such work.

Embedded with Risk: Technical Communication and Risk from Colonization through Industrialization (1500s to 1890s)

In this era, technical communication involved increasing numbers of people in systems of knowledge production as increasing literacy rates, empirical research, and the development of plain forms of writing that expanded access to knowledge. Technical communicators began to embrace vernacular language and styles meant for nonspecialist audiences. While technical communication researchers' historicizing has proved accurate, as the burgeoning scientific revolution and the desire for textual representations of empirically verifiable actions grew substantially, this broadening of technical knowledge emerged alongside regimes of colonialism and imperialism. While technical communication is not synonymous with these abusive systems, it blossomed within them, becoming embedded with systemic, state-sanctioned control over people and the environment.

Though not necessarily intended to be used in instructional contexts, Shen Kuo's work from 1088 explained the processes used in numerous technical operations (also see box 2.2 for additional starting points to this history). Shen Kuo lived during the Northern Song dynasty, held court positions, and had the opportunity to both travel and discuss some of the technological and cultural changes happening during this time. The Northern Song dynasty (960–1127 AD) was a time of immense development in China, with widespread agricultural expansion, the creation of mechanical clocks, the distribution of paper money, and the invention, perhaps most famously, of gunpowder (Liu 2015). As well as assisting in the development of several technologies, Shen Kuo's major contribution was a series of conversations he documented with tradespeople, written in a casual style and collected in a volume called *Brush Talks from Dream Brook* (alternatively translated as *Dream Pool Essays* or *Dream Torrent Essays*). *Brush Talks* contains discussions of astronomy, meteorology, and geology, but also moveable type printing, the magnetic compass, mining, and metallurgy. Shen Kuo described the process of forging cast iron (later called the Bessemer process), explained the value of using petroleum as a lighting and fuel source, and described geomorphology and paleoclimatology. Most significantly, however, *Brush Talks* was written for nontrades experts—marking a significant change in how technical communication was practiced.

Box 2.2
The Complex History of Technical and Professional Communication

At the risk of overwhelming readers with caveats about historiography early on in a chapter on technical communication history, we venture one more concerning the myriad and multiple sources for the history of TPC.

We acknowledge that TPC predates Shen Kuo's work, as we showcase below. Kathryn Rosser Raign's *The Origins of the Art and Practice of Professional Writing* (2024) has expanded on alternative origins beyond those investigated by previous TPC historians. While we value Raign's contributions, our approach differs: we take a pan-historical, diachronic approach to trace TPC's ties to extractive industries rather than its alignment with liberatory ideals. Though strains of TPC have aligned with social justice, our focus is on its role in perpetuating unequal distributions of harm.

We could have begun our history chapter with the emergence of Sumerian writing, which "emerged as the main outcome of abstract counting, taking off when abstract counting dissociated the concept of numbers from that of the commodity accounted" (Schmandt-Besserat 1997, 122). Sumerian clay tokens replaced marks for quantity, and therefore created abstract technical writing procedures leading to written accounts of debt and inequality. Similarly, the Canaanite turquoise miners at Serabit el-Khadem in the Sinai Peninsula may have created alphabetic script under conditions of severe exploitation and isolation (Rainey 2009). We might also examine the oldest known topographical map—the Turin Papyrus Map—drawn around 1150 BCE, which details quarrying and mining operations in Egypt's Wadi Hammamat (Harrell and Brown 1992, 8). Or we could highlight the Laurion mines, which produced silver, copper, and lead, contributing to Athen's wealth and, as some scholars argue, shaping Greek rhetoric through the labor of enslaved workers. These are just a few examples of the long-standing relationship between TPC, risk, and extractive industries.

While not a technical manual, *Brush Talks* described technical processes in detail for a nontechnical audience—a radical idea in an era dominated by guild-oriented knowledge and Confucian beliefs. Zhang (2013) explained that this era was influenced by Confucian philosophy, wherein "social elites in Northern Song still considered science, technology, and any activities that involved technical specialty and that lead to building things as 'lowly skills,' " with the exception of medicine (368). Science in this era was deeply institutionalized and rarely explained or described to the public; as Zhang noted, "court scientists were not interested in adopting popular views and values, nor were they committed to making scientific knowledge available to the public" (369). Shen Kuo's significance, then, was twofold: "First, as a literati, he gave science and technology due acknowledgment for their importance to the society. Second, he not only made science and technology accessible to the public, but also enabled the public to participate in the creation of scientific knowledge" (369). Shen's efforts resulted in short descriptions of technical advancements, such as talk #56, the way of making steel, which described steel production in everyday language and compared the process to making bread: "Usually iron contains steel just as the dough contains the gluten. The gluten appears only after the flour of the wheat is washed to remove the starch. The steel is made in a similar way" (2011, 40). Shen Kuo also described the process of collecting petroleum and why the burning of petroleum as a substitute for wood could help save pine trees in the Qi and Lu regions, as they were rapidly being cut down for fuel (341–42).

The practice of making technical material accessible to a wider audience also happened elsewhere. For example, technical communication historians have suggested that Geoffrey Chaucer authored one of the earliest technical documents in English. His *A Treatise on the Astrolabe* (1391–1393) is cited as one of the first English technical manuals (Moran 1985). Chaucer framed his instruction manual for using an astrolabe as being written for his ten-year-old son, so he wrote in clear, simple vernacular English, carefully controlled sentence length, and included useful metadiscourse. He also structured the document by first describing the mechanism and then offering procedures for its use (Hager and Nelson 1993). This manual, if we can call it that, marked an important moment in the development of technical writing, focused as it was on making complex materials understandable to a wider audience, though Chaucer was hardly alone in performing this kind of writing (Hagge 1990). For context, Chaucer's source material for *A Treatise* was a Latin translation of eighth-century Persian astrologer Mashallah ibn Athari's work *Construction and Operation of Astrolabes*, which was initially written in Arabic and later translated into Latin. Technical writing in this era meant writing for an audience that had less immediate contextual knowledge to bring to bear on the technical situation—a major shift toward the systemization of informational and educational writing strategies.

Bernadette Longo (2000) has described the emergence of technical writing in this era as a practice of discourse accompanying the scientific (and later industrial) revolution, a discourse that needed to emphasize clarity if it were to make its content useful to humanity. In *Spurious Coin* (2000), Longo explained how a primary goal of technical and scientific works, like Agricola's mining manual *De re Metallica* (1556), or Moxon's manual on smithing and printing, *Mechanick Exercises* (1687), was to present complex procedures and knowledge in simpler language, so as to have "the Secrets of all Trades lye open" (as cited in Longo 2000, 45). The development of scientific processes in the West emphasized the shift from protected knowledge to a broader dissemination of printed works on a range of technical topics—such was science's purported goal in an emergent modernity—to expand the world's share of knowledge and to do so faithfully, accurately, clearly, and concisely. Unlike Hermetic texts, where "recipes for manipulating nature through revealed knowledge" were coded for a group of readers already within an "initiated group of magi," and later in insular guilds and trades, technical communication shifted to report on experiential and experimental knowledge in the service of knowledge dissemination (Longo 26). Technical communication in this era became the lingua franca of technical and scientific knowledge.

Much has also been made of *De re Metallica,* a twelve-volume compilation about mining practices, published in 1556. Agricola's work is especially notable because it functioned as a transition point between Hermetic alchemical texts, such as *Physica et Mystica*, and empirical explanations. Longo explained that Agricola "presented recipes for manipulating nature, just as previous authors of books of secrets had done," but also synthesized this information with experimental knowledge that was both more recent and less associated with Hermetic and magical beliefs (30). Agricola presented these latter sources of information, but built authority for his own writing with details from modern practitioners and subject matter experts. *De Re Metallica* valued empirical knowledge and connected it to past traditions of cloistered, less-robustly empirical knowledge practices. As Longo explained, "Agricola's philosophic position embraced the idea that scientific knowledge could be gained more readily through practical experience and observation than through logic and speculation in the Aristotelian (or scholastic) tradition" (36).

Yet, what was the consequence of democratizing knowledge about mining through technical communication? How did the emphasis on writing for nonexpert audiences generate additional harm toward the environment and the people who worked within it? Less often mentioned in these early technical materials, and in the commentary on these materials, are the concurrent impacts of mining—on the people who were working in the mines and on the environments that were abused to extract resources from the earth. Foremost, mining required fuel, and the easiest available source of fuel had not changed since Sumerian kilns. Trees were the source of fuel for farming, shipbuilding, and construction, but mining was especially timber-intensive, and the destruction of Europe's forests in this era was difficult to ignore. Estimates show a decline of forests in France from about 30 million hectares in 800 to about 13 million hectares in 1300; across Germany and central Europe, roughly 70% of the land was forested in 900, but only 25% remained by the end of the nineteenth century (Kwiatkowska 2007). Where mines were established, for example, when copper became mined extensively in the foothills of the Alps, the surrounding hillsides were stripped bare to supply fuel for smelting. In *The Underground Wealth of Nations* (2019), Jeanette Graulau explained that by the eleventh century, timber shortages were widespread throughout Europe, with little left to build shelter: "High wood prices led to a rapid spread of the timber industry and increased the pace of deforestation. The situation favored capitalists from abroad: Venetian merchants bought timber in the Adriatic and sold wood to ore-processing factories located in Lombardy. Local mining and smelting factories also imported charcoal from as far as Crete, a move that increased the running costs of production of a diverse group of industries" (79). By the fifteenth century, wood demand in Europe was at an all-time high, and that demand led to financial exploitation by outside interests (79).

Not only was the environment being disrupted by mining, but people were too. Graulau noted that "the mining roots of capitalism were violent, and poor miners, including women, paid the highest price. The wage laborer that slowly emerged from the mining feodum had a predatory past; his alienation from the means of production was not eliminated with the displacement of feudal lord by corporations. Rather, alienation was reinforced and reinvented by new ways of digging underground wealth" (272). Those who emigrated for work, or who had mining imposed upon their area, once a rich ore was discovered, had to navigate flooding, deforestation, and metal pollution (Kempter and Frenzel 2000, 71).

As someone writing about the practice of mining, Agricola was aware of these environmental and humanitarian risks and appreciated the potential impacts of technical communication. However, Agricola *explicitly dismissed* fears over the environmental destruction that resulted from mining. He noted the concerns of others about the poor conditions found in mining-intensive regions:

> The woods and groves are cut down, for there is need of an endless amount of wood for timbers, machines, and the smelting of metals. And when the woods and groves are felled, then are exterminated the beasts and birds, very many of which furnish a pleasant and agreeable food for man. Further, when the ores are washed, the water which has been used poisons the brooks and streams, and either destroys the fish or drives them away. Therefore the inhabitants of these regions, on account of the devastation of their fields, woods, groves, brooks and rivers, find great difficulty in procuring the necessaries of life. (8)

While Agricola acknowledged these widespread harms, he viewed them as largely inconsequential, claiming that these mountains were "otherwise unproductive" and would go unused without mining. He argued that because these mines were situated

> in valleys invested in gloom, they [mines] do either slight damage to the fields or none at all. Lastly, where woods and glades are cut down, they may be sown with grain after they have been cleared from the roots of shrubs and trees. These new fields soon produce rich crops, so that they repair the losses which the inhabitants suffer from increased cost of timber. Moreover, with the metals which are melted from the ore, birds without number, edible beasts and fish can be purchased elsewhere and brought to these mountainous regions. (14)

Apparently, no ecosystem destruction is so bad that it cannot be restored with a few cartloads of agricultural plants and animals. Furthermore, Agricola was also aware of the risks to the mine workers, and described those risks in some detail: "The critics say further that mining is a perilous occupation to pursue, because the miners are sometimes killed by the pestilential air which they breathe; sometimes their lungs rot away; sometimes the men perish by being crushed in masses of rock; sometimes, falling from the ladders into the shafts, they break their arms, legs, or necks; and it is added there is no compensation which should be thought great enough to equalize the extreme dangers to safety and life" (6). He *again dismissed these safety concerns*, arguing that "things like this rarely happen, and only in so far as workmen are careless," and further suggested that miners are rarely bothered by these incidents (6). The manifestations of risk in dangerous mines, Agricola claimed, "do not deter miners from carrying on their trade any more than it would deter a carpenter from his, because one of his mates has acted incautiously and lost his life by falling from a high building" (6). Agricola blamed miners for their own deaths, argued that the environmental destruction caused by mining is ultimately worth it, and refused to see the structural forces within mining economies that contribute to widespread risk. Technical communication and mining became deeply linked in this era, as the dissemination of technical knowledge occurred alongside the complex technical activities of the industry. Of course, because technical communication was so deeply embedded with mining, it also supported the continued exploitation of the environment and the increased disbursement of harm to disempowered people.

Agricola's observations on the impacts of mining to the environment were not new—mining was well known to disrupt lives and livelihoods—but his callous disregard for the people and ecologies disrupted by mining coincided with a sea change in how Europeans thought about nature. As Carolyn Merchant (1989) explained in her feminist history of Western beliefs about nature, most sixteenth-century Europeans would have believed in an organismic metaphor for the interdependence of life. The earth was conceptualized as a nurturing mother that provided for people as long as people took care not to overexploit nature. This conception changed, however, with the emergence of the scientific revolution and the coming of a mechanistic and rational worldview. With the development of empirical science, nature was seen to exist in a disordered state that needed to be mastered if resources were to be realized: "Whereas the nurturing earth image can be viewed as a cultural constraint restricting the types of socially and morally sanctioned human actions allowable with respect to the earth, the new images of mastery and domination functioned as cultural sanctions for the denudation of nature" (Merchant 1989, 2). In the more organismic worldview, metals were seen as quasi-living elements of mother nature's body—or in other metaphors—grown in the world as if from a tree (29).

In a mechanistic worldview, however, we see rationales for the exploitation of the earth's resources, a systematic exploitation that was supported by a rationale of utilitarian human need. Exemplifying this rationale, Agricola summarized his rejection of any ethical concerns over mining with an instrumental argument emphasizing human identity and moral right:

> If there were no metals, men would pass a horrible and wretched existence in the midst of wild beasts; they would return to the acorns and fruits and berries of the forest. They would feed upon the herbs and roots which they plucked up with their nails. They would dig out caves in which to lie down at night, and by day they would rove in the woods and plains at random like beasts, and inasmuch as this condition is utterly unworthy of humanity, with its splendid and glorious natural endowment, will anyone be so foolish or obstinate as not to allow that metals are necessary for food and clothing and that they tend to preserve life? (14)

In this new paradigm, not only was nature hiding valuable resources from humankind, who were justified in wrenching them from the earth, but the development of scientific methods also promoted the continued extraction of resources (and knowledge) from a passive nature (which, as Merchant explained, was continually depicted as female).

Along with a more instrumental, mechanistic perspective on nature came the development of non-Aristotelian modes of logic, empirical research methods, abstract reasoning, an emphasis on quantitative data, and "plain" forms of technical writing. These, and other qualities, amounted to the formation of a new worldview in western Europe throughout the sixteenth and seventeenth centuries and eventually led to the formation of Royal Society of London for Improving Natural Knowledge (1662) and the Académie des Sciences of Paris (1666). Independent disciplines of discovery were developed within these scientific approaches to knowledge—all guided by an inductive form of reasoning championed by writers and experimenters such as Francis Bacon and Robert Boyle. Bacon's work and thought defined the spirit of the new science and his understanding of nature was likewise emblematic of the changes that Merchant described. Merchant likened Bacon's perspective on nature as an inquisition of sorts, noting that Bacon framed his method of inquiry as one where nature must be put "under the trials and vexations of art" (169). In this formation, man must interrogate nature and learn the secrets of all *her* inner workings. The misogynist tones to these explanations were intentional and helped explain Western man's actions toward an opaque, confusing, and passive nature that concealed more than it revealed. Historian Sarah Irving affirmed that "Bacon's aim was adopted by the exponents of the new natural philosophy. . . . Robert Boyle, John Locke and other founding members of the Royal Society of London aimed to use natural philosophy to restore man's original dominion over nature" (2008, 2). A narrower question that arose within this framing of the world as passive and exploitable is how, exactly, should these inquiries into nature be communicated?

This scientific revolution was aided by a style of writing, often called plain style, that allowed for a more unadorned, stylistically sparse representation of nature—a style that aligned with the views taken up in the "new" science. Such simplified prose was intended to present information without elaborate or metaphysical argumentative framing. The Royal Society provided perhaps the most famous representation of the plain style of writing in the service of larger scientific goals, and Thomas Sprat's *History of the Royal Society* (1667) described how plain style functioned. Sprat argued for a norm in scientific and technical writing, in part by framing the new science as hostile to ornate and florid abuses of rhetoric. According to Denise Tillery, "The *History of the Royal Society* repeatedly draws its readers' attention to what Sprat wants to depict as the austere, masculine beauties inherent in the plain style" (2005, 276) in a larger effort to root out emotions from a more objective approach to knowledge. For Tillery, "The Royal Society members were particularly concerned with maintaining the proper hierarchy of reason over emotions as they engaged in the new experimental science, the advancement of learning instantiated by Francis Bacon" (277). This language must also be "abstract, repeatable, and iterable, which means it is reliant on language that is fixed, not subject to personal interpretation or introduction of error through the careless use of synonyms and metaphors" (282).

The larger implications of these assumptions about writing are impossible to extract from the assumptions made in this manner of thinking—writing mirrored the mode of thought. Representing nature in writing as if it were passive, irrational, gendered as feminine, and available for Western, male, capitalist manipulation engendered a range of potential exploitations (see box 2.3). We can observe these connections in the work of Robert Boyle in *New Experiments Physico-Mechanical, Touching the Spring of the Air and Its Effects* (1660), the book in which Boyle described the theory behind the creation of an air pump able to create a vacuum, detailed numerous experiments he carried out with the air pump, and offered descriptions about the nature of air. As Steven Shapin and Simon Schaffer explained in *Leviathan and the Air-Pump* (1985), Boyle engaged in a "naked way of writing," "in a philosophical rather than a rhetorical strain" (66). Shapin and Schaffer explained that "the 'florid' style to be avoided was a hindrance to the clear provision of virtual witness: it was, Boyle stated, like painting 'the eye-glasses of a telescope' " (66). The appropriate tone, style, and form of writing must accompany the assumptions about the world that Boyle (and other scientists) were trying to convey.

Box 2.3
Scientific and Colonial Interests Often Pursued Simultaneously

Our long-standing narrative about the emergence of Western science via a revolution in empirical thinking often forgets to include the colonial and imperial aims of the same nation-states that promoted scientific ways of thinking. Science was exported as a powerful new method, one justified by technical communication, because, as this narrative was told, science would be good for all.

Belief in the power of empirical science also manifested itself alongside the ambitions of nation-states in the seventeenth and eighteenth centuries—and were contributors to the rationale for expanded European colonial endeavors. Beliefs in human capacity to dominate the natural world also fueled exploration, biopiracy, and slavery. Sarah Irving has argued that Robert Boyle in particular was one of the first people to "put forward a programmatic suggestion for the way in which man's dominion over nature could be restored by fostering a relationship between naturalists and the English colonies. This relationship would enable England to harness a wealth of information from the New World that would improve natural philosophy" (Irving 2008, 21). The colonies became portals to extraction, and the North and South American continents, as part of the "New World," were likewise emblematic of the age of scientific and geographic discovery. For Francis Bacon, and others, the global expansion of European power was justified, because all humanity deserved to benefit from the expansion of the (technical and scientific) arts. The colonial powers felt similarly justified in the subjugation of

Indigenous populations because, as Mauro Scalercio explained, imperiality became "an epistemological and philosophical manner of interpreting and giving sense to the world," where imperiality was not understood to be "something given but something to be made through the work of [the] human race" via new technologies and arts (2018, 1080). This perspective held largely true for both the British and the Spanish, the two dominant colonial forces for hundreds of years.

Antonio Barrera-Osorio, in *Experiencing Nature* (2006), argued that Spanish scientific perspectives were founded before their English and French counterparts, as they sharpened knowledge in the New World via the "the exploitation of natural resources for commerce, especially minerals, tropical commodities, and medicinal plants" (Barrera-Osorio 2006, 10). In such colonial pursuits, the emergence of empirical science provided the rationale for the exploitation of people and environments, and the exponential production and displacement of risk. The dominant forms of technical communication in this era were deeply embedded within these imperial practices as both the means of representing the knowledge gained and as one of the arts that could be practiced in the accumulation of European colonial wealth.

Because plain language forms of technical communication were meant to be a practical accompaniment to, and therefore intentionally embedded within, scientific and technical practices, these same forms of writing were carried outside of Europe through colonialism. The logics underlying technical communication allowed for this; seen as a useful, practical, and productive art, technical writing became one of the many technical arts that were lauded as beneficial for all, even though this knowledge assumed a universal conception of truth where the determination of facts required categorization according to a rational scheme. The environment, including the "New World" and every being in it, became available for Western classification and alignment within a system of empirical knowledge. As Stephen Mrozowski explained, this form of thinking provided "a cultural rationale for seeing nature in the abstract, an essential step in its classification as a commodity" (1999, 156). This is a cultural rationale that Walter Mignolo has articulated as a "second revolution" that sits alongside the scientific revolution; though this one established a new formation of time and space. Mignolo referred to this as a "hidden dimension of events that were taking place at the same time, both in the sphere of economy and in the sphere of knowledge: the dispensability (or expendability) of human life and of life in general" (2011, 6). Western powers shifted to acknowledge a regime that disqualified "all coexisting and equally valid concepts of knowledge and by ignoring concepts that contradicted their own understanding of nature. At the same time, they engaged in an economy of brutal resource extraction (gold and silver and other metals) for a new type of global market" (11). Powered by colonialism, mobilized by oceangoing vessels and mining technology, western European powers turned all of nature into "natural resources" (12).

This Western epistemic project was furthered by plain language, insofar as it was meant to be a vehicle for neutral, repeatable truth, regardless of cultural context. While it is often direct and concise, the feigned neutrality of technical writing was designed to generalize, educate, and create the conditions for the repetition of certain forms of work—and embed the conditions for risk into that same language. For example, Elizabeth Tebeaux's work on shipbuilding (2008) emphasized that after the mid-seventeenth century, the craft of shipbuilding moved toward written rather than oral discourse, facilitating the reach of English industry, increasing agriculture, forestry, whaling, and other colonial aspirations, including the forcible enslavement of human beings (which her work ignores). Roughly 3.1 million people from Africa were transported on British ships between 1640 and 1807, when the Abolition of the Slave Trade Act was passed (National Archives n.d.). In this context, "risk" encircled financial or pecuniary issues, as those with the means to finance slave trading, commercial expeditions, or the widespread plundering of Indigenous land wanted to see a return on their investments as their ships returned to port. Yet technical writing was also inextricably tied to the risks that those colonized and enslaved experienced; like mining examples in earlier eras, these writing methods did not cause such harm but were instead embedded within and facilitated by those practices.

For another example of technical communication's embedded status, we can consider where and when the Spanish colonizers developed their methods for the systematic exploitation of Central and South America. When Columbus led the colonization of Hispaniola in 1492, his diaries record his primary goal—to find gold. Allison Margaret Bigelow (2021) explained that within weeks after landing, he located information that changed his understanding of gold production, and the Spanish technical language of mining and metallurgy changed along with it. A pattern of forcible Spanish appropriation of Indigenous mining terms and practices set the tone for this extractive practice for centuries to come. Bigelow explained that Indigenous knowledge and culture contained systems for mining that specified how techniques, tools, and buildings should be used in culturally significant mining practices. The Spanish technical texts that recorded these practices for duplication in other locations, like royal gold refiner Oviedo y Valdés's *De la natural hystoria de las Indias* (1526), gave no credit to the Indigenous workers' knowledge or its cultural significance, and his diagrams left out the technical work led by Indigenous women and by enslaved West Africans. This appropriation of knowledge and erasure of agency coincided with the genocide of the Indigenous Taíno and the first mass movement of enslaved African peoples across the Atlantic.

Elsewhere, the centers of the mining world in the mid-sixteenth century became the cities of Potosí, now in present-day Peru, and Huancavelica, now in present-day Bolivia. Potosí was a silver mine and Huancavelica was a mercury mine, and most of the mercury mined at Huancavelica went straight to Potosí, as mercury was key in the process of mining silver. Mercury was added to rock that contained silver, bonding to the metal in an amalgam, after which it was heated and melted away, leaving the silver (and Potosí was the site of a Spanish silver mint for hundreds of years). This process was intensely dangerous to the workers, surrounding villages, and ecosystems downstream from these cities. The mercury mine at Huancavelica was known as mina de la muerte (the mine of death) (Brown 2001, 468). Workers at Huancavelica were exposed to cave-ins, floods, malnutrition, silicosis, tuberculosis, pneumonia, carbon monoxide poisoning, and perhaps the most prevalent, rampant mercury poisoning. While those working at the mine included free workers, many were conscripted under a system of *mita*, which existed in earlier Inca communities as a system of shared labor, but was exploited by the Spanish as a system of compulsory labor for men aged 15–50. So dangerous and deadly was the mine at Huancavelica that even the *mita* system began to fail, as the mine killed a third of those who worked there (495).

For a complete geographic contrast, we can also look toward nineteenth-century mining practices in the American West, the forcible removal and genocide of Indigenous groups, and the eventual development of large-scale mining practices (see chapter 3 for a more detailed case study). Unlike the romantic notion of solitary miners panning for gold with a mule, the process of high-pressure hydraulic mining throughout the latter half of the nineteenth century created enormous wealth, but also significant environmental damage. Supported by technical material in new journals like *The Mining and Scientific Press* and the *Engineering and Mining Journal*, and technical books like *A Practical Treatise on Hydraulic Mining in California* (1885), hydraulic mining created hundreds of millions of tons of debris, destroyed ecosystems, caused flooding, and created mercury contamination of California's waterways that continues to be a problem today. While these narratives have evolved within this period of technical communication, technical communication was embedded alongside extractive industry to facilitate the exploitation of natural resources while dispossessing Indigenous groups, enslaving others, and forcing still others into wage slavery or multigenerational poverty. The environmental conditions under which these people labored, unsurprisingly, were all too dangerous.

Indebted to Risk: Technical Communication and Risk in American Universities (1890s to 1980)

In this era of technical communication and risk, technical writing developed as a teaching practice and nascent academic field within American colleges and universities. It was an era in which TPC was deeply indebted to, and frequently justified itself by, the industrial practices that were emerging and thereafter flourished. The establishment of land grant universities throughout the US was a major contributing factor. These institutions, which were founded in 1862 and after on land seized from Indigenous people, and again later in 1890, focused on practical and technical fields that were deemed useful and necessary for a growing capitalist economy. Many of these technical fields, including mining engineering, required students to write in styles and genres that universities were less equipped to support, as existing writing courses inherited from the nineteenth century emphasized belletristic writing for a smaller, educated, East Coast, white elite. Emerging from this pedagogical pressure, newly developed technical writing courses became a requirement for many degrees.

Throughout eighteenth- and nineteenth-century America, higher education had been dominated by religious and private colleges and universities, which predominantly specialized in educating white male students for law, the clergy, and medicine. The impetus for educating a wider array of students for other, more explicitly practical professions—ones designed to exploit the resources of a vast geographic area—took root in the institutions developed from the Morrill Land-Grant Acts (which expropriated Indigenous land and gave it to states), as they emphasized technical degrees in science, technology, engineering, and mathematics (STEM), often with a stress on engineering and agriculture. As Teresa Kynell-Hunt explained, it was in this milieu that engineering faculty attempted to justify their status within the academy by increasing both the volume of scientific and technical content in their courses and the number of these courses within their curricula, thereby leaving less room for humanities courses, including writing (2000, 15). Similarly, Robert J. Connors noted that "before 1870 an engineer graduated with a good bit of knowledge of the 'humane subjects.' But the engineering discipline was rapidly being awakened by the fantastically rapid industrial development of the Gilded Age, and new engineering materials were not long in appearing in curricula" (1982, 331). By the 1870s, Connors observed, few humanities courses were left in engineering-specific schools and programs.

Eventually, the narrowing focus of engineering programs pushed writing and communication to the margins, with the freshman writing course operating as the only exposure to explicit writing instruction most students would experience. As Connors explained, while "freshman composition requirements were almost universal . . . the tacit assumption in engineering schools between 1880 and 1905 or so was that these first-year courses were all the introduction to writing that engineers needed" (1982, 331). Of course, engineers needed more than freshman composition, taught in a mixture of belletristic writing, literature, and (falsely) Standard Written English (SWE) grammar instruction. By 1900, engineering faculty across the country had realized something was amiss—and by some accounts, this was a "rather dark time in the history of engineering education, a time when, by the schools' own later admissions, they turned out a large number of otherwise competent engineers who were near-illiterates" (Connors 1982, 331). Solutions to this supposed problem came via further influence from the Society for the Promotion of Engineering Education, the emergence of current-traditional rhetoric, new technical writing textbooks, the reintroduction of other English literature courses, and an emphasis on grammar skills in the writing classroom. Unfortunately, these courses were almost universally undervalued by English and engineering faculty alike. Historically, composition was taught by those who had spent their careers attending to the advanced study of literature. Courses in writing instruction were also seen as a "service" begrudgingly performed by English departments and similarly denigrated by the engineering schools as only marginally acceptable (Kynell-Hunt 2000, 32). Literature professors "tended to regard first-year composition and technical communication with condescension and hostility" (Longo 2000, 171).

The first explicit technical writing textbook, *A Guide to Technical Writing* (1908), was created by a mining engineer, Thomas Arthur Rickard. A former editor of the *Engineering and Mining Journal* and owner of the Mining and Scientific Press, Rickard created a textbook founded on SWE grammar and mechanics' rules and drills—drilling information into students as well as resources out of the earth. Rickard's book was also framed by linguistic imperialism and portrayed any casual, regional, or "nonstandard" language as incorrect, deficient, and evolutionarily primordial. His book taught students that colloquial terms were improper for the accomplished technical writing student and that "there remains scant excuse for the employment of terms that come from the uneducated" (1908, 16). He argued that language derived from mine workers was improper to use in this context, but also ill-befitting the racially coded superiority of precise technical communication in English. In this same textbook, Rickard argued for a standard language:

> The English language is the common heritage of the people of not one mining district, nor one region, nor one country, nor one continent; it is the heritage of the race to which Englishmen, Americans, Canadians, Australians, and Afrikanders all belong, and also of the various races that they have assimilated in the course of their effort to conquer nature the world over. The mere fact that a word is distinctively Western Australian or Californian, is peculiar to Michigan or New Zealand, is reason enough for rejecting it. Let us have a mintage that will pass current at full value throughout the English-speaking world; let it be the refined gold of human speech. (19)

For Rickard, language was minted akin to metals, purity was paramount, and strict, objective control—over language, people, or the environment—was the goal.

Rickard's beliefs about technical writing emerged from his experience as a mining engineer, and his other books, including *Man and Metals* (1932), covered a range of societal beliefs, including his definitions of civilization and his connections to Thomas Henry Huxley, his former teacher. Huxley, a noted biologist, championed technical innovations because they were necessary for the stability of Western culture. Huxley asserted that technical education was needed for the "preservation of that stable and sound condition of the whole social organism which is the essential condition of real progress" (Longo 2000, 59). "It was also his remedy," Longo explained, "for maintaining a strong British colonial rule throughout the world, thus enabling English progress to continue through social evolution" (59). In Huxley's view—and in Rickard's—"technical education led to sound reasoning, social stability, a sound English economy based on colonial resources, and progress through the manipulation of nature" (60). Rickard believed that TPC's purpose was to spread technical knowledge broadly, a claim that was based on the assumed superiority of Western culture and white normative logics. In the second edition of his textbook, he argued that "the intent of technical writing is to transmit accurate information, whether as fact or theory, from one man to another, to the gain of all" (1910, 128), and that to keep industry secrets is to "be today as the [racial epithets redacted]; civilization has been evolved by the free exchange of thought and the frank transmission of experience" (130). In this formation, technical communication is used to support the idea that Western industrial knowledge created a better world for all, though it conveniently ignored the role of capitalism in encouraging inequality, competition, and secrecy.

This position shifted somewhat after World War II, when the goals of technical communication merged with those of the US government. Post–World War II technical communication was, as David R. Russell argued, when technical communication emerged as an identifiable field, both inside and outside the academy (2002, 121). This academic formation was in part due to "rapid technological growth coupled with the postwar economic boom [which] led to a strong demand for technical writers in government and in industry, fueling an increase in technical communication courses and teaching staff" (Werry 2001, n.p.). Miles A. Kimball likewise called this moment in technical communication "The Brass Age" to denote the influence of military spending and increasingly complex military technology on the field (2017, 335). Also contributing to this emphasis on technical writing, the Society for the Promotion of Engineering Education's Committee on the Aims and Scope of Engineering Curricula released its findings, documents better known as the Hammond Reports (1940 and 1944), which condemned narrow vocationalism and emphasized humanistic courses. Bolstered by increased college attendance assisted by the GI Bill, technical writing courses thrived, even though neither engineering faculty nor English faculty supported technical writing or composition as a humanistic course (Connors 1982, 340). The result of technical writing's emergence was threefold: (1) it solidified the teaching of technical writing as a current-traditional approach grounded in SWE, thereby continuing to harm students; (2) it justified this pedagogy through the logics of industry; and (3) it aligned the teaching of writing with arguments for industrialized warfare.

In part because of the continuing frustrations experienced between engineering faculty, who wanted students to be more "precise" in their writing according to SWE conventions, and English literature faculty, who saw technical communication courses as a vocational backwater, technical writing pedagogy coalesced around current-traditional pedagogy. As Robert J. Connors explained, "Although technical writing had by this time a long and honorable history and was obviously in English departments to stay, it got as little welcome from literary departments in 1959 as it had in 1929. Still considered a low-level service course, technical writing was still assigned to graduate students and instructors" (1982, 344). Engineering schools supported this approach to teaching writing, because current-traditional rhetoric validated the "skill and drill" approach to writing. Here, grammar knowledge and falsely nonideological, clear, concise writing techniques must be drilled into students to establish habit. Teresa Kynell-Hunt reported that the Society for the Promotion of Engineering Education encouraged this approach, and also noted that composition's own focus on mechanical correctness may have delayed the emergence of unique technical writing courses, because the focus on "the concept of *drilling*—forcing, if you will, the rules of English grammar into students' heads," was abhorred by student and teacher alike. Yet engineering faculty felt that something must be done; "the worse engineering students wrote, the more educators called for drills and mechanics, leaving engineering students, in particular, with a flawed introduction to such an important subject—writing" (Kynell-Hunt 2000, 28). The harms of this pedagogy upon students in this vicious cycle have been well documented (for further elaboration, see box 2.4). Connors described the ascent of current-traditional rhetoric as "The Dark Ages of Composition" (1981, 216), and James Berlin explained how current-traditional pedagogy "reduces the composing act to a concern for exposition" (Berlin 1984, 66), which was often represented in corporate, sterile, and disinterested prose.

Box 2.4
Standardizing Technical Writing Style

The style guides that proliferated after World War II were devised to systematize style, primarily through a form of Standard Written English dialect that was acceptable to white American industry and business.

William Strunk's style guide, *The Elements of Style*, originally written in 1918, showcased just how a current-traditional writing pedagogy enforcing a writing style based in linguistic white supremacy flourished. Prompted by the National Defense Education Act (1958) and robust congressional funding for English education, William Strunk and E. B. White's rigid style guide promoted a "more politically ideological and educationally pragmatic vision of Western culture" (Lisabeth 2021, 92). *The Elements of Style* was greatly enlarged by White in 1959 and the guide was used alongside, or closely imitated in, hundreds of textbooks across tens of thousands of courses throughout the twentieth century (Lisabeth 2021, 92). Much of the unstated rationale behind the use of Strunk and White's style guide are the assumptions it made about what qualities constituted a literate American citizen in the Cold War era. As Laura Lisabeth explained, educational acceptance of *The Elements of Style* is directly connected to lobbying of Congress by the National Council of Teachers of English via *The National Interest and the Teaching of English* report, which argued for "English as a crucial site of American cultural stability" (Lisabeth 2021, 94). Arguments for cultural norms might have found a sympathetic ear at the time (and Congress did provide additional funding in 1962), but they were also rationales for the extension of current-traditional pedagogy and white language supremacy, a strategy that was, and continues to be, a tool to maintain social and racial hierarchies.

Nearly all technical writing textbooks of this time emphasized adherence to SWE even more stringently than composition textbooks. Strict adherence to SWE undeniably harmed students who had not been previously exposed to these linguistic and cultural expectations, and it forced, at best, a challenging code-switching exercise that left students demoralized about the many non-SWE dialects and styles in which they communicated. This practice has long created emotional, psychological, and material harm in students, especially when they have been penalized, failed, or rejected as not literate, based on SWE expectations, in technical communication writing contexts where white language supremacy, and a falsely nonideological belief in objective language, has been enforced.

Most technical writing teachers of the time saw the technical writing classroom as a largely neutral space, one where the focus on precise language construction and adherence in descriptive writing and naïve realism were dominant. This belief functioned in concert with strict SWE style guides, but it was also bolstered by the long-standing vocational focus in technical writing courses and impacted by the manner in which English departments taught technical writing. In part because technical writing teachers were more likely to be staffed by contingent faculty—early career faculty, limited term instructors, or graduate students—they were functionally controlled by literature-dominant forces within their own departments. As a result the teaching and research of technical writing was stunted. Technical writing courses were seen as practical, vocational exercises in precise SWE writing, but not courses that contributed to students' humanistic growth. As Miller (1979) argued, "Technical writing as it is commonly taught is shot through with positivist assumptions, which destroy its aspirations toward disciplinary respectability and relegates it to its status as a skills course" (613). The combination of a lack of disciplinary formation, academic devaluation, and pressures from other academic stakeholders led to vocationalism instead of an ideological and epistemological exploration. This positioning also led to the popularization of abstract quantitative models for writing, including Claude Shannon and Warren Weaver's mathematical approach to communication and Rudolf Flesch's "scientific rhetoric" for writing, a staggeringly popular method that led to numerous popular-press books, textbooks, and the "objective" formations of valuation like the Flesch-Kincaid reading test.

This positivist lean in technical writing also facilitated a new form of apologia present in many technical writing textbooks. Following from earlier exhortations justifying technical writing via industry, these apologia looked explicitly toward modern industry for justification. Kynell-Hunt mentioned that different textbooks of the postwar era based their textbook materials on just these American industrial assumptions. Gordon Mills and John Walter's popular *Technical Writing* (1954) explained to students that it "was based on a comprehensive survey of over 300 writing situations in industry" and James Souther's *Technical Report Writing* (1957) boasted of being justified by how it was based upon writing processes done at IBM, GE, and Westinghouse (Kynell-Hunt 2000, 105). The trade-off for this justification for the field was an indebtedness to industry, and likewise the adoption of an ethos from corporations—corporations that were aggressively placing huge amounts of risk on underrepresented minorities, the poor, and vulnerable ecosystems. Examples of industry orientations toward environmental risk abound: IBM was staggeringly careless in handling of cancerous solvents, including trichloroethylene; GE was largely responsible for increasing the Hudson River's toxicity throughout the 1950s; Westinghouse dumped toxic PCB-laced oil in landfills. Technical communication, caught in a milieu of utility, became indebted to twentieth-century Western industrialization and the configurations of risk that emerged from those same locations.

Perhaps the most damning indictment of technical writing in twentieth-century America may come from its tacit support of the military-industrial complex. Richard Ohmann, in *English in America: A Radical View of the Profession* (1976), argued that writing had been taught in a manner that sustained capitalism, Western imperialism, militaristic thinking, and the same logics used to support the Vietnam War. Ohmann claimed that regardless of the sympathies of educators, and their "esthetic contempt for the language of businessmen, bureaucrats, advertisers," writing courses were "framed in response to the needs of the industrial estate and its governing class" (94). The writing that took place in writing classrooms, Ohmann argued, was emblematic of the same thinking happening in boardrooms and war rooms:

> Organizing information, drawing conclusions from it, making reports, using Standard English (i.e., the language of the bourgeois elites), solving problems (assignments), keeping one's audience in mind, seeking objectivity and detachment, conducting persuasive arguments, reading either quickly or closely, as circumstances demand, producing work on request and under pressure, valuing the intellect and its achievements. These are all abilities that are clearly useful to the new industrial state, and, to the extent that English departments nourish them—even if only through the agency of graduate assistants—they are giving value for society's money. . . . It is enough that both the skills (fluency, organization, analysis) and the attitudes (caution, detachment, cooperation) that we encourage in the young are essential to the technostructure and to the smooth functioning of liberal (not liberated) society. (301–2)

In Cold War American education, Ohmann accused writing courses of teaching students to become unthinking bureaucrats.

For Ohmann, writing students were trained in abstract problem-solving activities, and he described how memoranda were the main form in which this writing and thinking occurred. He argued that memo-based writing encouraged students to abstract reality, determine a future that relates to the writer's own interests, and connect that abstraction to a future state via one or more clearly demarcated acts. Because of the "severe technical restrictions it lays on argument, [the memo] makes people into elements of the problem, to be manipulated conceptually as well as physically. It abstracts them in strange and repellent ways." (202). Problem-solving writing of this sort, Ohmann claimed, is complicit in seeing the world as a problem to be solved. He eloquently argued that "as soon as you identify a situation as a problem you have endorsed the perspective from which it is problematic" (315). However, while problem-solving was undoubtedly taught in composition courses, memo-driven problem solving was even more firmly established within technical writing courses (205–6). The real object of Ohmann's disgust, whether he realized it or not, was *technical writing*, not composition. Ohman's thoughts on writing were indicative of the unwitting pact that technical writing had formed with industry throughout the twentieth century—from racist assumptions built into technical writing textbooks and skill-and-drill current-traditional pedagogy to alignments with Western capitalism.

Ohmann ended his wide-ranging critique of writing instruction in higher education with a startlingly prescient argument about the environmental impacts of abstract positivism. Highlighting the dominance of Western capitalism, he argued that extractive industries are likely to "destroy human lungs or human society in time," and without better planning, humanity "will make little headway toward maintaining civilized life into the 21st century" (308). To demonstrate the problems of memo-based abstract problem-solving, Ohmann offered the example of the Santa Barbara oil spill—the largest oil spill in the US at the time (and still the third largest). In 1969, a Union Oil offshore oil field platform had partially exploded, spilling roughly 100,000 barrels into the waters off the coast of Santa Barbara County, fouling the water, killing wildlife, and highlighting the extremely substandard oil cleanup abilities of public and private industry (this oil spill also contributed to the naming of Earth Day in 1970). Ohmann related that the deputy attorney general of California expressed his frustration over the lack of assistance from university experts, complaining that they "all seem to be working on grants from the oil industry" (326). One Berkeley professor confirmed he was an industry-aligned, (falsely) ideologically neutral, vocationally focused professional, and explained that his "interest is serving the petroleum industry.

I view my obligation to the community as supplying it with well-trained petroleum engineers' " (326–27).

Divested from Risk: Technical Communication as a Research Field (1980 to 2010s)

Toward the end of the twentieth century, the teaching of technical writing in American colleges and universities became more firmly established. One survey noted that by 1973 about a third of all English departments in the US were offering at least one technical writing course, and by 1976 nineteen institutions offered academic degrees in technical communication (Brereton 1989). Also by the 1970s, four technical communication journals were publishing articles (*IEEE Transactions on Professional Communication*, *Technical Communication*, the *Technical Writing Teacher*, and the *Journal of Technical Writing and Communication*), the field had sprouted an academic professional society (the Association of Teachers of Technical Writing), and created a major professional organization (the Society for Technical Communication). However, the conversation within these spaces was not initially focused on research—at least not critical, self-reflective research that explored questions central to the theory and practice of technical communication. Up to this era, journals mostly contained "articles by nonacademics and consisted largely of tips, teaching pointers and other forms of what [Stephen] North classified as 'lore' " (Werry 2001, n.p.). Regardless, in the academy, technical communication was developing into a humanities (or at least a humanities-adjacent) discipline, after roughly a century of focus on pedagogy in service of industry.

The shift toward research in academic technical communication circles had been slowly building. For instance, Janice Redish's work was a research-oriented touchstone (certainly her founding of the Document Design Centre at the American Institutes for Research in 1979 is significant), but the field grappled with exactly what orientation it would take in a series of articles in the pages of *College English*. Carolyn Miller's "A Humanistic Rationale for Technical Writing" argued that the dominant models of how we teach and think about technical writing are often based upon positivist, aggressively pragmatic, and industry-oriented assumptions that will "destroy [technical writing's] aspirations toward disciplinary respectability and relegate it to its status [to a] skills course" (Miller 1979, 613). Miller argued against a naïve realist "windowpane" view of knowledge where rhetoric is told to get out of the way of the production of objective reality. By pointing out that a positivist view of science "is no longer held by most philosophers of science or by most thoughtful scientists," Miller demonstrated that "facts do not exist independently, waiting to be found and collected and systematized; facts are human constructions which presuppose theories. We bring to the world a set of innate and learned concepts which help us select, organize, and understand what we encounter" (1979, 615). Following this logic, Miller asserted that technical and scientific writing could be humanistic, especially if we "ground our teaching and our discipline in a communal rationality rather than in contextless logic" (1979, 617). Over time, numerous scholars—and nearly the entire academic field of technical communication in the US—would come to agree with Miller's stance.

However, when they were voiced, Miller's perspective on a complex, humanities-oriented technical writing course was immediately attacked. Elizabeth Tebeaux argued that "the point of view of the business and industrial world of which the student will become a part is the *only criterion* which should be used to plan and teach the course" (1980, 823 emphasis ours). Tebeaux believed "what an English professor thinks should be included in technical writing is not important. The requirements of the real world and the departments whose students take the course should determine what is taught" (1980, 824). Here, Tebeaux was not alone (see Mitchell 1976; Smith 1985; Pinelli 1985; Carliner 1995; Moore 1997), but the argument that the teaching of technical writing had no innate rhetorical, ethical, or humanistic responsibility had been largely dismissed by the mid-1990s. Tebeaux's perspective was ultimately rooted in the previous era of technical communication, and similar to Mitchell (1976), who had argued that technical writing instructors should indoctrinate "students in the forms appropriate to their employers," because "students know they must dance with the guy that brung them, and they elect our courses to learn his dance steps" (1976, 5). There may be no clearer representation of a sexist, slavish industry devotion.

Precipitated by a century of educational frustrations, the field evolved toward an approach that had been clearly voiced by Miller—that modern technical writing is a form of social action, a praxis that equips students with both technical writing ability and a sense of how writing interacts with power. Throughout this era of technical communication, the field became increasingly self-reflective about its ethical positioning in relation to the industry connections it had fostered over the previous century. Additional calls for humanistic forms of technical communication came from Dale

Sullivan, who lamented the paradox faced by many technical writing teachers as they taught styles and genres that allowed students entrance into industry, but likewise wanted to push them "to responsible social action" (1990, 377). Similarly, Carl Herndl asked how TPC could turn from a field that too often "described the production of meaning but not the social, political and economic sources of power, which authorize this production" (1993, 351), and Paul Dombrowski explained that the field's additional attention to humanism in technical writing was simply "the growing recognition of previously unacknowledged aspects of what has always been there" (1994, 4). This era of technical communication attempted to avoid the recent mistakes of the twentieth century, and rejected the calls for increased focus on the demands of industry, an orientation where TPC had been indebted to capitalist, industry-based assumptions, and its associated risks, for disciplinary validation.

Since the 1980s, *most* perspectives on academic technical communication have focused on expanding technical communication, broadening the methods and practices that we teach students, developing relationships between technical communication and critical theory, performing histories of our field, offering a critical lens through which we can view technical communication practices, engaging with risk communication and theory, and laying an ethical foundation for the teaching and research of technical communication. These last two areas of study would take center stage, and questions of ethics would expand (though codes of ethics had existed for some time; see Hamlett 1956), perhaps best represented by Steven Katz's "The Ethic of Expediency: Classical Rhetoric, Technology, and the Holocaust" (1992) and Paul Dombrowski's *Ethics in Technical Communication* (2000). TPC was forming a more robust critical, humanist, and ethical foundation, and in doing so, was also pushing back against the industry-oriented rationales for its existence.

However, around the same time that TPC was formulating its humanist foundations, the political climate in the US began changing, especially concerning environmental and occupational health and safety laws. Notable environmental success was achieved in the 1970s, with the National Environmental Policy Act (NEPA), the formation of the Environmental Protection Agency (EPA), the Mine Safety and Health Act (MSHA), the Clean Air Act amendments, the Clean Water Act, and the Comprehensive Environmental Response, Compensation, and Liability Act (CERCLA). Still, these successes were juxtaposed to environmental and industrial disasters, such as the Times Beach Dioxin Spill, the Seveso disaster, Love Canal, the

Willow Island cooling tower collapse, Three Mile Island, the Warren County PCB landfill, Bhopal, and Chernobyl, among others. Amid these visible environmental and public health disasters, President Reagan's conservative government began defunding federal environmental oversight and dismantling occupational health and safety laws. Reagan, influenced by the conservative Heritage Foundation's *Mandate for Leadership* report, cut the EPA's budget by three million dollars (Omnibus Budget Reconciliation Act), and, just to add insult to injury, pulled President Carter's solar panels from the White House roof. Reagan's presidency was a concerted effort to remove corporate regulatory restrictions and implement cost-based analyses or Christian ethical mandates to justify all regulations.

Technical communication researchers and teachers were well aware of these contradictions. While the energy, chemical, and industrial sectors experienced significant, high-profile disasters that led to environmental and public health impacts, the environmental and workplace protections gained in the previous decade were either being rolled back or made ineffective via conservative government actions that protected corporate interests over ecology or public health. Within this growing awareness, Reagan did "little to enforce existing laws and had no interest in giving support to environmentalists who called on the government to do more to combat issues such as pollution, acid rain, or toxic waste" (Kruse and Zelizer 2019, 179–80). Environmental justice, as both a community movement and an academic concern, developed in the US following protests over the PCB landfill in Warren County, NC—and other protests exposed the cruel conditions of environmental risk people were being forced to endure. TPC's response to this era occurred alongside the emergence of TPC as an academic field with its own research agenda and the development of methods, theories, and values—the same ones that confounded Tebeaux and that she would call "selfish" (in a now-retracted article) for not being adherent to the desires of industry.

Perhaps most importantly, TPC's dominant understanding of risk and risk communication emerged from this same era, with the first studies on risk emerging in the 1990s (see: Mirel 1994; Katz and Miller 1996; Grabill and Simmons 1998). According to Leiss (1996), risk communication was also awakening from an era (1975–1984) in which risk analysts were "openly contemptuous" about the public's beliefs about risk and risk taking (89) and now realizing that risk was a rhetorical act. This era of risk communication research (roughly 1985–1994) acknowledged that "statements about risk situations ought to be regarded as acts of persuasive communication, that is, as messages intended to persuade a listener of the correctness of a point of view" (89). TPC scholars, likewise influenced by these same historical trends, but working hard to establish the credibility of TPC as a research field, would incorporate some concepts from risk communication, though not fully.

TPC's lack of deep engagement with risk communication was largely due to the historical circumstances: because of their attention to neoliberal deregulation, accompanied by notable environmental disasters, TPC connected to Foucauldian critiques of institutional power, but missed opportunities to engage with both risk communication (as a field of practice) and broader social and structural conceptions of risk. In practice, this meant that many of the events technical communicators studied throughout this era are of a certain kind. Almost all are article-length case studies of recent environmental or industrial disasters (Beverly Sauer's book-length work stands out here), where risk could be analyzed from the perspective of hindsight, and where risk communication was subsumed into the logics and concerns of TPC (exactly what a developing field of study, looking to consolidate its position in the academy and stabilize its critical methodology, would do). This work, *which was deeply insightful and valuable*, developed as a means to distance the field from the previous era, where TPC was strongly connected to industries and institutions.

In chapter 1, we explained additional context for TPC's response to these historical circumstances, noting how Grabill and Simmons's (1998) article on the social construction of risk set the tone for much of the critical work that would come thereafter. Their work focused on local conditions and community settings and responded to technocratic abuses and environmental disasters with humanist-influenced, rhetorical critiques of institutional power. We also explained how insights into institutional configurations of risk gave TPC scholars the ability to examine how power was wielded by influential organizations, albeit at the expense of the additional ability to employ insights from the closely adjacent field of risk communication (see Mirel 1994; Reamer 2015). Explaining how TPC's response to the *Challenger* disaster is fairly emblematic of the field's considerations of risk, we described this response as occurring primarily via article-length case studies, analyses of communication and miscommunication, and articulations of how the TPC methodologies could have been used (and could be revised) by technical communicators to avoid calamity.

We can clearly identify this transitional moment for TPC in a specific study—James Paradis, David Dobrin, and Richard Miller's oft-cited ethnographic account of technical writing among researchers and writers at Exxon. They studied the typically tacit writing activities of thirty-three research and development engineers and scientists to answer how they wrote internal materials and discovered that companies like Exxon could improve their in-house writing education, develop better mentoring, and improve their editorial cycle. Their article is often seen as the first in the field to document how writing in the workplace could serve purposes beyond "information transfer," such as "establishing accountability, managing employees and work processes, and strengthening the social network" (Read 2019, 235). In the mid-1980s, the work of Paradis and his colleagues was fairly revolutionary for a field that was starting to determine its own research methods and learn how to generate verifiable knowledge about writing in technical environments. The study was therefore rather emblematic of TPC in transition—an empirically robust ethnographic account of how a closed system created knowledge through writing and how writing activities created meaning beyond simple communicative goals.

Paradis et al.'s study straddled two eras of technical writing; it was both an extension of the industry-aligned TPC of the era mentioned above—that which is indebted to industry for its existence—and an extension of the era marked by increasing attention to rhetoric, humanism, and ethical analysis. Connections to the first era are clear in the framework for the study. Their article is likewise reflective of a field locating its own research approaches, yet Paradis et al. had access to the Exxon Corporation's research and development teams and were provided with travel, expenses, and company time; they explicitly thank Exxon for such funds and access in the acknowledgments. They're indebted to this extractive corporation.

Dobrin would later disavow the results of the article, calling them false generalizations created to contribute to an emergent field of study. "In retrospect," Dobrin explained, "I wish we had been able to write a different report, one more true to the facts. . . . The interest of such a report would not be that it contributed new specialized knowledge to a discipline. . . . It would be a confession that our knowledge about technical writing or business writing is quintessentially localized" (Dobrin 1987, 7). Dobrin identified how this landmark study was an explicit attempt to contribute to a field moving from one concerned only with teaching to one with a developing research corpus. Paradis et al.'s study (1985) would be unthinkable today, primarily because of their lack of acknowledgment that Exxon perpetrated decades of disproportionate levels of harm to people and environments. For example, Paradis et al. failed to mention that when they visited Baton

Rouge for their study, Exxon was still doing business in apartheid South Africa, and would continue to do so for another two years after the study was published (Potts 1986). The chemicals that the research and development team at Exxon was developing—phthalate esters, which are used to manufacture polyvinyl chloride—are also not critiqued (Paradis et al. 1985, 282). Phthalates are endocrine disruptors that have been linked to a wide range of major health risks (Giulivo et al. 2016), including attention deficit hyperactivity disorder, endometriosis, fibroids, obesity, and death (Trasande et al. 2016). Even at the time of the Paradis et al. study, phthalates were known to cause negative environmental impacts (Wolfe et al. 1980) and human health effects (see National Toxicology Program 1981; Ganning et al. 1984; Nielsen et al. 1985), and their danger had been suspected at least since 1953 (Carpenter et al. 1953).

Moreover, Paradis et al. overlooked the staggering environmental racism in Louisiana, where the Exxon plant was located. While broader information about what would become known as "cancer alley" was still developing at the time, there was clear evidence in research journals, much of it published by Marise S. Gottlieb, a public health researcher, throughout the 1970s and '80s (1980). By 1985, links between the petroleum industry in Louisiana and cancer in underrepresented minority populations would have been evident. It had been clear enough by 1988 to inspire residents to hold the Great Louisiana Toxics March from Baton Rouge to New Orleans. Earlier in the year, the *LA Times* explained the situation quite simply: "The air, ground and water along this corridor are so full of carcinogens, mutagens and embryotoxins that an environmental-health specialist defined living here as 'a massive human experiment,' the state attorney general called the pollution "a modern form of barbarism," and a chemical-union leader now refers to it as 'the national sacrifice zone' " (Maraniss and Weiskopf 1988). There are no references to any environmental, human health, or race-based decisions about industrial pollution in Paradis et al.'s article.

Ultimately, the lack of references to the many risks that are irreconcilably part of Exxon's research and development further positions the Paradis et al. article as one firmly rooted within the transition—between TPC's indebtedness to industry and need to create its own research methods. However, their article represents neither a field self-reflectively divesting from its previous industrial collusions, nor one critically engaging with industrial disasters. Of course, our critique of Paradis et al. is in some senses unfair. Can we hold this article accountable for failing to include information on risk any more than we can hold it accountable for not knowing that Exxon researchers knew about global warming as far back as 1977 (Hall 2015) or that their safety rules would be so lax as to eventually lead to the Valdez oil spill? In some ways, the answer is no, we cannot hold researchers accountable for paradigm changes that would eventually emerge in a disciplinary arena. However, our point is that this study could never be completed in this same way by anyone in TPC today, largely because of these forms of risk involved, which should be obvious to anyone even considering this work. To fail to do so now, we argue, would be an ethical failing.

Implications: Confronting the History of Risk in TPC

In this chapter, we've attempted to describe some of the dominant historical relationships between technical communication and risk, focusing on employing a diachronic, pan-historiographic approach. This approach refuses a complete, scholastic view of technical and professional communication, but instead offers us glimpses into major historical and cultural moments that brought technical communication into, alongside of, or against various regimes of power—and traces its strong and lasting connections to extractive industries.

- The first era described TPC as embedded with colonial and imperial formations of power that made risk manifest against certain peoples and environments.
- The second located TPC as indebted to power and risk, as the justification for teaching TPC was made via connections to industrial capitalism.
- The third era showcased attempts to divest TPC from the structures that govern who and what is placed at greatest risk of harm, and while not fully successful, is certainly ongoing.

In the later era, TPC researchers and teachers have worked to distance themselves from these systems of exploitation and incorporate a social construction of risk that could emphasize the power of local communities and empower people. Each of these historical eras provides us with an opportunity to identify where our existing attention to the historical details of our field has missed substantive connections to extractive and exploitative nation-states and industries.

Ultimately, TPC needs to confront this contentious history if it is to continue doing the work of aligning with the tenets of social justice. Without, as Cecilia D. Shelton and Sarah Warren-Riley explained, "naming the Consequences of the Historical Desire for Power and Legitimacy," our field cannot fully move on and adequately address ongoing power imbalances (2022, 7). We are attempting, via an historiographic approach and through a diachronic narrative, to move toward "the task of discovering . . . the available means of constructing better social worlds" (Russell and Babrow 2011, 256). We also take seriously those who have already highlighted connections between TPC and hegemonic power—Scott, Longo, and Wills (2006) among others—and this chapter has worked to even more fully excavate those relationships. Our goal in doing this history has been to undermine one specific set of relations that connect TPC and articulations of risk. The history of TPC accompanies a history of human and environmental exploitation, though we blame no individual technical or professional communicator for their role in these historical power formations. Likewise, our history is not fully "owned" by those in academia, insofar as the field of TPC has been a long-standing practice and profession far longer than it has been a teaching field or an academic discipline. Because we don't control this past, we assertively recognize the necessity of excavating relationships that proliferated in the history of TPC, especially when those relationships undermine the coherence that many have sought in our current-day discipline.

In chapter 1, we defined risk as "the unequal distribution of the likelihood of harm" and we self-consciously articulated risk in such a way to connect the study of risk by technical and professional communicators with an orientation toward social justice. Defining risk in this way allows for additional questions from those who study risk and risk communication, namely questions concerning how power is implicated in the distribution of harm. Questions relating to power are perhaps the most significant, and our approach to the history of our field showcases how risk, power, and the communication of that risk have led to the critical and social justice turns presently informing the theory and practice of TPC (Simmons 2007; Haas and Eble 2018; Walton, Moore, and Jones 2019; Haas and Frost 2017). The following chapter will build upon these historical connections and locate the applicability of both structural violence and considerations of scope and scale for theorizing an approach to doing risk communication work in TPC.

Chapter Three

Moving Beyond the Industrial Present in Risk Communication

Rethinking Models and Methodology

> Many of my colleagues at EPA, along with the rest of the developed world, think we're mad to try this. Some countries are angry at us because they are certain they are going to be dragged in behind us and will have to wrestle with their publics as we are with ours.
>
> —William D. Ruckelshaus, former administrator, US Environmental Protection Agency (EPA), 1986

The epigraph above comes from the first ever National Conference on Risk Communication. Ruckelshaus was well known for including public voices in conversations about risk, most notably for his work in Tacoma, Washington, which incorporated the community within decision-making processes about air pollution from a smelter. His language of "wrestling" with the public exemplifies the themes explored at this event, which related to empowering the public to advocate for themselves and giving the power, so to speak, back to the public in policy decision-making pertaining to risks, including but not limited to cardiovascular disease, hazardous waste siting, nuclear energy, and ethylene dibromide (EDB). Situated in an ethos of public advocacy, this dialogic push was inherently a rhetorical move and reminds us that previous work in risk communication was not always steeped in information deficit models, but that communicators, all the way up to the EPA, believed in the importance of public perspectives on risk decision-making.

In this chapter, we provide an overview of industrial and governmental models of risk communication, highlight variances between models, and describe the rhetorical features of the models—which are, perhaps, more rhetorical than our field has recognized. Despite this positive reframing, we posit that a major limitation of these models is their narrow focus on the "industrial/historical past" or "present." As such, we explain that mainstream, industrial, and governmental models of risk communication, by focusing on hazard probability in a region, organization, or event, while useful and indeed rhetorically savvy, illustrate the problem of scope and scale we discussed in chapters 1 and 2. We argue that conceptions of risk that do not take into account both the history of inequality and the scope of injustice—for people and ecosystems—apprehend but a portion of risk. Thereafter, we offer a methodological frame that expands our conception of risk. This methodology draws from Beck's (1992) historicization of risk, Haas and Frost's (2017) apparent decolonial feminist rhetoric of risk, scale theory as it emerged from ecology (Levin 1992) and evolutionary biology (Chave 2013), and theories of structural violence from Fanon ([1961] 2004), Galtung (1969), Farmer (2006), Berlant (2007), Yusoff (2012), and Nixon (2013). The result is an approach that can be applied to the research and practice of risk assessment, communication, and management in technical and professional communication. Specifically, in this chapter we articulate a scalar model for methodologically framing studies of risk in TPC before we apply the approach to three cases in chapters 4, 5, and 6.

The Field of Risk Communication

For TPC to move toward more justice-oriented approaches to risk, we argue that it must first wrestle with the affordances and limitations of existing industrial models of risk. The first section of this chapter details the contours of mainstream models of risk communication—models established in the arenas of government, industry, political science, and risk analysis and management. We do this because, first, the field of TPC has not adequately grappled with the contributions in these arenas and has too often dismissed existing models. Not enough work from within TPC has engaged with risk communication, nor has it adequately addressed the work that risk communication practitioners perform. While TPC has castigated many industrial models for promulgating an "information deficit" approach, many of these existing models are unabashedly dialogic, consider the distribution of harm, address trust and credibility in perception-based and nontechnocratic ways, and are far more rhetorical and audience-centric than our field has acknowledged. Certainly, these models have limitations, as approaches within TPC do, since they have similarly emphasized perspectives that privilege work within a particular scope or rhetorical feature, like ethos or audience, at the expense of others.

Put simply: our application of scale as a concept does not work as effectively unless we adequately demonstrate *how* current models outside our field do in fact focus on the industrial/historical past or present. Certainly, there is a disconnect between TPC researchers writing the history of TPC and the origins or formations of risk and risk communication about which they could be more aware. But the reasons for this disconnect have as much to do with the development of various academic disciplines as they do with historical neglect. In this section, we explore models of risk communication (and their associated conceptions of risk) outside the field of TPC.

History and Evolution of Risk Communication

On January 29, 1986, over five hundred risk communication practitioners met in Washington, DC, for the National Conference on Risk Communication—the first of its kind, as the attendees understood it. At that point, many risk communication professionals had been acting alone at their organization or agency, as risk communication hadn't yet assembled as a cohesive field of study or practice. The Conservation Foundation (a non-profit research and communications organization dedicated to encouraging human conduct to sustain and enrich life on earth, which did not engage in political lobbying and eventually merged into the World Wildlife Fund in 1990) was the primary sponsor of the event and published proceedings a year later (Davies et al. 1987). In these proceedings we note *three* key observations in terms of how the meeting and its exigencies were framed.

In the introductory remarks to the conference, J. Clarence Davies, a representative of the Conservation Foundation, crafted the exigence for the event as the widespread recognition of risk communication as an important subject. In doing so, he acknowledged the corollary that the event would not cover risk assessment. He explained: "If we begin talking about that, then we are doing the wrong thing and we'll be off on a different subject. . . . What we want to focus on here is the process of trying to communicate risks, not the evaluation of risks" (Davies et al., 1–2). Attempting some field-building, Davies cordoned off assessment from communication. The separation of risk assessment from risk communication, lamented in our own early field-building, might have emerged because we were arguing for a spot at the table with communication specialists. For example, Grabill and Simmons (1998) argued that "the failure to see risk as socially constructed leads to an artificial separation of risk assessment from risk communication. This separation can lead to unethical and oppressive risk communication practices because the public is separated from fundamental risk decision making processes" (416). The public and the communicators of risk are intimately involved in the assessment of risk, but the early events that brought scholars and practitioners together required more separation in order to leave space for an exclusive focus on communication processes and practices. This trade-off was not a failure to see risk as socially constructed, but a concerted effort to focus energies on the communicative practices to engage in field-building.

The second observation is starker. William Ruckelshaus, a longtime administrator at the EPA, framed in his opening remarks at the National Conference on Risk Communication the effective communication of risk as a "take-back of power" (1987, 5) after the unsettling and trust-eroding eras of the Vietnam War and Watergate: "The public response to these two national traumas," Ruckelshaus explained, "was to take back power that had been delegated to the government" (4). This move to share power between the government and the American people was described as part of a participation in the management of risk and the larger structure from which risk communication would emerge. At this time Ruckelshaus, and others, fought tooth and nail for the right to include the public in dialogue about risks to their livelihoods, but in turn expected a steady commitment, and appealed to citizenship to do so, because "the bottom line is forcing the public to be responsive to the real issues. The public must then ultimately take the responsibility for the decision that is finally made. The public can't have it both ways" (8). Taking back the power, so to speak, came with a rather clear-throated expectation of consistent, diligent, and informed citizen participation. Early approaches to risk communication, however institutionalized, fought for dialogic participation and conceived of the public not just as an audience to clarify science *to* but rather an informed force to be reckoned *with*.

Our third observation builds on the above as it concerns our shared belief in the primacy of audience. The majority of the proceedings were case studies, and ranged in topics from cardiovascular diseases to hazardous waste siting to EDB. Ruckelshaus noted that "we" (read: regulators in the federal government) had learned that it is "crucial to start with the raw material[s, which are,] in this case, public attitudes towards what we are talking about. If we don't start with an understanding of the view of the receptor, we are doomed to failure" (3). Ruckelshaus explained that the American people think of risk as "micro risk," while the EPA administrator framed risk as "macro risk." While still hierarchical, Ruckelshaus made unprecedented efforts to foreground audience in the risk communication process and made an unprecedented effort to involve the Tacoma, Washington community in the decision-making process about what to do with arsenic air pollution standards to impose on a smelter owned by the ASARCO mining corporation (6).

Why share so much discourse by Ruckelshaus? This EPA keynote came about around the same time the field of risk communication was solidifying into a research discipline. Risk communication seems to have arrived somewhere in the 1980s, as the term "risk communication" first appeared in relation to an academic field and an industry practice in 1986 (Leiss 1996, 86). In their history of risk communication, Alonzo Plough and Sheldon Krimsky (1987, 4) explain there are few mentions of the term until the mid-1980s, but they acknowledge that the broader concept of risk communication emerged from public health assessments and military risk assessment strategies in the twentieth century; and they also note the foundational work the EPA did in advancing risk communication, specifically Ruckelshaus's promotion of risk communication (3). Plough and Krimsky write that risk assessment achieved greater support in the US stemming from the National Environmental Policy Act (1970), the Occupational Safety and Health Act (1970), and the subsequent Occupational Safety and Health Administration (OSHA) Hazard Communication Standard regulation of 1983, when risk evaluation was made an official part of numerous practices. Since then, they argue, risk communication has been primarily concerned with the tensions between public risk perception and expert risk assessment and management.

William Leiss's (1996) own history of the field of risk communication articulated three main paradigms in the brief history of modern risk communication. Phase 1 (about 1975 to 1984) stressed quantitative expressions of risk. Phase 2 (about 1985 to 1994) emphasized that risk communication, like all communication, was a rhetorical act, taking place in a particular context. The first phase indicates a focus on risk as the outcome of "objective," "expert" risk assessment processes, whereas "lay" perspectives were considered "subjective and irrational" and where a deficit model was most likely dominant (Balog-Way et al. 2020). The second phase considered how "risk began to be widely recognized as a social construct" and where social, cultural, or psychological influences could be identified (Balog-Way et al. 2020). Phase 3, where Leiss historically located the field at the time of his writing, was "characterized by an emphasis on social context, that is, on the social interrelations between the players in the game of risk management" (90). Such a history also aligns with Robert Heath and H. Dan O'Hair's summary of risk communication (itself borrowed from Hadden 1989): an "old" version where risk communication had been impeded by risk perception, and a "new" version where dialogue has been meaningfully engaged by institutions and involved parties and where institutional barriers stand in the way of such efforts (2009, 12).

Other histories, such as Roger E. Kasperson and Pieter Jan Stallen's (1991), took a comparative approach to the history of risk, positioning the emergence of risk communication as an inevitability "as the United States discovered the limits of regulatory control over the seemingly unending parade of technological hazards," which made it "apparent that regulation was not a panacea for public and worker protection" (1). They historicized explicit interest in risk communication, as a political phenomenon, to the early 1950s, specifically the "Atoms for Peace" campaign that sought to study the potential negative response to the civil use of nuclear energy: "With the increase in commercial prospects of nuclear power, the interest of researchers [shifted] to the response of opponents exclusively, as the opposition [became] more and more seen as the deviant response" (3). In discovering the complex psychological factors taken into account by the public, Kasperson and Stallen (1991) argued that the

> rush to risk communication strategies in the United States (and increasingly Europe) has proceeded as if risk communication were born *au nouveau*. In the United States, risk communication fit the temper of the times; it has been a preferred strategy for a political conservatism during the Reagan years that sought to minimize safety and health regulation during the 1980s. A number of governmental and industry bench-marks [for example: ambitious programs by the chemical industry after the Bhopal accident; SARA (Superfund Amendments and Reauthorization Act) Title 3 amendments in the U.S. requiring chemical plants to disclose emissions to the public; and the publication of the UNEP (United Nations Environment Program) handbook "Awareness

> and Preparedness for Emergencies at the Local Level] indicates the rapid emergence of risk communication as a preferred form of risk management during this decade. (3)

Ultimately, they perceived the burgeoning of risk communication as a necessary complement to the limits of regulatory control. More cynical than Ruckelshaus, who framed risk communication movements as "taking back the power" from the government, Kasperson and Stallen contended that this shift in balance was less about power calibration and more about pragmatic necessity, more about an exigent response to intense deregulations. What's clear in the history of risk communication, however, is that many industry-oriented risk communication professionals have sought to consider rhetorical issues and attempted to understand the power of the public as influential stakeholders. Further, much of this theoretical and methodological framing was responding to historical and cultural events throughout the twentieth century.

Models and Approaches in Industry

The theorizing of risk described so far in no way constitutes a monolith. To understand the landscape of risk communication outside of TPC, we offer a modest overview (table 3.1) of the areas of risk communication to ensure consistency in language and stasis in our questions. The most notable and well-read risk communication handbook has likely been Regina E. Lundgren and Andrea H. McMakin's *Risk Communication: A Handbook for Communicating Environmental, Safety and Health Risks* (2018), now in its sixth edition with IEEE Press. The authors have covered the various principles, legal constraints and mandates, and best practices of communicating risks in a slew of settings but also, quite helpfully, have delineated the various approaches to communicating risk—which vary by field, purpose, and philosophy. In all, they identify fourteen distinct approaches to communicating risk, and we'll abstract them here. The first column, "Framework," and the third column, "Rhetorical Feature," are unique to us. By "Framework" we mean the larger operating philosophy driving the work of risk communication. In the "Rhetorical Feature" column we aim to showcase a core rhetorical component of the approach, something that scholars in our field could use to match the approach that might be appropriate for their own work. In doing so, we highlight the rhetorical features that TPC scholars would recognize and appreciate in existing models outside our field, where

Table 3.1. Various Models of Risk Communication

Framework	Approaches	Rhetorical Feature	Key Texts
Evolutionist	Extended Parallel Process Model	Fear and Denial: Humans assess hazard in terms of relevance to them; as it escalates and control decreases, humans control fear through denial or hostility instead of controlling the hazard.	Witte et al. (2001)
	Evolutionary Theory	Survival: How we evolved shapes how we perceive risk; natural selection resulted in people who valued fairness—humans are accustomed to negotiating different categories of risks in group settings.	Tucker and Ferson (2008)
Rationalist	Communication Process	Gestalt: Rational approach concerned with the interplay between all components of a communicative model (e.g., channel, receiver).	Sadar and Shull (2000)
	Three-Challenge	Structuralism: Challenges of knowledge, process, and communications skills are discrete in their characteristics and goals.	Rowan (1991)
	Crisis Communication	Pragmatism: Occurring in the face of sudden danger, predictable or not; only communicate what is needed to accomplish immediate goal.	Walaski (2011)
	Hazard Plus Outrage	Balance: Controversy emerges when the hazard (technical information) is not the same level as the outrage (public emotion). Centering the public's emotions is critical.	Sandman (1987)

Framework	Approaches	Rhetorical Feature	Key Texts
Constructionist	Social Constructionist	Values: Focuses on the bi-directional flow of technical information and values, beliefs, and emotions between scientists and the public.	Waddell (1995)
	Social Network Contagion	Conformity: Who audiences spend time with affects their views of the world; audiences adopt behaviors of their social networks.	Scherer and Cho (2003)
	Social Amplification of Risk	Consequences: Social activities amplify risks in unexpected ways. Anticipate secondary scenes of risk to avoid outrage.	Kasperson et al. (1988) Leiss and Powell (2004)
	Convergence Communication	Iteration: Long-term, culturally situated process where organization and audience cycle information back and forth until convergence.	Rogers and Kincaid (1981)
	National Research Council	Reciprocity: Risk communication is a process of disseminating scientific information and gathering public opinion in the earliest stages.	National Research Council (1989)
Cognitivist	Mental Models	Empiricism: Effective risk communication must be founded in careful empirical study of audiences' existing mental schemas.	Morgan et al. (2001)
	Mental Noise	Sensitivity: Understanding the threshold of technical cognition in stressful environments; messages should be simple and repeated.	Covello (2020)
	Social Trust	Ethos: Trust and credibility need to be established first; audiences will trust messages from institutions they understand and align with.	Cvetkovich et al. (2008)

considerations of scope and scale are already emergent, if not robust, and also where there is room to develop and expand upon these concepts.

Lundgren and McMakin framed their risk communication approaches as each having three types: care, consensus, or crisis. For example, there could be a care-based model for the "Hazard + Outrage" approach, or a crisis model for the "Social Trust" approach. This leaves a good deal of room to think about timing and scale for each approach—especially if one is thinking about crisis and immediacy within each of these approaches. As such, they don't divide risk from crisis. The *when* is secondary to the *how*. In terms of the three types, they defined each in turn, where care communication "is communication about risks for which the danger and the way to manage it have already been well determined through scientific research that is accepted by most of the audience" (4). Consensus communication helps groups with disparate perspectives work together, and crisis communication fits situations of more immediate threat (4–5). We might identify doxa, stasis, and kairos as the rhetorical concepts most fitting to care, consensus, and crisis, respectively.

Further, in these broad, "functional" categories, Lundgren and McMakin also created three topics (environmental, safety, and health) where care, consensus, and crisis purposes can be applied (3). For example, focusing on "the safe use of pesticides" is an example where care communication can be applied to an environmental issue (3). They acknowledged that the risks addressed by applying these communication approaches to different topics results in a risk communication tailored to a specific time and space, but many of their examples are firmly in the industrial/historical past or present. Of course, we would expect their examples to have such a focus, as those contexts are most directly applicable for industry.

Lundgren and McMakin created categories covering the bulk of accepted "textbook" methods for engaging in risk communication. One category is designed to make sense of risk via broadly "anthropological" approaches to risk, where conceptions of risk communication are based upon understandings of how all humans process information and emotion. The *evolutionary theory* approaches to risk communication emphasize human biological and psychological features that make us more or less susceptible to certain messages. The evolutionary theory risk communication method, perhaps uniquely, considers how human beings, as a species, have evolved "hardwired" traits that control how we share resources and avoid risk (20). Likewise, the *extended parallel process* approach assumes that all people will evaluate risk based on relevance and severity, before considering recommended actions.

In contrast to risk communication methods that take into account biological or evolutionary traits, others incorporate a more linear, "rational" process to communication itself, assuming that some features of risk communication should follow expected guidelines. These approaches are founded upon uncomplicated and directional communication models, and could be represented, for example, by how a "a regulatory agency (the source) may decide that a chemical poses an unacceptable risk to the public (the message) and issue a press release (the channel) published as a story by the news media (another channel) that is read by members of the local community (the receivers)" (12). Whether this *communication process* model has ever actually worked as intended (and it may have never done so), it is still quite common, as is the broad *three-challenge* model, in which risk communication can be broken down into challenges where the audience needs to understand the risk, feel involved, and then communicate well with those who hold knowledge about the risk. Many of the models named here assume knowledge about risk to be largely within the control of experts who need to determine the best way to overcome challenges presented by panic, human evolution, or lack of adherence to communication models. For these time-constrained situations, nuance and context have been less valued than rational expediency for the sake of minimizing harm. In this group we see *crisis communication*, perhaps most obviously, but additional audience-centric approaches to risk communication that attempt to address how messages spread among a community, but can be distinguished by whether they stress audience trust or emphasize detailed research into audience beliefs and ideologies. Of the former, we see the *hazard plus outrage* approach, in which "the audience's view of risk reflects not just the action (hazard) but what emotions they feel about the action (their outrage)" (17).

Social constructionist models, the ones that helped initiate TPC's integration of risk communication, disrupt the neat binary between experts and nonexpert publics and stakeholders. In these models, the goal is to facilitate the exchange of knowledge so that the cultural values of the scientific community are placed in context and the technical knowledge of the public can be incorporated into a risk communication context. Also heavily focused on social context is the *social network contagion* approach, which, despite its unappealing name, refers to how explicit and implicit influences from one's social network can impact attitudes and behaviors toward risk. Likewise, the *social amplification* approach holds that social activities can impact risk communication situations in unexpected ways. When there's a lack of expert-oriented risk information, for example, other information sources, sometimes promoting misinformation, can fill the void (19). Some risk communication approaches emphasize risk to the extent that responding to audiences, or providing specialized messages to different kinds of audiences, becomes the goal of research. The *National Research Council* approach is perhaps the oldest of these, and considers social context, typically by involving "audience feedback before and after risk information is distributed" (13). Also crossing over with the models that emphasize the complexity of cultural issues is the *convergence communication* approach to risk communication, which assumes that the back-and-forth of messages about risk between experts and publics eventually converge into a kind of stasis. This model avoids being simply an experts versus stakeholders standoff because continuous feedback and interpretation of audience responses is part of the dialogue.

The framework we have termed "cognitivist" includes approaches that involve more robust forms of audience research alongside an intensive conception of how people process thoughts and emotions. Included here is the popular *mental models* approach, which investigates what segment of the population will be targeted with risk communication messages, and then identifies the concerns, beliefs, lifestyles, and psychological characteristics of that specific audience. Similarly, the *social trust approach* is bolstered by social science research and considers the kinds of institutions that people believe in and how, when confronted by risk, they lean toward existing structures they trust. Also included in a cognitivist structure is the *mental noise* approach, which focuses on the human ability to comprehend and retain information when under duress. Cognitivist risk communication models also work well in time-constrained communication contexts and can be said to function alongside crisis communication approaches.

All of these risk communication approaches are rhetorical, though each grouping emphasizes different rhetorical features. Some focus on the significance of right timing and kairos, some consider embodied biological or psychological traits, others address audience trust in institutions, while still others place emotion, affect, and interpersonal relationships at the center of risk communication efforts.

Further, it should be noted that the categories provided by Lundgren and McMakin are by no means exhaustive. For example, Paul Slovic (2010) helped cultivate the theoretical framework called "risk as feelings." Feelings serve as an important cue for risk/benefits judgments and decisions; cognitive methods that are part of the "psychometric paradigm" are used to gauge this "affect heuristic" (xxv). This framework has borrowed heavily from psychological research and "assumes that risk is subjectively defined by individuals who may be influenced by a wide array of psychological, social, institutional and cultural factors. The paradigm assumes that, with appropriate design of survey instruments, many of these factors and their interrelationships can be quantified and modelled in order to illuminate the responses of individuals and their societies to the hazards that confront them" (xxv). While connected to Peter Sandman's (1993) "risk = hazard + outrage" model that focused on affect and emotion, and the work done in the mental noise and social constructionist camps, this paradigm is distinguished by its experimental and empirical methods. The methods used include rigorous survey instruments, psychometric surveys, and the observation of effects of various textual and visual stimuli. Where mental models work outwardly to establish persona-based patterns of a social group, research in the psychometric paradigm works inwardly on the psychological perceptions of stimuli and messages in a smaller group of individuals.

Scholars outside of TPC also understood on a deep level that many issues around risk and risk communication could be described as issues of rhetorical framing, undergirded by an awareness of the rhetorics of science. William Leiss and Douglas Powell's *Mad Cows and Mother's Milk* (2004) contended that the popular misunderstanding of science stemmed not from shoddy peer review or fraudulent work, but rather that misunderstanding is "found in the failure to understand that science results are, like every other product of the human imagination, an *interpretation* of some body of evidence, not 'facts' as such; that all such interpretations are of necessity limited by the existing overall state of knowledge" (xiv). They explained that the nuances of science, that it is cumulative and never complete, are often lost on the public (xiv). They continued: "Above all, the popular misunderstanding often overlooks the reality that science is cumulative, tentative, always incomplete, and never-ending"; improved rhetorical framing in media and journalism is what constitutes and potentially cultivates "risk literacy" in the public (xv).

Yet, despite attempts to broaden their research implications, many fields related to risk communication are wedded to the industrial/historical past or present, and few would deny this framing. To make such a claim is far from a damning criticism—focusing on the industrial/historical past or present foregrounds the material living conditions of people living now, and working within the industrial/historical past or present means the critique and development of risk communication strategies can focus on industrial-era harms and advocate for people and ecosystems experiencing those harms. Plough and Krimsky explained that for risk communication to emerge as a discipline, it required three conditions: a modern state with responsibility for social welfare; public health agencies, namely sanitation and water; and decision analysis, namely operations research and systems analysis (1987, 5). In part, modern risk communication approaches were born from the present and therefore largely speak to the present; the scale of risk communication has been synthesized from within the conditions to which it can respond. Risk researchers in TPC who dismiss industry risk communication as overly focused on artificially constrained quantitative measures may have a point, but they have likewise struggled to anticipate risk beyond the present, in part because TPC emerged from, and reacted to, these same conditions.

Expanding Risk

The field of risk communication outside of TPC is and always has been far more rhetorical than our field perhaps has given it credit for; perhaps we are even guilty of strawmanning industry-based models to make space for a more localized approach that justifies our work. That said, scholarship in risk communication, while more rhetorical and audience-centered than it is given credit for, still confines itself to more immediate and apparent risks. The rhetorical situations modeled by risk communication scholars are quite human-centered and segmented by isolated moments of interaction. To expand risk communication, we need to expand our conceptualizations of risk first.

In chapter 1 we forwarded Leiss and Powell's (2004) expansive definition of risk, where they framed risk as "the probability of harm in any given situation . . . determined by two factors: (a) the nature of a hazard and (b) the extent of anyone's exposure to that hazard" (33). This definition broadly accords with our sense of risk as "the unequal distribution of the likelihood of harm," and aligns with the related concept of precarity. Precarity was initially considered by French sociologists in connection to tenuous labor practices, but was soon developed into an intersectional approach to understand how complex harms are felt by people who have been marginalized, sometimes intergenerationally. Johnson and Johnson (2020) described studies of precarity as investigations "into uneven distributions of risk, exclusion, and exploitation that reproduce inequality," an explanation that aligns with our own understanding of risk (371). Judith Butler emphasized that precarity "designates that politically induced condition in which certain populations suffer from failing social and economic networks of support and become differentially exposed to injury, violence, and death" (Butler 2009, ii). Here we perceive a strong connection between the way that time and space are stretched in descriptions of precarity and how risk operates. That is, we see risk functioning in multiple valances, throughout time, and often through people and environments. Much of this conception of risk relies on an understanding that recognizes risk as material and rhetorical forces that accumulate over time that can be felt by those directly and indirectly related to acts of violence.

The work of Ulrich Beck (1992, 2006) is valuable in understanding risk as distributed—neither because he was especially accurate about how risk functions, nor because of his claims about reflexive modernity, but rather because he read risk in two expansive ways. Beck understood risk as fluid in temporal scale and geographic scope—scale because he read risk across time and scope because he sees newer human-instigated risks able to escape the immediate localities where the behavior causing such risk was initially generated. Beck described this formation of risk in *Risk Society: Towards a New Modernity* (1992) and explained that our current society, dominated by calculations of risk, is distinct from an industrial society, where risk was contained to those marginalized by indices of wealth, race, and status. Risk, in a reflexive modernity, might have been produced by an earlier industrial era but now takes the form of "irreversible threats to the life of plants, animals, and human beings" (13). However, as Beck explained, "unlike the factory-related or occupational hazards of the nineteenth and the first half of the twentieth centuries, these [risks] can no longer be limited to certain localities or groups, but rather exhibit a tendency to globalization which spans production and reproduction as much as national borders" (13). According to Beck, in our reflexive modernity, we all face the overwhelming "latent side effects" of modernity (12). At the time, Beck was concerned with how the risks and impacts of industrial pollution, nuclear radiation, acid rain, and ozone depletion would echo for generations to come.

Beck's main insight about reflexive modernity was that risk was no longer limited to exploited workers who toiled in unsafe conditions, or even to their families and communities, who were forced to reckon with the immediate impacts of generational poverty, systemic racism, and human and environmental exploitation. He explained that wealth, which once insulated people and communities from industrial-level risk, no longer provided such security, and current-day risk not only overwhelms national borders but also eclipses the monetary benefits for those who previously left others to deal with the risk generated by industry. Of course, while Beck read risk as global and incalculable (1992, 23), he acknowledged that wealth still offers a measure of insulation from dispersed, worldwide risks. That is, Beck acknowledged the existence of class or privilege-specific risks and explained that "poverty attracts an unfortunate abundance of risk" (35)—certainly an understatement. He illustrated the global, planetary nature of risk, explaining that, short of not breathing and eating, it is simply impossible to escape the exponential growth of risk, and where the only defense is to become more educated about risk and the political struggles that result. While we do not accept that risk is as radically dispersed as his work suggests, we appreciate Beck's critique of industrial-era risk, which pulls it from quantitative evaluation, or geographically isolated assumptions, and allows risk to be seen as an ongoing construction of material and rhetorical factors.

Beck's historicization of risk acknowledged its fluid nature, where impacts of risk can be (and have been) intentionally manipulated, and where risk is not bound to temporal or geographic frames. Beck recognized the state of risk through considerations of radioactivity and pollution, his quintessential examples of how harm can escape the geographic confines of the previous industrial era. We agree that risk operates in a similar way, yet we see risk (as the unequal distribution of harm) as present in countless other acts. Other forms of harm can appear as cultural violence or structural violence, sometimes called "slow" or "invisible" violence, because they fail to (not only) produce health statistics or result in mass death, but very much count in our understanding of risk. However, Beck doesn't read risk as structural violence; others have made these connections more explicit.

For example, Frantz Fanon, who rarely, if ever, appears in literature about risk, articulated the means by which risk has been unfairly distributed by colonial powers upon those they colonized. In *The Wretched of the Earth* ([1961] 2004), Fanon famously argued for the necessity of violence against oppressive colonial powers, because violence by the oppressed is one of the first steps in breaking colonial oppression. For Fanon, anticolonial violence is required because violence is how the state maintains control. Fanon made this clear when he wrote that in colonial regions, "the proximity and frequent, direct intervention by the police and the military ensure the colonized are kept under close scrutiny and contained by rifle butts and napalm. We have seen how the government's agent uses a language of pure violence" (4). However, this violence, which the oppressed must reject to enact anticolonial power, did not always mean an explicit physical violence.

Fanon also argued that this violence governed "the ordering of the colonial world which tirelessly punctuated the destruction of the indigenous social fabric, and demolished unchecked the systems of reference of the country's economy, lifestyles, and modes of dress," and so on (6). This form of violence is structural violence, a violence that often exists alongside explicitly physical violence, and likewise leads to bodily and environmental harm, but comprises another manifestation of that harm.

When Fanon wrote of violence between colonial powers and those they colonized, he also identified massive power imbalances and "enormous disparities in lifestyles," locating the source of Western complacency about colonialism and social injustice in the structural violences that constitute wealth disparity (5). The structures that maintain this disparity in favor of the colonizer come in many forms, though most often through the intentional limitation of resources, combined with the environmental and health damages from resource extraction:

> The masses battle with the same poverty, wrestle with the same age-old gestures, and delineate what we could call the geography of hunger with their shrunken bellies. A world of underdevelopment, a world of poverty and inhumanity. But also a world without doctors, without engineers, without administrators. Facing this world, the European nations wallow in the most ostentatious opulence. This European opulence is literally a scandal for it was built on the backs of slaves, it fed on the blood of slaves, and owes its very existence to the soil and subsoil of the underdeveloped world. Europe's well-being and progress were built with the sweat and corpses of blacks, Arabs, Indians, and Asians. This we are determined never to forget. (53)

These intentional harms arrive via policies that create living conditions—for all life—where the likelihood of harm is increased and where these violences are waged through systems and organized actions, but are unlikely to be as dramatically represented as the physical violence of warfare.

The literal concept of structural violence was named in Johan Galtung's early work in peace studies, and stemmed primarily from a distinction he made between literal, structural, and cultural violence while working at the International Peace Research Institute in Oslo. His short article "Violence, Peace, and Peace Research" defined violence broadly before identifying the many manifestations that violence could take. Galtung defined violence as "that which increases the distance between the potential and the actual, and that which impedes the decrease of this distance" (1969, 168). This useful definition allows for an elastic reading of violence that accommodates harms that have been imposed over longer time frames and in less centralized geographies. According to Galtung, the causes of this less immediate form of violence include when "resources are unevenly distributed, as when income distributions are heavily skewed, literacy/education unevenly distributed, medical services existent in some districts and for some groups only, and so on" (171). Galtung would further describe structural violence as "silent," almost "static" in nature, where such violence can seem as natural or inevitable as "the air around us" (173). Of course, Galtung was far from the first or only writer to articulate the violence of structural, social injustice, as Hannah Arendt ([1963] 2006), Martin Luther King (1967), Paulo Freire ([1968] 2000), Audre Lorde (1984), and Patricia Hill Collins (1990), among others, have contributed to the development of the concept.

Paul Farmer, a medical anthropologist by training, later expanded upon Galtung's work, often locating the material consequences of structural violence within global poverty and human health. Specifically, Farmer et al. (2006) connected structural violence and risk, explaining that "risk has never been determined solely by individual behavior: susceptibility to infection and poor outcomes is aggravated by social factors such as poverty, gender inequality, and racism" (1687). Farmer and his colleagues showed how the AIDS epidemic disproportionately impacted those in poverty, "many of whom engaged in 'risk behaviors' at a far lower rate than others who were not at heightened risk of infection with sexually transmitted diseases" (1687; see also Scott 2003), and later Farmer would explain how humanitarian failures following the 2010 Haitian earthquake were precipitated by deeply pervasive, structured inequities and largely avoidable circumstances (Rylko-Bauer and Farmer 2016).

Structural violence and cultural violence (wherein violent actions are endorsed more broadly in cultural representations) have also been utilized by modern critical theorists as they seek to describe the conditions of harm that pervade everyday life. Notably, Lauren Berlant outlined the impacts of structural violence in her description of "slow death," the "physical wearing out of a population and the deterioration of people in that population that is very nearly a defining condition of their experience and historical existence. The general emphasis of the phrase 'slow death' is on the phenomenon of mass physical attenuation under global/national regimes of capitalist structural subordination and governmentality" (2007, 754). Rejecting how some activists will reconceive structural violence into an immediate crisis, Berlant instead considered the condensed time constraints of risk-as-crisis to be a "distorting or misdirecting gesture that aspires to make an environmental phenomenon appear suddenly as an event because as a structural or predictable condition it has not engendered the kinds of historic action we associate with the heroic agency a crisis seems already to have called for" (760). Slow death, as opposed to a crisis, happens via numerous mechanisms and impacts people in various ways, few of which are identifiable as crisis events. These forms of everyday violences, measured often through longer stretches of time, can be difficult for researchers and activists to highlight—precisely because they are not often dramatic nor do they lend themselves to breathless reportage. They are what Kathryn Yusoff, intentionally pulling from Hannah Arendt's work, has described as "banal violence." Instead of measuring violence only in physical harm or visible, wholesale habitat destruction, for example, she located violence directly within the practices of the everyday, seeing the banality of violence in the palm oil used in shampoos and the impacts of hardware store herbicides on amphibians (2012, 580).

But perhaps the most impactful recent articulation of structural violence is that of Rob Nixon's (2013) "slow violence" from his book of the same name. Nixon similarly rejected the immediacy of crisis as the only form of risk worth attending, and describes slow violence as "a violence that is neither spectacular nor instantaneous, but rather incremental and accretive, its calamitous repercussions playing out across a range of temporal scales" (3). Nixon blamed the media, in part, for focusing only on the startling events of violence, and missing opportunities to explain what he described as the more invisible forms of violence, like "toxic buildup, massing greenhouse gases, and accelerated species loss due to ravaged habitats" because media experts are less deft at telling "scientifically convoluted cataclysms in which casualties are postponed, often for generations" (3). Yet Nixon's work has been critiqued for suggesting just this "invisibility," as the people who live with the impacts of environmental racism, in "cancer alley" in Louisiana, for example, are often quite aware of the effects of industrial pollution on their bodies and communities (for more insight into "invisible" violence, see box 3.1). Framing this slow violence as "invisible" is somewhat disingenuous, as it is invisible only to those whose media fails to present these stories, or to those who benefit from the inequitable distribution of harm. Thom Davies suggested that those who are the victims of slow violence live with the "situated knowledges" of everyday violences because the "interactions with contested toxic places can encompass a wide range of embodied ways of knowing polluted environments" (2022, 418).

Closer to TPC, Erin Clark (2023) took additional inspiration, and exception, to Nixon's concept of "slow violence," and instead posited a "slow crisis" as more accurate for identifying how harm can be distributed, often without clear agency, over time (78). Clark agreed that " 'slow' patterns actually constitute crisis under some conditions—conditions that might include, for example, not only spouse battering but also systematic assaults on reproductive rights, human health effects of slowly unfolding environmental disasters, and shifts in what is considered 'standard practice' over time" (74). However, Clark distinguished slow violence, and its precursors that rely on structural violence, as not focused enough on energy and speed, especially as those valences coincide with feminist theory and practice. "I differ from Nixon in that I find the term slow crisis to be more instructive and useful than slow violence," Clark argued. "Women have long recognized the horror of slow violence; violence has always happened at many speeds for us. Crisis, though, suggests urgency and speed" (Clark, 77). This reconceptualizing of crisis also helps push back against the all-too-typical construction of risk in TPC. Technical communicators, Clark contended, "must do a better job of recognizing and resisting this rush to efficient resolution of obvious crises and instead recognize that slow patterns can also constitute crisis" (77). Clark explained the relevance of "slow crisis" via the examples of the Deepwater Horizon oil spill and its impact on human health and of how battered woman syndrome is defined, treated, and argued about in legal discourse, and how both examples challenge definitions of immediacy and crisis.

Box 3.1
"Invisible Violence" and Environmental Racism

The forms of structural violence that Rob Nixon (2013) called "invisible" can be invisible within the broader public media landscape, but are unlikely to be invisible to communities, community leaders, and activists who are in touch with the conditions that face people and ecosystems worldwide.

While we can point to an array of different contexts in which "invisible" forms of structural violence have been rendered visible, many have been rendered visible through the efforts of environmental justice activists. The most notable example in the US is perhaps that of the polychlorinated biphenyls (PCB) protests in Warren County, North Carolina.

When owners of the PCB Transformer Company wanted to avoid EPA regulations (the disposal of PCBs was governed by the 1976 Resource Conservation and Recovery Act), they secretly dumped thirty-one thousand gallons of PCB-contaminated oil along the roadways throughout North Carolina. Discovered in 1978, the soil wasn't cleaned up until 1982, at which point people living along those roadways were reporting higher levels of miscarriages and birth defects (Exchange Project n.d.). As part of the effort to clean up those roadways, soil was removed and a landfill site in Warren County, a rural site with a largely poor, Black population, was chosen, and the state was granted multiple safety waivers to use that specific location for PCB-contaminated soil. In the resulting conflict over the landfill site, over five hundred people were arrested in protests that lasted for more than six weeks; those responsible for dumping PCBs were variously tried, convicted, sentenced to prison, or fined (United States v. Ward 1980; Webb 1982) and the NAACP would file an ultimately unsuccessful lawsuit (NAACP 1982). By 1997 the state of North Carolina admitted that the landfill was improperly contained and began cleanup efforts. While there had been previous protests overlapping issues concerning the environment, race, and class, the Warren County PCB protests galvanized the emergence of the environmental justice movement (Natural Resources Defense Council 2023). The protests in Warren County galvanized national attention toward environmental issues in a new way. Previously, issues of race and poverty were sidelined in conversations about environmental issues, but the clear links between race and environmental risk helped create a more inclusive sense of environmental awareness and emphasized that the slow violence of environmental harms often impacted Black and Indigenous communities first.

There are far too many examples of these forms of supposedly invisible violence to reference here—some the work of specific individuals, some based on racist assumptions built into governmental policies and laws (Hill Collins 1990; Williams and Pemental 2014), some the accumulated activities of entire industries. Structural violence can occur via many different physical, legal, social, and rhetorical structures. It can emerge in the hostile architecture of cities, where park benches are impossible to sleep on, where windowsills are sloped to disallow resting, or where underpasses have concrete anticamping spikes installed. It can occur in the practice of redlining neighborhoods along racial lines, demarcated locations where banks would refuse mortgages, cities would withhold basic services, and where healthcare institutions and businesses would refuse to build, compounding risk in unequitable ways. The location of steam cracking plants, fracking sites, waste incinerators, and other industrial sites participate in this same violence, as do historical practices of eminent domain, the neglect of infrastructure, the placement of oil pipelines, the structure of city zoning laws, and legal restrictions on labor, water breaks, rights to assemble, the design of algorithms and biometrics . . . and dozens of additional examples. These forms of slow violence are branded into the landscape and reinforced through the structures and infrastructures of modern nation-states. Our goal here is less to point out that such structural violences exist but more to argue that they should be integrated into how we conceptualize risk. In order to do so, we need to rethink how TPC engages in work that concerns risk. The topoi we articulate in the following section for mapping risk and rhetoric should not act as a template, but rather as entry points for reconsidering the scalar variability of risk. Researchers in TPC can engage risk at multiple points and continue investigating what additional theories and methods help make sense of the conditions for risk—in fields such as risk communication, risk management, risk perception, environmental humanities, environmental justice, social geography, and political ecology. This broader approach to risk could very well result in short, article-length case studies, as the field of TPC has sustained itself on, and as we offer later in this book, but intentionally frame such an approach within a broader sphere of choice. The field of TPC should expand the scope and scale of how it can conceptualize risk and choose topoi from a much larger paradigm.

Scaling Theory

In chapter 1, we described Jeffrey Grabill and W. Michele Simmons's groundbreaking work on the social and rhetorical construction of risk. We explained how their 1998 article, "Toward a Critical Rhetoric of Risk Communication: Producing Citizens and the Role of Technical Communicators," was central to articulating a critical rhetoric of risk and locating what that critical perspective offers for user-, community-, and participant-focused methods in general and TPC specifically. We also described their work as being rooted within an era in which TPC was experiencing some significant changes, focused on responding to the field's previous inattention to risk, developing as a humanities-oriented field, and reacting to the neoliberal politics of three consecutive regressive administrations. These historical pressures would come to shape how risk was to be investigated in the field. However, we can also describe these pressures as part of the larger contextual forces that encouraged a certain scalar framing of risk in relation to the work that could be conducted by those in TPC. That is, the field of TPC approached risk research according to a certain scale and scope.

However, models from the 1980s, 1990s, and 2000s demonstrate that researchers outside TPC appreciated the role of audience but often struggled with scale. That is, while TPC performed localized case study work pretty much right away (Grabill and Simmons 1998; Herndl, Fennell, and Miller 1991), likely because it fit our ethos and suited the qualitative methodologies we use, other fields attempted to scale up to try and aggregate a broader but still rich sense of risk communication. For example, developments were made to scale up the mental models approach to risk communication (Morgan et al. 2001), a comparative method that seeks to articulate alignment and divergence between the cognitive schemas held by the general public and those mental models of causes and effects held by scientists.

In emphasizing "scale" here, we mean to articulate that TPC researchers and practitioners have engaged and could yet engage different levels of risk investigation. As mentioned in chapter 1, the field of TPC can usefully expand by considering risk beyond regional-level, user-focused, participant research and retrospective, after-the-fact analyses of disasters, crises, and failures. The temporal scale and spatial scope in which the field has conceptualized risk has, up until very recently, focused on specific localities and recent or currently unfolding events—an approach that has certainly created a wealth of knowledge. Yet we want to contextualize these efforts with a much broader sense of scope and scale and, in doing so, critique the field's existing range of approaches to understanding risk and engaging in risk analysis and communication. What we offer, then, is a paradigm for more expansive orientations to risk and toward more clearly defined senses of the boundaries that enrich what risk *is* or *means* (or should mean) to those in TPC. Again, this approach is not intended to be monolithic, but expansive; we want to broaden the field's working conceptions of how it might approach risk (and for an approach to disaster communication, see box 3.2).

Box 3.2
The Legacy of Disaster Studies

It can be tricky to consider the forms of time-expanded risk that we have introduced here without also considering its opposite: the time-constrained issues related to crisis communication and disaster research. We cover crisis communication earlier (see table 3.1), but disaster research can involve multiple fields of study and a surprisingly expansive sense of risk.

Disaster research in America is in many ways indebted to an increase in post–World War II funding for various civil defense strategies and emergency management policies. Here, we often think of the Emergency Broadcast System and films produced for schoolchildren to "duck and cover" in case of an atomic attack. It is also indebted to Anthony Giddens (1991) and Ulrich Beck (1992), in part because disaster studies often embraced their concerns that "one of the consequences of modernity is a commitment to 'colonize the future' as a means to control risk"—meaning that because expert knowledge has increased throughout modernity, local or regional understandings of risk were displaced by such centralized forms of expertise (Mohun 2016, 35). Modern expertise became granted through formal education, and the trust built around such education and knowledge was legitimized in quantified definitions of risk. "As expert knowledge about risk replaces local knowledge," Arwen Mohun explained, "credentialing rather than community status defines whose ideas about risk can be trusted" (35). The impetus to "colonize the future" can then emerge as expert-driven disaster recovery and preparedness efforts impact future action (Giddens 1991).

Other histories of disasters emerged from analyses of structural inequity. Perhaps most notable is Theodore Steinberg's *Acts of God: The Unnatural History of Natural Disaster in America* (2000), where he argued that disasters almost always impact disempowered communities more than those with resources to avoid them. Instead of seeing disasters as "natural," we should see their impacts as replicating the cultural and economic inequalities that permeate American life, most often impacting America's poor, elderly, or minoritized populations. In recent memory, we could highlight Hurricane Katrina, a natural disaster, and the decidedly "unnatural," unequal impacts on people and ecosystems that followed.

Also emergent from Giddens's and Beck's work was the field of safety history. David Rosner and Gerald Markowitz detailed workplace safety in *Dying for Work: Workers Safety and Health in Twentieth Century America* (1987) and industrial pollution in *Deceit and Denial: The Deadly Politics of Industrial Pollution* (2013); other studies in safety history have tackled the cultural and historical contexts for industrial and transportation-related accidents.

For us, the origins of the conversation on scope and scale arise out of questions that developed in the ecological sciences, perhaps most notably from the work of Simon Levin, a professor of ecology and evolutionary biology, and his lecture given in acceptance of the 1989 Robert H. Macarthur Award. In that paper, published in *Ecology* in 1992, Levin outlined a major problem in ecology research—what he called "the fundamental conceptual problem in ecology, if not in all of science"—the problem of scale (Levin 1992, 1944). For Levin, the problem of scale was the problem of conceptualizing the populations, time, or geography about which ecologists do their work. Levin explained that the chasm between the levels in which different fields are able to make claims is sometimes vast; the differences between scale in evolutionary biology and ecosystems science, for example, "is a wide one, and there is little overlap between the two in journals or scientific meetings. Yet neither discipline can afford to ignore the other: evolutionary changes take place within the context of ecosystems, and an evolutionary perspective is critical for understanding organisms' behavioral and physiological responses to environmental change" (Levin 1992, 1944). Ecologists had been making claims that spoke to very different scales, some focusing on global migratory patterns, populations, or climate models and some on much more granular details from location-precise field research. Levin wasn't the first to note the concern over scale, as Marten (1972) and Wiens (1973) had referenced the concept almost two decades earlier, but he did emphasize the growing problem of scale—a concern that would garner worldwide attention.

Scales can function as a methodological lens through which ecological systems can be studied, and when ill-fitting scales are chosen, the data that results can be distorted. Levin, as Jérôme Chave argued, prompted the realization that it is "essential to study ecological questions across scales," even though substantial problems in aligning spatial and geographical scales would invariably remain (2013, 13). Levin carefully noted the source of these scalar problems, too, and recognized that there is no clear grand unified theory for ecology in part because the many different models that exist highlight different details. "Because there is no single scale at which ecosystems should be described, there is no single scale at which models should be constructed," Levin noted, so we "need to have available a suite of models of different levels of complexity, and to understand the consequences of suppressing or incorporating detail" (1992, 1960). While problems arise, not only in applying scales without careful consideration but also in attempting to merge scales, there have been advances in building bridges between scalar approaches. Highlighting these approaches, Chave recognized how we can bridge research at different scales, though thinking in scalar modes is necessary to identify these opportunities (13).

Yet scale is not only applicable to ecologists trying to have conversations across research methodologies. Scale can also be used to understand the changing sociopolitical landscape that has framed the work of TPC. Erik Swyngedouw's work (1997a, 1997b, 2000) has identified a derangement of scale in much sociopolitical discourse. Swyngedouw argued that as neoliberal capitalism shifted toward a "globalization" scalar framing in the 1980s, national economies became international trade zones. Important to this process, however, was how the scale of political and social life was correspondingly altered alongside this economic and cultural shift. Specifically, Swyngedouw explained how the dominant neoliberal scale became one of "glocalization"—a term that has suggested the interrelation between global and local forces. Still, Swyngedouw viewed this emergent era as an alteration where "the contested restructuring of the institutional level from the national scale" forces itself "both upwards to supranational or global scales and downwards to the scale of the individual body or the local, urban or regional configurations" (2004, 37). Essentially, thinking that occurred only within one scale—the institutional or corporate scale—dominated other possibilities of thinking, manipulating both much larger international concerns and local/regional issues, threatening to subsume those scalar concerns within "new territorial scales of governance [that redefined] the regulation and organisation of social, political and economic power relations" (2004, 26). Of course, Swyngedouw was expressly concerned with how increased attention to scale and its manipulations can be used to respond to these developments, and more recent work has provided some of these tools.

How can we recognize and respond to these "derangements of scale," as Timothy Clark (2012) described the phenomenon? One way would be to identify, as we have done in previous chapters, how a profession or field of practice has concentrated its work within a certain scale, for example, in how TPC has generated article-length case studies of recent disasters and therefore how the field has neglected certain scalar formations of risk. Clark placed our attention to scale in a different, but extremely helpful structure as he read Raymond Carver's story "The Elephant" at three different levels of scale—levels that broadly mirror Swyngedouw's description above. Clark explained that most forms of analysis and criticism "are blind to scale effects in ways that now need to be addressed" and that most critics are stuck in what he described as a "middle scale" of "methodological nationalism," a term he borrowed from Beck (2006, 150, 159). This scale of analysis addressed "a national culture and its inhabitants, with a time frame of perhaps a few decades, a "historical period of some kind" (158). The problem with reading (fiction in this example, but any set of "texts") solely within a single scalar formation is that such analysis manifests the connection between culture and nation-state as overwhelmingly dominant; Clark explained that "we often still think, interpret and judge as if the territorial bounds of the nation state acted as a self-evident principle of overall coherence and intelligibility within which a history and culture can be understood—ignoring anything that does not fit such a narrative" (159). Clark then asked "what, then, is being held off?" when we read only within one scalar frame. In turn, we ask: What is being held off in risk theory and communication when we limit our work to disaster-based case studies?

In order to determine what is missed when we work within only one scale, we can perform further analysis through (at least) two additional scales. The first, the "personal," argued Clark, is perhaps of limited value and is often critically naïve; this is a scale "that takes into account only the narrator's immediate circle of family and acquaintances over a time scale of several years" (2012, 157–58). Such a scale is immediate, inter/personal, and humanist, and may deserve more attention than Clark offered in his reading. He spent more time addressing another scale, that of a third, hypothetical scale that "could be, spatially, that of the whole earth and its inhabitants, [one that places us] in the middle of a, let us say, six hundred year time frame i.e., from three hundred years before [the event in question, to] three hundred after, and bearing in mind authoritative plausible scenarios for the habitability of the planet at that time" (158). In these "very long time scales, human history and culture can take on unfamiliar shapes, as work in environmental history repeatedly demonstrates, altering conceptions of what makes something 'important' and what does not" (p 159). Within this scale, we recognize that any event can be plotted within an expanse of geographical space and chronological time, where a specific, hypothetical moment of crisis can be seen as an accumulation of centuries of causes and effects—and often through the accumulation of the intentional unequal distribution of harm.

Zachary Horton (2021) has recognized this, explaining that such scalar fixedness can be aligned with the formations of slow violence described earlier. He argued that "*Slow violence is not accidental; it is the result of weaponized scalar difference*. How trans-scalar flows are managed and put to work, and what they produce for whom, are questions any contemporary analytic of power must ask" (6; italics ours). Slow violence, itself a manifestation of risk, is enabled when those in power operate within a single frame of scalar difference or perform scalar transactions that intentionally disempower or disadvantage certain entities. Horton explained how "scalar transactions" can be manipulated, for example, to focus on individual actions instead of emphasizing governmental or institutional roles in pollution, hide sweatshop labor in regions geographically remote from consumers, or displace the consequences of climate change upon people and ecosystems.

So how do we move away from the calcification or manipulation of scalar logics? How does TPC, as a field of study, research risk outside of the scalar equivalent of a time-constrained regionalism—the scale where most of its attention to risk has been? In order to break the cycle of scalar assumptions, we have to first recognize that scalar decisions are natural when *creating* knowledge. In *Scale Theory: A Nondisciplinary Inquiry* (2021), Joshua DiCaglio explained that in order to identify scalar issues, we need to see scale as natural to any human research endeavor. "Because scale underlies observation," DiCaglio argued, "it is implicit within our ways of dividing, grouping, and relating together the various aspects of the world. When we speak about society, culture, language, evolution, humanity, objects, matter, economics—we are working with certain assumptions about scale" (3). Human knowledge creation requires some scalar stability, as the work of disciplinary knowledge-making further "produces intensifications within its constructed continuity, authorizing human access and mastery as normalized medial encounter. This arrangement perpetuates itself: because knowledge is scale-disciplined, it only ever concerns itself with a small slice of the scalar spectrum, and thus the illusion of scalar contiguity is maintained" (34). To break this cycle, we need to, circling back to Horton, enumerate how scale, "as an attribute of an already unified subject or object, profoundly disturbs this scalar pact of humanist thought. . . . At the very least we will need to change our default question: instead of asking which scales are occupied or accessed by a conceptually preconstituted human, we'll need to ask how the human emerges—along with many other objects and subjects—out of the dynamics of scale" (Horton 2021, 7). This disruption also requires questioning the neoliberal accumulation of capital. Because the expansion of human scalar assumptions is tied to "ever increasing scales of accumulation," asking questions about scale similarly means questioning how our research assumptions are configured within neoliberal capitalism (8).

Mapping Risk

Unlike ecologists, we are not particularly interested in unified theories for all investigations of risk in TPC, nor are we necessarily focused on obtaining a predictive model for the field. However, we are interested in identifying a range of approaches that can be explicitly and critically applied by those doing work on risk in TPC (and perhaps in related fields). To facilitate these choices, we might need to adopt how scale theory has been integrated into humanities and social science disciplines and develop those ideas with the technical communication of risk in mind. We need tools—in this case, a set of topoi—designed to function as heuristic entry points for reconsidering the variability in risk between hazards and exposures. In other words, we're hoping researchers are able to use these topoi to "track and narrate, rather than capture and catalogue" how risk can be scaled (Carr and Lempert 2016, 21). Researchers in TPC can then engage risk at multiple points and continue investigating what additional theories and methods—in fields such as risk communication, risk management, risk perception, environmental humanities, environmental justice, health communication, and political ecology—are able to help make sense of the conditions for risk. This broader approach to risk could result in short case studies, as we offer in the following chapters, but it intentionally frames this approach within a broader sphere of choice. The field of TPC should expand the scope and scale of how it can conceptualize risk and choose neglected topoi from a larger paradigm.

The topoi we present here (see table 3.2, initially developed in Pflugfelder et al. [2023]) have been influenced by Ehrenfeld (2020) and Jones (2021), who have argued that rhetoric's ecological turn has produced spatiotemporal problems that emphasize flux within networked systems while deemphasizing historical specificity. Jones offered the metaphor of an ecologist suspending a temporal slice (kairos) and a spatial slice (scale) between a microscope coverslip. This allows the ecologist to study a system at the expense of an understanding of space and time. We argue that both temporal and spatial historicity and flux matter. Jones noted that ecologists

Table 3.2. Spatiotemporal Table Highlighting the Relationship Between Time and Place as a Means of Understanding Risk

	Deep Time	**Industrial/ Historical Past**	**Present**	**Immediate Future**	**Long-Term Futures**
Macroscopic Risk (Global) Mesoscopic Risk (Regional) Microscopic Risk (Local)	How do material formations and past risks create the conditions for risk in the future?	How has the Industrial Revolution and westward expansion tied to colonialism based upon material formations of the past and notions of value in the present created risks related to material dependencies?	How is risk around water currently perceived in relation to everyday, mundane activities (for example, watering lawns, showering, agriculture)?	How are activities in the present understood to contribute to episodic moments of risk in the immediate future that have the potential to return to risk levels of the present or a sense of normalcy?	How is risk perceived in relation to catastrophic scenarios?

rely on "a particular space/time to reduce complexity in order to make holistic modeling possible . . . These cuts allow ecologists to study systems, but they also displace and derange our sense of place and time" (341). Much like scholarship in rhetorical ecologies, approaches to risk necessitate focusing on specific spatiotemporal configurations that reduce complexity to understand the relations that create risk. These deliberate choices have allowed scholars of risk to see certain kinds of risk at the expense of others, but have also limited the resulting studies in both scale and methodological diversity. While synchronicity (locating the relations that exist when things occur at the same time) is often seen as a necessity, we believe there are affordances to moving diachronically—identifying change and causation occurring throughout time—in making sense of risk.

In hopes that TPC scholars studying risk might productively consider new spatiotemporal dimensions in risk research, these topoi could be used to identify prominent gaps in our approach, as well as usefully contextualize and reorient the views in previous TPC studies of risk. These topoi privilege diachronic and trans-spatial logics for accounting for how climate risk affects people, nonhuman animals, and environments across generations and geopolitical borders. With respect to time, we ask what risk means at specific moments and places. Across the temporal plane, we have articulated five topoi that reflect variance in temporal scale: "Deep Time," "Industrial/Historical Past," "Present," "Immediate Future," and "Long-Term Futures." Along a geographic plane, we have articulated three points that reflect variance in scope: "Macroscopic risk," "Mesoscopic risk," and "Microscopic risk." These points allow us to move across global, regional, and local scales in terms of understanding the development of risk. Table 3.3 showcases how these topoi

Table 3.3. Spatiotemporal Heuristic Highlighting the Relationship Between Time and Place as a Means of Understanding Risk at a Finer Level

	Macroscopic (global: mining at national and international levels)	**Mesoscopic (regional: San Juan Mountains; Bonita Peak Mining District; Animas River Watershed; Uinta Basin)**	**Microscopic (specific: Gold King Mine; American Tunnel; bulkhead; sediment in riverbed)**
Deep Time (Geologic and prehistoric time)			
Industrial/Historical Past (Time as multigenerational history)			
Present (Time as generational history)			
Immediate/Future (The moments when a crisis or disaster is acutely perceived)			
Long-Term Futures (Time as legacy moments that will influence multiple generations)			

could be engaged at different levels of scale, opening up new framings for how we can approach risk in TPC. (Audiences interested in an example of this table populated as a heuristic for considering risk across such scales are encouraged to review Pflugfelder et al. 2023. This example corresponded to the initial work we performed for the case study that appears in chapter 5.)

These topoi may seem somewhat overwhelming at first glance, as they represent a huge expanse of both time and geography; no one single study of risk could—or should—consider all of these scales at once. Instead, we encourage researchers to examine past investigations of risk in their chosen area of study and ask whether, much like Timothy Clark's (2012) overview of literary analysis, the topic has previously been approached from within a "methodological nationalism," where institutional-level considerations have overwhelmed other scalar opportunities. This "methodological nationalism" scale of investigation is represented in our set of topoi by the bottom-center portions of the table—mostly as these studies have considered the local or regional impacts of recent risk events. This is the scale of institutional power. In chapter 1 we explained that, following Grabill and Simmons's work, most TPC investigations of risk have been built (explicitly or implicitly) upon Foucault's framing of institutional and disciplinary power relations. In TPC, risk communication has been seen as a practice engaged by people, through texts that construct power within institutions, where, crucially, communication is also an inherent element of the process of creating and reproducing power. TPC's approach to risk became its limiting scope: risk became almost entirely seen as the negotiation of meaning between institutions and people, containing much risk research to the present or the immediate future and to mesoscopic (regional) or microscopic (local) impacts.

Not all investigations of risk have to emerge from a dominant scalar position of risk in relation to human institutions, and we see value in questioning scale from the start. The opportunities in doing so offer TPC researchers an increased range of observation and inquiry that "reveals relationships that were previously not apparent simply because they were not discernible; and . . . provides new possibilities for comprehending these aggregates and relations" (DiCaglio 2021, 7). Making scalar decisions is transformative and rhetorical; by considering the scale at which our research proceeds, we not only change how we represent the forces involved in risk, we change the relations involved in risk. As DiCaglio reminds us, thinking in scale "requires a transformation or reconfiguration of our understanding of reality. As the study of persuasion, rhetoric focuses us on both the descriptive power of scale for objects and the transformative power of scale for those attending to these descriptions. Different rhetorical strategies are needed for us to follow out this transformation and permit scale to properly transform and reorient ourselves" (10–11). Increased attention to scale is also essential for identifying the structural violences that damage people, ecosystems, and communities, because reconsidering scale allows for expanded conceptions of cause and effect. Such an approach can also better value a diachronic sense of events, where change and causation can be followed over time, and lead to better understandings of structural violence. As Horton explained, by assigning damaging processes to other scales, either geographically or temporally, we run the risk of putting them out of sight of researchers, functionally perpetuating those violences (Horton 2021, 6). Just because causes and effects are sometimes out of sight, they should not be out of mind.

The TPC scholars we feel most indebted to for our approach to mapping risk across geographic and temporal scale have been Angela Haas and Erin Frost; their work argued how apparent decolonial feminism (ADF) can be used to make sense of the events in a "slow crisis." As Clark (2023) explained, the term "apparent" signals the need for purposeful strategies, actions, and practices that make feminism visible. In fact, we consider Frost's work as key to understanding a difficult-to-represent "Z axis" on our currently two-dimensional representations. Frost focused attention on the events surrounding the aftermath of the 2010 BP Deepwater Horizon explosion and resultant oil spill. She argued that while many documents were distributed about the ongoing crisis,

> the delivery methods of these artifacts are ironic in that international and national entities utilized local spaces whereas regional and local communicators turned to globalized digital sites to narrate the disaster; they also narrated different versions of it. Specifically, government- and BP-authored documents were inserted into physical spaces on Dauphin Island and sponsored largely economic understandings of the effects of the spreading oil; regional and local sources used online spaces to discuss the disaster and engaged in more nuanced constructions of combined and interdependent economic and ecologic risk. (2013, 50)

Frost described how documents offered different versions of the disaster and explained why this is precisely the kind of scenario that TPC research should engage. We agree. Complex risk scenarios like the aftermath of the Deepwater Horizon explosion ask us "to pay attention to complex transcultural flows of communication that move between local and global cultural spaces as they participate in constructing both the risks and the histories of particular events" (2013, 51). Frost's work critiqued risk communication documents from an apparent decolonial feminist framework, identifying how "efficiency" had been mobilized by corporate actors in order to focus on the economy and ecology of the region—at the expense of the human health implications of the oil spill. These intentionally manipulative forms of risk communication disseminated after the Deepwater Horizon explosion and during the spreading ecological and human health emergencies that occurred afterwards could also be described as a form of scalar deferral, or weaponized scalar difference. As we note above, Horton explained that because scale is "a set of political tactics for aggregating and disaggregating assemblages," it can be used to displace "undesirable consequences" for certain agencies (Horton 2021, 6). Asking how the documents establish risk, in distinct scales, helps researchers identify this scalar manipulation at work.

In order to locate a critical approach to risk communication, Frost read the attention to "efficiency" via a structural apparent feminist approach, and identified how a transcultural lens could be used to make apparent additional "perspectives that are only evident when we take into account the multiple networks and communicators with stakes in the situation" (2013, 52). For Clark, "transcultural communication is a way of getting at intersectionality, as it allows us to see across (some, limited) cultural divides and to interrogate the efficiencies that undergird differing perspectives on the [Deepwater Horizon disaster]" (2023, 106). Frost's approach to understanding the trajectories used to articulate risk in the instance of the Deepwater Horizon disaster can be employed in numerous other scenarios because a transcultural, intersectional approach can be used as a way to keep researcher bias at bay and recognize the multiple, sometimes overlapping, sometimes competing forms of shared experiences that exist in a specific time and place. Referencing the groundbreaking work of Linda Flower (2002), Frost described transcultural inquiry as being about "reaching across a lack of shared experience to discover 'rival readings of that issue that have the potential to transform both the inquirers and their interpretations of problematic issues in the world' " (Flower 2002, 186, cited in Clark 2023, 120). This intersectional approach functions as a necessary critical Z-axis in our topoi-focused scalar approach to risk.

After a researcher chooses the geographic and temporal scale of their approach to risk, in response to the rhetorical analysis of that risk, they then need to consider which agents will form the intercultural cut from within that scalar consideration. This imaginary "Z axis" emerges from our two-dimensional model. It might help to think of this as a relief map of sorts, with the Z axis jutting out from the page, but instead of geologic detail, it presents us with those agents within the scale who are able to express a particular risk narrative. Here we build from how Clark described her account of the Deepwater Horizon disaster as "selected, localized . . . as noted in the title of the time line I include." Clark asked us to imagine

> what a time line might look like if written by an individual living on the Gulf Coast. It would be more localized; they might note many things I did not, such as the date the federal government banned fishing, the date the beaches started to empty of tourists, the dates local states of emergency were declared, the dates when local fishers began to elect to work cleanup, the date when a rash first appeared on their skin. Such an account would be very different from the one I include but also still very traditional chronologically. We might also imagine a disaster time line with slow crisis as its underlying value, a time line that sees efficiency as a longer-term project. That time line might include a history of the Macondo area, the dates on which BP made strategic decisions leading to the deepwater rig being in the Gulf, the dates of legislation that enabled offshore drilling near Louisiana. (Clark 2023, 104)

For our purposes, we perceive Clark asking questions of scale, and while she didn't explicitly ask questions that expand scale from the same extremes as our topoi model, the goals are aligned—to question the trajectories of agential narratives that are able to leap off the two-dimensional page and highlight the construction of risk within an intentionally chosen scale.

Implications for TPC Studying Risk

Theoretically and methodologically, our table of topoi (you can call it a tool, heuristic, or framework—whichever you like) infuses ideas and practices from a swath of other fields. It does not itself represent a new *method.* Perhaps it is a primer, a pre-methodological diagnostic, or even a conceptual framework in the sense that Ravitch and Riggan (2016) mean: as a guide that ensures alignment between theory, research questions, method, and implications. In our own methodological backyard, we find our work here as being "developmental" and "theoretical," if using Hayhoe and Brewer's (2021) classification system of research goals in TPC, especially since the former "focuses on the invention and improvement of creative approaches to enhancing technical communication through the use of technology and theory" (7). Our priming table of topoi might engender qualitative work that uses document or content analysis as methods, or it might guide quantitative work on mental models in a given community. The point is not to overdetermine methods or research questions but to help researchers locate them and find consistency across scope and scale.

In their own book on research methods, Carradini and Swarts (2023) argued that "corpus analysis offers a way to approach the work of technical communication at the source material's level of scale by allowing analysis of more texts than an individual or team could read alone" (6). For TPC, considerations of scale allow us to make sense of an activity, a history, or a field, and offer us insight into a certain volume of work. Scale in TPC also plays a role in how we go about studying the source material. For risk-based case studies, the source material can be expansive—global and ancient or widespread and multilayered. Implementing a scalar model for risk analysis gets us closer to the true nature of the "source material," rather than cordoning off certain features of a much larger data set by genre (for example, accident reports, news coverage, fault tree analyses), community (for example, flood survivors, climate refugees, at-risk workers), or perceived impact (for example, groundwater chemical leaching, toxic shock, mine subsidence).

In hopes that TPC scholars studying risk might productively trouble the spatiotemporal limitations characteristic in risk research, our topoi in tables 3.4 and 3.5 could be used to identify prominent gaps in our approach, as well as usefully contextualize and reorient the views in previous TPC studies of risk. We believe that these spatiotemporal topoi can be used in conjunction with the topoi Haas and Frost (2017) forwarded to productively advance work that engages in climate justice, as these topoi can

1. promot[e] a deeper understanding of the interdependencies between local, global, and international risks and across economic, environmental, geopolitical, cultural, and technological risks;
2. mak[e]s connections between historical, contemporary, and future risks;

3. requir[e]s responsible and ethical engagement of underrepresented rhetorics and realities of risks. (169)

Moreover, our topoi privilege diachronic and trans-spatial logics for accounting for how climate risk affects people, animals, and environments across generations and geopolitical borders. With respect to time, we ask what risk means at specific moments and places. Across the temporal plane, we have articulated five topoi that reflect variance in temporal scale: "Deep Time," "Industrial/Historical Past," "Present," "Immediate Future," and "Long-Term Futures." On a geographic-plane, we have articulated three points that reflect variance in scope: "Macroscopic risk," "Mesoscopic risk," and "Microscopic risk." These points allow us to move across global, regional, and local scales in terms of understanding the development of risk. We encourage others to scale these periods and spaces into units appropriate to their projects, while also noting that they must be operationalized within an apparent decolonial feminist approach to work toward the aims of climate, social, and environmental justice.

Further, we hope that the following three chapters illustrate three different approaches to scalar choice through these topoi—choices that we feel bring out useful and appropriate analyses in each of the cases on offer. Each of the cases approach these topoi in different ways. In chapter 4, we attend to the riskscapes of the Gold King Mine collapse and wastewater spill. We consider how issues of space complicate the reconfiguration of geographies and develop a case study to bring about different conceptions of risk. Certain risks are global, while others are more local in scope; yet both are connected. Connecting risk across scales allows us to complicate our relationship to risk across these multiple locations that shape our lives in confluent and diffluent ways. Chapter 5 switches to emphasize time in order to trace applied risk relationally across global, transnational, and ecological nexuses. To illustrate the spatial limitations of present approaches toward risk, we apply topoi to "The Law of the River" (US Bureau of Reclamation 2008), a series of legal documents assigning water rights in the Colorado River Basin, contrasting the articulation of climate risk within the documents to the manifest flux in risk. Finally, in chapter 6, we consider how risk is made to travel, across time and space, through energy extraction, transportation, and refinement. This movement of energy creates what we call "contradictory risk flows" and we follow them along the proposed Uinta Basin Railway, a railway that would connect waxy crude extraction fields in Utah's Uinta Basin to the national rail network. These chapters serve as examples of how researchers might work to expand the scope and scale of risk in technical and professional communication.

Chapter Four

Riskscapes

The Bonita Peak Mining District and the Displacement of Native Americans in the San Juan Mountains

> It is tempting in times of crisis to point fingers and place blame. Attempts to blame single agencies or individuals are pointless and ignore the scale and complexity of the problem that needs to be addressed.
>
> —Senator Barbara Boxer, quoting Mayor Dean Brookie of Durango following the Gold King Mine Spill

Scholars interested in risk communication have long studied the mining industry as a useful contextual site of inquiry for studies in technical and professional communication (e.g., Clark 2023; Frost 2013; Reamer 2015; Sauer 1994, 1996, 2002; Stratman et al. 1995), environmental communication (e.g., Haas and Frost 2017; Spoel and Den Hoed 2014; Paliewicz 2018), and rhetoric (e.g., Paliewicz 2023; Spoel and Barriault 2011). Particularly influential have been Beverly Sauer's wide-reaching examinations of the rhetorical construction of risk within the mining industry, which considered topics ranging from the representation of risk in technical documentation, the role of gesture (and other forms of embodied knowledge) to communicate risk, as well as feminist, cross- and transcultural approaches to risk communication. Consistent with the larger trend discussed in chapter 2, much of this scholarship has been locally and temporally bounded to offer a detailed contextualized analysis of various phenomena surrounding the construction of risk in a particular site, event, or organization. That is, this work thoughtfully enriches our understanding of how risk operates within particular spatial scales, and in the case of those studies using cross- and transcultural approaches (Clark 2023; Frost 2013; Haas and Frost 2017; Sauer 1994, 1996, 2002), has problematized how constructions of risk might be in tension across cultural locations.

We are particularly influenced by an approach to transcultural risk communication that Angela Haas and Erin Frost have termed an *apparent decolonial feminist rhetoric* of risk (Haas and Frost 2017, 169). Following this approach, we seek to cast light upon the various "interdependencies" that influence the materiality of risk across geographic locations (WEF 2014, 9, cited in Haas and Frost 2017, 169). Specifically, this chapter considers "the colonial effects of risk" in relation to a Superfund Site that the EPA designated the Bonita Peak Mining District (BPMD) in 2016, following the 2015 Gold King Mine Spill (GKMS). Despite the significant attention that mining has received within TPC as a site for studies of risk, few studies have directly considered how the materiality of risk in this industry has been influenced by the aims of colonial expansion. Moran's (2005) study of the persuasive strategies utilized within the Raleigh Reports, for example, briefly observed that the reports' authors outlined opportunities for mining to attract settlers to form a colony in Virginia in the late 1500s.

Similarly, Gregory Wickliff's (1997) study of the use of the emerging technology of chemical photography within geological surveys of the American West in the 1800s illustrated how these technical documents forwarded arguments that served the interrelated epistemic and economic goals of technological progress, westward expansion, and American exceptionalism. These geological surveys contain passages and imagery, Wickliff pointed out, that demonstrate how such progress sought to overwrite—both symbolically and materially—the presence of and relations between Native Americans and Western lands through practices such as re*placing* names that had been given to locations in the West by Native Americans indigenous to these lands, complemented by systemic and military campaigns that sought to dispossess Native Americans from their ancestral lands. Portrayals of the American West, then, re*presented* such lands as desirable and profitable places for tourism, settlement, and economic development: "Images of developing villages . . . [portrayed] agricultural and mining industry successes [that] seemed to promise wealth and 'culture,' that is, culture in the sense of nature worked over, shaped by human labor into a materially profitable technological construct" (42). Here, Wickliff's approach toward tracing the material risks associated with mining anticipated the approach that Haas and Frost later described, as it directly named the broader epistemic and relational shifts toward lands and lifeways imbricated within the socio-technical networks that cultivated the development of mining as an industry aligned with the aims of coloniality.

Outside of TPC, the works of Endres (2009, 2023), Castro-Sotomayor (2020), De Onís (2021), and Cram (2022) have illustrated how we might more meaningfully engage with the role colonialism has with and for risk in this industry. These scholars have emphasized how extracting, producing, and consuming petrochemicals, nuclear energy, and critical minerals foment violent intersecting colonialities that negatively influence our understanding of place, time, race, gender, and sexuality. Mining has only ever been associated with violence, dispossession of land, and ecological destruction. The extractive economy grows and sustains itself by pooling wealth at the expense of periphery economies, which struggle with environmental degradation and socioeconomic instability. Some scholars have advocated alternative forms of development (Bernauer 2019; Zografos 2022). However, even so-called *green* approaches in pursuit of a *just energy transition* still further neocolonial logics as they continue the trend of encouraging the transition of peasant economies into extractive economies that create new hierarchies of labor in which people are made to work on behalf of others while receiving little to no benefit from greener energy technologies, particularly in the Majority World (covered in more detail in chapter 6). Simply put, as long as mining continues to benefit external interests, it will always be a colonial enterprise.

Extending the work of these earlier scholars, then, we expand on our consideration of the matrix of risks encircling the Colorado River Basin, turning toward the legacy of Colorado's hard-rock mining industry upon the watershed. We offer a case study of the BPMD, including the GKMS, a disaster that released over three million gallons of acid mine drainage trapped within the Gold King mine into Cement Creek on August 5, 2015. The toxic plume of effluent continued to flow downstream through the Animas, San Juan, and Colorado Rivers until it reached Lake Powell a week later (US EPA 2017). While we zoom into an event associated with a particular time and location—the GKMS occurred approximately twelve miles northeast of what is known today as Silverton, Colorado—more broadly this case study problematizes the spatial and temporal complexity surrounding risk in this geography. Here we trace a series of historical events distant from the immediacy of the GKMS that nevertheless had a significant influence on the growth and decline of the mining industry within the BPMD. We work from these distant events—settler-colonialists traveling westward to expand the US, the evolution of the mining industry in Colorado, the US Treasury's gold standard, and World War II—toward the shaping force they have had in underwriting risk within and across geographies encircling the BPMD. The events illustrate the boom-and-bust cycles affecting the social and economic viability of mining in the BPMD, leading eventually to the abandonment of mines in the region by various property owners, the problem of persistent acid mine drainage from the abandoned mines affecting Colorado River tributaries, the GKMS, and the addition of this location to the Superfund National Priority List.

In this chapter, we forward the concept of *riskscapes* (Müller-Mahn and Everts 2012). While time remains important to our analysis, we emphasize the significance of spatial considerations in TPC practices. By extending the discussion of risk beyond the specific incident of the GKMS to the larger BPMD, we argue that how we conceptualize risk is deeply intertwined with our understanding of space. Our analysis aligns with Rachel Luft's (2009, 2016) notion of moving "beyond disaster exceptionalism," urging a broader perspective that includes adjacent spaces and moments critical to understanding the historical, structural, and cultural dimensions of risk. While our initial focus on the GKMS led us to analyze numerous technical reports, we consciously shifted our approach to interrogate the spatial frames that shape risk discourse, particularly through the lens of the Senate Committee on Environment and Public Works oversight meeting held on September 16, 2015. Here, we analyze how government officials, including US senators and EPA director Gina McCarthy, navigated competing spatializations of risk to serve their rhetorical objectives, revealing complexities often flattened in official narratives. We propose that a nuanced understanding of these spatial dimensions can enhance technical and professional communicators' ability to prepare for and respond to risks associated with extractive industry. In sum, readers will find that we seek to address the following interrelated questions:

- How does the concept of riskscape expand our understanding of the relationship between risk and space?
- What is the overall riskscape of this region, of a specific location, in this case, Colorado?
- How does risk within this riskscape cascade into surrounding regions?

- What other (un)seen practices within the riskscape of resource extraction add to the complexity of how we might conceptualize interrelationships between risk and space?
- How does the GKMS help us to understand the way that riskscapes are rhetorically constructed via maps, memos, after-incident analyses, and other risk-communication-associated genres forwarded by experts?

Our aim is to illuminate how risk compounds across space and time, and in ways that have differentially and inequitably impacted humans, animals, and ecosystems that rely on the life-sustaining water that the Colorado River provides. In relation to the next chapter, this specific case study offers an acute look at how an event that might otherwise be framed or regarded as a fairly localized crisis exacerbates the cascading disasters that contribute to the precarity of accessing water that communities located across the Colorado River Basin face; the GKMS unfolded during a historic twenty-two-year drought that brought water levels in Lake Mead and Lake Powell to their lowest levels in history. Events such as the GKMS exacerbate water scarcity within the region that have further cascading impacts beyond these geographies. The United States Department of Agriculture, for example, has observed that water scarcity threatens the sustainability of agricultural industries located across the American Southwest that generate over $30 billion annually and serve as critical nodes within local and global foodways (USDA n.d.).

Thus, this case study illustrates how conceptualizations of risk surrounding the development of mining in the BPMD connect to and are influenced by broader social, political, and economic events within history. In this case, we zoom into a moment when American colonists sought to realize the westward expansion of the country. Even though the history of mining practices predates the discovery of gold in the West, gold, as we illustrate, might nevertheless be seen as a critical catalyst for both the industrialization of the mining industry and what becomes a successful expansion to the West for the United States. Indeed, as Carey McWilliams famously noted in *California: The Great Exception* (1949), the discovery of gold in California and the subsequent California Gold Rush attracted prospectors from across the world and accelerated the settlement of lands that came to be known as the western United States. One historical entry point, then, into the story of risk in the Bonita Peak Mining District is the discovery of gold in the western United States.

Space, Scale, and Risk

Space and spatial scales matter to our practices of technical and professional communication. Here we want to extend that line of reasoning to suggest that conceptualizations of risk—whether those manifest within genres utilized to perceive, assess, mitigate, manage, or communicate—also hinge upon the ways we think about space. Tracing arguments forwarded within work from Walton, Moore, and Jones (2019), Agboka (2013), Richards (2018), and Haas and Eble (2018), Banazek et al. (2022) recently argued that spatial scales influence conceptualizations of ethics. For example, Kerry Banazek and her colleagues pointed to a distinction that Walton, Moore, and Jones have drawn between *individuated conceptualizations of ethics* and *systemic conceptualizations of ethics*. Indeed, Walton, Moore, and Jones (2019) have insightfully highlighted that ethics is not only shaped at both individual and systemic levels, but more importantly that ethics that fail to attend to systemic levels can fall short of realizing progress toward the aims of social justice. Similarly, Banazek et al. (2022) directed audiences to Haas and Eble's (2018) arguments about the critical importance of considering equity across *global* and *local* scales, as shifts across these scales influence the quality of equity that manifests at these different levels. When we apply such thinking to scholarship on risk within TPC, we would like to suggest a move beyond binary thinking. We are concerned with how terms we've used to describe differences within the world contribute to abstracting and offshoring problems: First and Third World, industrial and postindustrial nations, developed and undeveloped nations, Global North and South, and, more recently, Majority and Minority World. While we value the move that the latter makes to shift attention to the deep economic privilege that only a minority of the world's population enjoys, we also worry that there are ways that such binaries present inequity and injustice as distant problems—that those comprising the Minority World might live in nations where such problems have been solved. Challenging the tradition requires an antenarrative of spatial thinking that expands the problem space of risk by understanding the geography of risks at scale. Specifically, we are concerned with the antenarratives (Jones, Moore, and Walton 2016) that challenge contemporary and seemingly monolithic understandings of risk. We assert that the absence of histories from official government and industry representation of risk within these geographies must be understood as a form of rhetorical erasure that limits how we understand the complexity and span of risk encircling this location.

The spatial dimensions of risk are best represented through two separate but interrelated events that help to illustrate why we need to understand risk across several interrelated scales. On April 26, 1986, operators of the nuclear power plant in Chernobyl, Ukraine lost control of the Number Four reactor during a test at lower power. The resulting steam and fire released at least 5 percent of the reactors' radioactive core into the environment and deposited radioactive material across Europe. The results of this disaster have been far-reaching and clouded with uncertainty. Approximately 350,000 people were evacuated and resettled. The death toll remains contested. There is large agreement that thirty people died from either blast trauma or acute radiation syndrome in the moments and months after the explosion. However, it is debatable how many deaths in the decades since the explosion can be attributed to Chernobyl. If the Chernobyl event was enough to grow the antinuclear movement, then Fukushima's 2011 earthquake-tsunami-nuclear event helped to speed up denuclearization plans. In the aftermath of that event, Germany permanently shut down eight of seventeen reactors. Chernobyl and Fukushima work best to help us understand how risk must be understood as "cosmopolitical" in the way that they both successfully achieved global attention and disrupted social life across scale (Schillmeier 2008).

Comprehending the way risk varies in different locations helps us grasp how risks influence people's lives and their environments, often presenting conflicting and competing outcomes. A few corollaries undergird our understanding of how risk and space intersect. First, *risk is always multiple.* It should not be restricted to one place and one time. Often multiple risks exist simultaneously. Second, *being at risk* and *feeling at risk* are spatially determined and should matter. Dispositions to risk connect local and global events in innumerable ways. Overlapping risks and competing reactions across space make it difficult to plan. Isolation is easier. Connecting is hard.

Detlef Müller-Mahn and Jonathan Everts (2013) offered a compelling methodology for thinking about how to link spaces. They have used the work of Appadurai (1990), Schatzki (1996, 2002), and November (2004, 2008) to emphasize how understanding the complete intricacy of connections to other risk categories requires adopting a spatial perspective. Their concept of *riskscape* enjoined risk and landscape to encompass all the potential risks and hazards within a system. This includes both known risks that have been identified and assessed, as well as potential known risks that emerge. The concept of a riskscape emphasizes the complexity and interconnectedness of risk, recognizing that they can arise from various sources and interact with each other in unpredictable ways. For us, riskscape as a concept is particularly useful for engaging with complexity. First, it emphasizes the existence of multiple risks in relation to either a local or global event. For example, the 2010 Deepwater Horizon oil spill in the Gulf of Mexico had multiple risks as a glocal event. This disaster had significant environmental, economic, and social impacts on both local ecosystems and communities, as well as global implications. On the local level, fishing and tourism industries suffered severe economic losses. However, the economic consequences of the spill extended beyond the Gulf Coast region, affecting global oil markets and energy policies. Riskscape also focuses our attention on the complex relationships of places, people, and practices. Consider the Amazon rainforest in Brazil. It plays a significant role in regulating global climate patterns. One of the biggest threats to the region is deforestation, which often results from economic activities such as agriculture, logging, and mining. Deforestation reduces the forest's ability to absorb carbon, exacerbating climate change. Loss of habitat increases the precarity of Indigenous and local communities who can no longer access the resources that form the basis of their traditional lifeways. Large-scale agricultural expansion, particularly for soybean cultivation and cattle ranching, will generate revenue for local and international markets, but it will come at the expense of environmental and social sustainability.

Riskscapes also highlight how experts' sense of risk is neither local nor a substitution for risk at other scales. Dichlorodiphenyltrichloroethane (DDT) was once hailed for its effectiveness in controlling agricultural pests and combating malaria. However, experts initially downplayed the environmental and health risks associated with DDT. It was later revealed that DDT accumulates in the environment and bioaccumulates, posing significant risks to wildlife and human health. Finally, the concept of riskscape stresses that each riskscape requires a different route of navigation and that assembling risks across spaces allows for different interpretations, estimates for damage, and opportunities for advocacy. To date, the best example that illustrates competing narratives of risk is the 2015 Flint water crisis. Residents were the first to indicate problems with the city's water quality. Residents reported health problems (e.g., rashes, hair loss, and neurological symptoms), which they attributed to the contaminated water. While some researchers did confirm there might be a problem, officials from the Michigan Department of Environmental Quality and the Environmental Protection Agency insisted that the water met safety standards (Counts 2016). The differing perspectives on risk in the Flint water crisis highlight the complexities of environmental disasters and the challenges of communication, decision-making, and governance in such situations. Competing interests, power dynamics, and institutional factors can influence how risks are perceived, interpreted, and addressed by different stakeholders. When we think about the spatial dimensions of risk, we also must factor in individuals' understandings. Risk across space changes from person to person. Positionality is key. An event changes a place, but the understanding of risk is largely determined by who controls the narrative of how space should be seen. The same event could impact the same people, but the manifestation of risk occurs quite differently in how people have established their own riskscapes. Thus, we stipulate that any discussion of risk must frame risk as fragmented and unfinished, emergent and evolving, and polyvocal. The potentiality of riskscape to uncover antenarratives allows us to be responsive to context "that invites reinterpretation of the past [and present] so as to suggest—and enable—different possibilities for the future" (Jones, Moore, and Walton 2016, 212). Perhaps this is where we see the potential for antenarratives to help us be responsive to context.

In her work with disaster, Luft (2009, 2016) advanced the need for a perspective toward disaster that appreciates the broader networks and histories surrounding such events. From a rhetorical perspective, her work foregrounded the consequences of narratives, epistemological inclinations, and policy that understand disasters as solitary exceptional events, rather than spatially and temporally situated consequences that reflect a broader and ongoing orientation to place—in Indigenous epistemologies—and relations of lands, nature, and water: "Seeking to 'de-exceptionalize' disaster, it points to the way in which 'the challenges of life are a "permanent disaster"' for people already living with the effects of structural oppression . . . Studying disaster from a perspective beyond disaster exceptionalism reframes the analysis and re-centres race, nation and other social forces" (Luft 2016, 803). Our approach to creating a historical case study or GKMS riskscape shares a methodological affinity with Luft's notion of *beyond disaster exceptionalism,* as we have also sought to think beyond the locatedness of the GKMS toward spaces and moments adjacent to the Animas River Watershed or the BPMD that are pivotal for appreciating the historical, structural, technical, and cultural dimensions of risk. We hold that by understanding the complexity of the spatial dimensions of risk, policymakers can better prepare for, mitigate, and respond to potential threats, thereby improving resilience and reducing vulnerabilities.

Figure 4.1. Map of the San Juan mining district (Fischer et al. 1883). *Source:* Public domain.

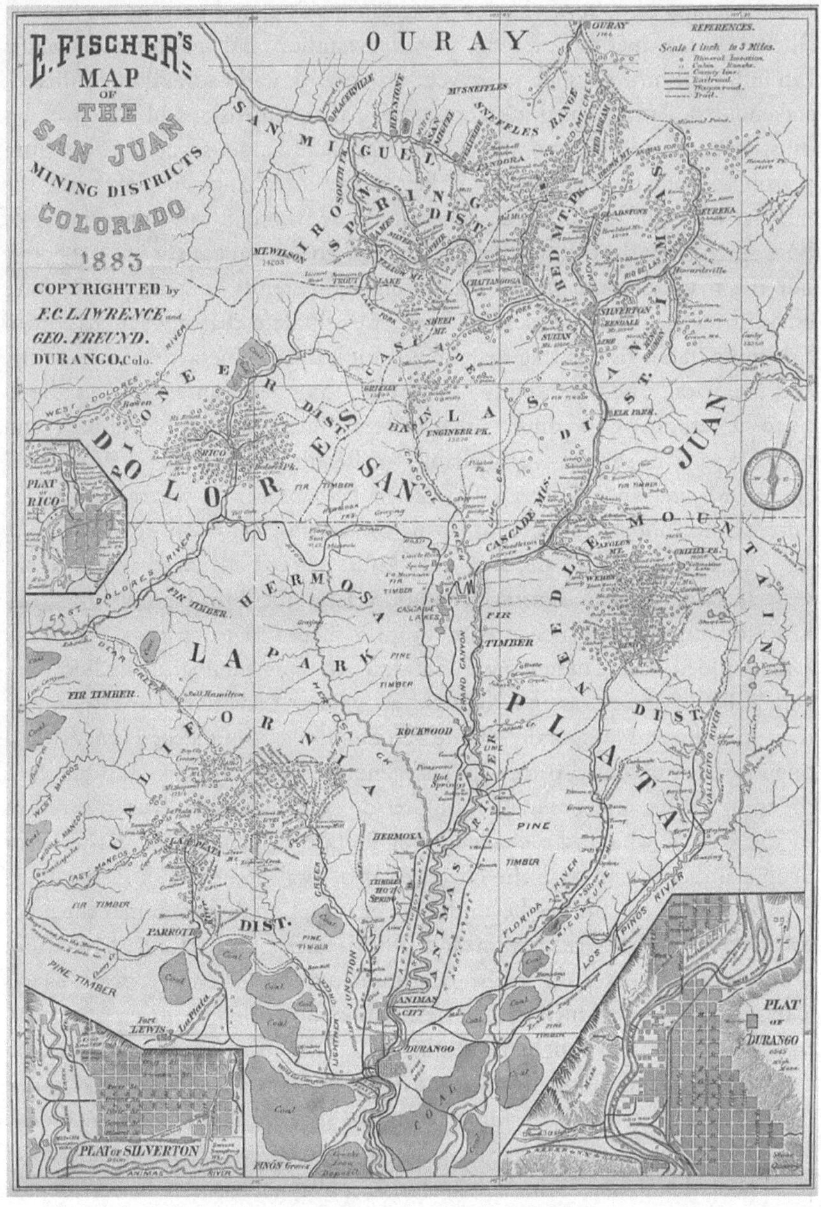

The Bonita Peak Mining District

The Bonita Peak Mining District, like many geographies in what is presently known as Colorado, is located upon the ancestral lands of allied bands of the Ute, amid the La Plata, as they were once referred to by Spanish colonists, or, as they are known today, the San Juan Mountains (see fig. 4.1). Places within this geography have been known by many names. The Animas River, or Rio de las Animas, as assigned by Juan Antonio María Rivera in the 1700s, while guided by Utes in search of silver, reflects the cascading and ongoing effects that the colonial quest for mineral resources has had upon this landscape. The Rocky Mountains have long been encircled by a mythos of abundant riches, as early settlers to the Colorado territory heard rumors of Rivera's earlier quests. Yet nearly two decades after the California Gold Rush of 1849, mining rushes spread to Colorado (Ellis 1996).

Flowing through the BPMD, the Mineral Creek, Cement Creek, and Animas River comprise the Upper Animas Watershed. Downstream from the BPMD, the Animas serves as a major tributary of the San Juan River, which, in turn, serves as a major tributary to the Colorado River. Like the rivers that flow downstream, however, the BPMD grows from the confluence of historical events shaping the promulgation and eventual abandonment of hundreds of hard-rock mines across the geography. Long before the first mines were established in the BPMD, the San Juan Mountains were inhabited by bands of Ute indigenous to the region. Indeed, allied bands of Ute, Arapaho, and Cheyenne fished, hunted, and resided across much of the geography that came to be known as the Colorado territory and later the state of Colorado. During the era of Spanish coloniality, Utes served as guides to explorers, such as Juan María de Rivera, who provided place names to many locations across the territory (Smith 1996). By the mid-1800s, after "acquiring" the territory through the Louisiana Purchase, the US government established several forts to encourage settlement. Following the passage of the Homestead Act of 1862, settlers were incentivized to venture further westward, expanding the imperialist aspirations of the US. Mining rushes intensified in Colorado during this decade, as the result of several loosely connected events that took place after surface deposits of gold that had been initially abundant during the earlier California Gold Rush had been depleted, so prospectors sought to identify new sites where valuable mineral deposits could be easily extracted (Smith 2009).

By the time the US Congress passed the General Mining Law of 1872, numerous small-scale gold and silver mining operations already dotted the southwestern Colorado landscape. According to Michael Lopez (2020), the passage of this law "stoke[d] national fervor for western settlement [and] . . . validated decades of wanton trespassing and unlawful prospecting on tribal and federal lands" (54). Existing white settlers, who were concerned over population decline within the Colorado Territory, especially along the Front Range, initiated booster campaigns that exaggerated the mineral resources of the Rocky Mountains to attract settlement (Berwanger 2007). These campaigns and increasing public demands persuaded the federal government to charge both the Army and Department of the Interior with expanding available topographic knowledge of the region to make Colorado's mountains more productive (see Bartlett 1980; USGS 2019).

Historical accounts denoted that gold in Colorado was first found in 1858 outside Denver. Upon news of the discovery, a subsequent group of prospectors rushed to establish claims outside of Boulder (Stene 1996) and near Pikes Peak outside of Colorado Springs (Smith 1996, 2009). While the US government had granted treaty lands to Native American nations, prospectors, often accompanied by US Army troops, disregarded these treaties, intruding upon these lands in search of resources. In 1860, for instance, hundreds of miners illegally established an encampment on Nez Pearce treaty lands; the Nez Perce were later coerced by the US government into a "steal treaty" that drastically reduced their access to ancestral lands (Lopez 2020). Similarly, in 1860, a group of prospectors led by US Army captain Charles Baker ventured into the San Juan Mountains on a reconnaissance mission. There the team discovered gold in the Animas River near Baker's Park, or at what is presently known as Silverton, Colorado (USGS 2007). Historical accounts suggest that early prospectors and homesteaders, including Baker's party, not only found the weather and remoteness of the San Juans hostile to settlement, but also caused conflict with the Ute, who had fished, farmed, hunted, and resided amid the San Juans for hundreds of years (Smith 1996; Denison 2017).

Following the conclusion of the Civil War, homesteaders and miners returned to the San Juans, intensifying conflicts with the allied bands of the Ute. Under the Brunot Treaty of 1873, the Ute secured a segment of territory located between Ouray and Durango, while ceding nearly 3.7 million acres of the San Juans to the federal government (see box 4.1 and fig. 4.2). Yet, according to Ellis (1996), the Ute were inaccurately led to believe that they were only ceding access to mining rights. Despite the rights the

Ute had secured to various territories via treaties, white settlers continued to press the government to remove the Ute from the region. Ultimately, tensions surrounding the use of assimilative tactics used by US government officials catalyzed the 1879 Meeker Incident (see box 4.1) and gave rise to yet another relocation that moved various bands of the Ute to either the Uintah Reservation in Utah or the southwestern corner of the state in the Four Corners region (Ellis 1996).

Box 4.1
Hard-Rock Mining and the Displacement of the Ute People

The legacy of hard-rock mining has had a profound impact on the riskscape encircling the San Juan Mountains. Native Americans, particularly the Ute People, have shouldered (and continue to shoulder) a disproportionate level of the material consequence associated with living within this riskscape.

Through a series of legislative and judicial acts, the US government systematically displaced and forcibly removed Native American People and Nations indigenous to this continent from their traditional and ancestral lands. In 1830, President Andrew Jackson signed the Indian Removal Act, granting sovereign nation status to Native American people and groups and enabling the US government to negotiate treaties that relocated Indigenous groups to Western territories. In the coming decades the US became increasingly interested in colonial, westward expansion, purchasing and creating territories. In 1861, following the gold rush in Colorado, Congress passed legislation forming the Territory of Colorado and President Lincoln established the Uintah Reservation for the Uintah bands of the Ute. The following year, Congress enacted the Homestead Act of 1862, and in 1863 the US negotiated the Conejos Treaty with the Tabeguache band of the Utes, led by Chief Ouray, granting the US government access to all land east of the Continental Divide. However, the desire for access to the minerals located in the central Rockies, including territory within the San Juans that would come to house the Bonita Peak Mining District, prompted the US to negotiate a subsequent treaty in 1868 that included the Capote/Caputa, Parinanuche, Mouache/Muache, Tabeguache/ Uncompahgre, Weeminuche, and Yampa bands. The Sabuagan, Uintah,

Timpanogos, Pahvant, Sanpits, and Seuvarits/Sherberetch bands of the Utes were not signatories to the 1868 treaty. A few years later, Congress passed the 1871 Indian Appropriations Act, which effectively ended the practice of recognizing Native American Nations as sovereign and independent. Despite this change, the US nevertheless sought to establish control of the San Juan Mountain area and negotiated the Brunot Agreement of 1873 with the Utes. While the Utes believed they were opening their hunting and fishing grounds to mining and granting mineral rights to the US, the agreement, since viewed by the Utes as fraudulent, ceded 3.7 million acres of the San Juans to the US government.

Constrained by the provisions of these various treaties and agreements and resistant to the attempts of Indian Agency representatives who sought to assimilate the Utes, tensions grew, culminating in the Meeker Incident of 1879. Following a conflict between Johnson Canavish, a Ute leader, and John Meeker, head of the US government's White River Indian Agency, Meeker enlisted the support of the 9th Cavalry, which entered the reservation of the Yampa and Parinanuche Utes. Despite warnings from the Utes that they would assert their sovereignty over the reservation, the soldiers invaded, kicking off a battle. The Meeker Incident served as a pretext for Governor Pitkin to mobilize racist rhetoric to build support for pushing the Utes out of the newly recognized state. The Utes entered into the compulsory Agreement with the Confederated Bands of Ute in 1880, which was ratified by Congress in 1881, as the Ute Removal Act. This act forced the Yampa, Parinauche, and Tabeguache/Uncompahgre bands onto the Uintah Reservation in Utah. The Mouache and Caputa bands of the Utes were moved to the Southern Ute Reservation, a narrow piece of land abutting the Four Corners area in the most southwestern corner of the state. The Weenuchi/Mountain Ute located within the westernmost area of this reservation; later this segment of the Southern Ute Reservation formally became reorganized as the Mountain Ute Reservation (O'Rourke 1980; Southern Ute n.d.; Ellis 1996).

Following the federalization of the San Juans, the first mines that would eventually comprise the larger BPMD were established. Two sites are particularly important to our discussion of the BPMD in the context of the GKS within the Upper Animas Watershed—the Sunnyside and Gold King Mines. In 1873, Ruben McNutt and George Howard forwarded a claim for the Sunnyside Mine situated near Lake Emma in the Upper Animas

Watershed and established the Eureka Mining District (Thompson 2016a). As additional claims proliferated, settlements sprung up across the watershed in Animas, Gladstone, Howardsville, and Silverton (Smith 1996; Vendel and Vendel 2015). Following pressure from silver mining companies, who sought to increase demand for the metal, Congress passed the Bland Allison Act in 1878, which drove the US Treasury to purchase $2 million to $4 million worth of silver per month (Stene 1996). While the act increased demand for silver, increasing production reduced the value of this metal. This signifies the first of what will be a series of successive boom-and-bust cycles surrounding the profitability of this industry in Colorado.

Operations began at the GKM nearly a decade after the establishment of Sunnyside. While working at the Sampson Mine in 1887, Olaf Arvid Nelson established the GKM (Kuhl 2022; US EPA 2023a). In 1890, the nearby Red and Bonita mine was established (US EPA n.d.), which was

Figure 4.2. Expatriation of the Ute from their traditional and ancestral territory, 1800 to present (Delayney 1974 in O'Rourke 1980). *Source:* Public domain.

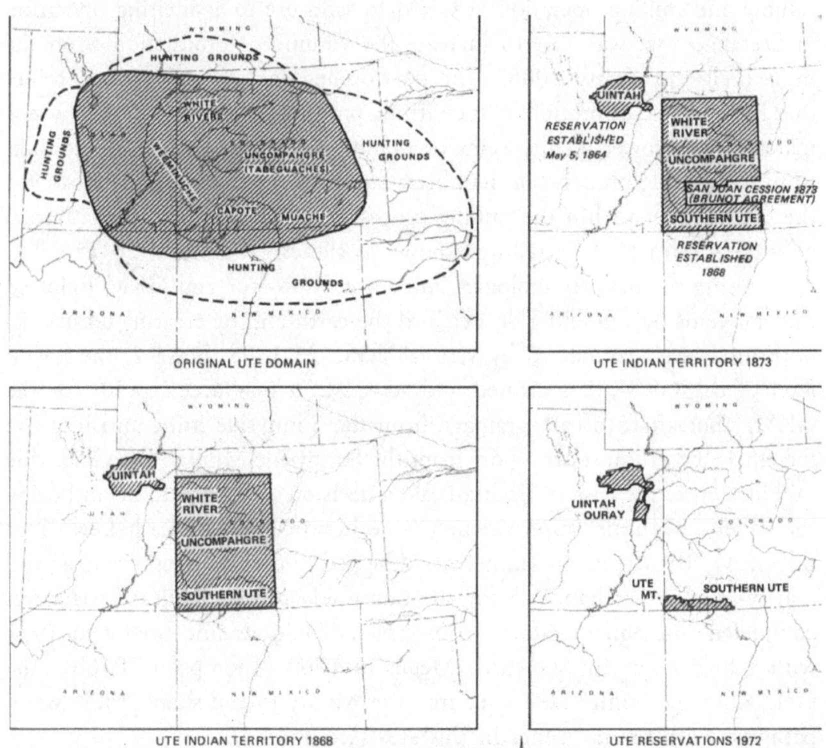

eventually expanded to contain forty nearby mines (Evans 2023). This moment also coincides with the increasing industrialization of mining technologies throughout the 1890s. The development of a hydropower mill and mechanized mining equipment led to increasing efficiency of extraction and caused, subsequently, the size, depth, and overall scope of mines such as GKM to grow; this corporatization had the effect of displacing smaller-scale prospecting practices. The silver mining industry experienced a boom cycle, as Congress passed the Sherman Silver Purchase Act of 1890, increasing the amount of silver that the US Treasury purchased monthly to 4.5 million ounces (Stene 1996). However, this boom would be short lived, as anxieties about the increased number of silver dollars issued by the US Treasury led to a run on the gold stock backing the dollar. In turn, Congress repealed the Sherman Silver Purchase Act in 1893, causing a decrease in the demand for and value of silver (Malone 1986; Stene 1996; Hoffman 2002; Taussig 1893).

Despite the devaluation of silver and the closure of some mines, the expanded efficiency of industrial extraction methods and railroad transportation were enough to buoy some mines within the industry. In particular, the extension of the Denver and Rio Grande Railway to Silverton enabled the mining and milling operation at GKM to send ore to a smelting operation in Durango that was able to increase the volume of production from the mine (Fell and Twitty 2008). The development of milling enabled mines that had become unprofitable to continue production by extracting new raw material from lower quality veins or milling the mine tailings, by-products from the mining process that had been discarded on mining sites. However, the use of water within the milling process resulted in a new concentrated, gelatinous form of toxic tailings known as slimes (Thompson 2018).

Using the new technologies, miners at Sunnyside and GKM followed mineral veins by tunneling deeper into the earth and by creating additional horizontal levels connected by vertical shafts. In 1898, Level 7, the lowest level of the GKM, was created and served as a new access point for the GKM. Thereafter, to ease drainage from the Sunnyside mine and improve the efficiency of transporting ore from the Sunnyside Mine to the Gladstone mill located at the base of Bonita Peak, a decision was made to begin boring the American Tunnel approximately nine hundred feet beneath Level 7 of the GKM. The American Tunnel was designed to provide deep drainage and gravity-assisted ore handling for the Sunnyside Mine. While it was never completed, subsequent efforts to extend it would resume briefly in 1921 with a final effort by Standards Metals in 1960 (Thompson 2016b). The Gold King and Sunnyside mines are in proximity to and share groundwater pathways with several mines in this area (see fig. 4.3).

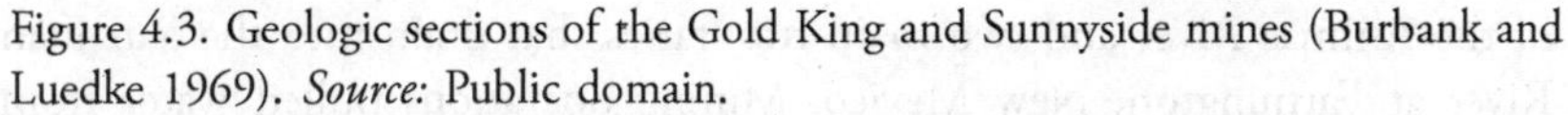

Figure 4.3. Geologic sections of the Gold King and Sunnyside mines (Burbank and Luedke 1969). *Source:* Public domain.

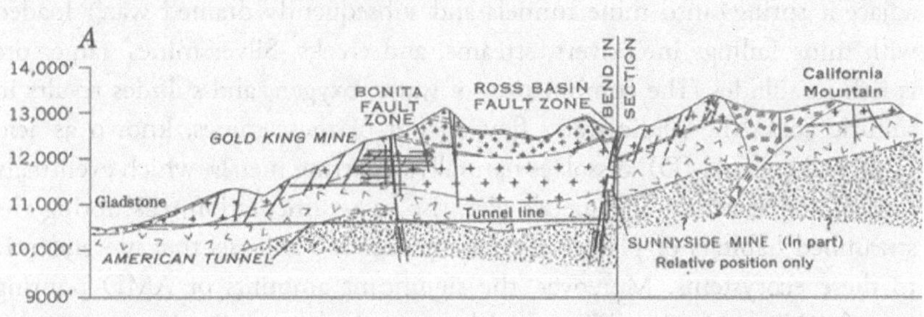

According to Malone (1986), several factors throughout the twentieth century—war, offshoring, globalization, and increasing environmental regulation—would contribute to the slow demise of the hard-rock-mining industry within the US. In the 1920s, US mining companies began broadening operations to the Global South, which offered mining companies access to new metals and minerals. This international shift, in turn, led to greater competition, weakening the dominance of mines located in the US. Thereafter, especially following the widespread promulgation of state and federal environmental regulations in the 1970s such as the Clean Water Act that placed responsibility for remediating the hazards mining companies had created within lands and watersheds, the economic feasibility of mining within the US declined as mining became offshored to Majority World nations.

By the 1970s the footprint of the Sunnyside Mine had considerably expanded beyond McNutt and Howard's original claim. Both the Gold King and Sunnyside Mines would pass hands from owner to owner on numerous occasions, following the boom-and-bust cycles of the US mining industry. In bust times, when mines in the US became unprofitable, they were often abandoned by owners, occasionally reopening when markets shifted, or technologies emerged that enabled the mines to produce profits again. Today, the Colorado Geological Survey has estimated that there are over twenty-three thousand abandoned mines in the state. GKM is one of at least two hundred abandoned and inactive mining sites within the BPMD and the Upper Animas Watershed. When considering the adjacent San Juan Watershed, this number doubles.

The environmental legacy of these mining operations within the BPMD is that they have had a deleterious impact on the hydrology of this watershed (Von Guerard et al. n.d.) (see box 4.2). The Upper Animas Watershed consists of the Animas River and two main tributaries that drain into the San Juan River at Farmington, New Mexico. Mining operations pulled water from adjacent springs into mine tunnels and subsequently drained water loaded with mine tailings into rivers, streams, and creeks. Silver mines' target ore is rich in sulfides. The combination of water, oxygen, and sulfides results in sulfuric acid. The acidic water flowing out of these mines, known as acid mine drainage (AMD), dissolves naturally occurring metals, which eventually load alpine streams. The metals give rise to sedimentation, disrupting the streambed habitats of plants, insects, and aquatic animals that are endemic to these ecosystems. Moreover, the significant amounts of AMD pouring into the Upper Animas Watershed have resulted in acidity levels too toxic for most species of trout to survive and causes the insects and invertebrates to absorb metals, in turn spreading up the food web.

Consequently, several techniques have been used to reduce the impacts of AMD flowing from the Gold King and Sunnyside Mines into the Upper Animas River (the distributed and interconnected forms of immediate, environmental risk in mining projects can be difficult to understand; for a brief explanation, see box 4.2). For instance, tailings ponds have been created to collect and treat contaminated AMD from both mines. The water is treated via a process where lime is added to raise the PH of water to a level where the metals are no longer soluble, thus the suspended metals settle at the bottom of the ponds and the clean water at the top flows out. The mines within the BPMD have had a harmful impact on this watershed, as the slow seepage of groundwater traveling through the mines, as well as the surface water combining with tailings piles that remain from mining and milling in the area, create AMD that flows into Cement and Mineral Creeks. Moreover, two catastrophic AMD spills occurred within the BPMD prior to the Gold King Mine disaster. The first occurred when a treatment pond that held tailings outside of the Mayflower Mill in Silverton owned by Standards Metals (the current owner of the Sunnyside Mine) collapsed in 1975 following heavy rains, releasing the toxic sludge into the Animas. The second catastrophic release occurred when, despite concerns from miners about the structural integrity, Standards Metals pushed on with work inside a shaft of the Sunnyside Mine that ran below Lake Emma. The roof of the shaft collapsed, allowing millions of gallons from Lake Emma to flood the mine, which, combined with tailings in the mine, sent a deluge of AMD into the watershed from the American Tunnel (Thompson 2015).

Box 4.2
Making Sense of Risk in Seemingly Dis/connected Systems

Understanding risk in relation to dis/connected systems, especially systems within the networks of industrial mining projects, involves many interconnected factors.

- *Hydrological Complexity*: A range of factors (e.g., soil type, rock formations, aquifer characteristics, and flow patterns) influence groundwater systems. It can be difficult to predict how contaminants move through a system as their impact can vary between short distances.
- *Contaminant Behavior*: Distinct contaminants behave differently in groundwater systems. Some contaminants move quickly; some may bind to soil; others may degrade over time. It is necessary to understand the chemical properties of contaminants to predict their behavior. Contaminants from mining operations, such as heavy metals and acid mine drainage, behave differently in the environment (Jha et al. 2016).
- *Weather Events*: Natural events (e.g., heavy rain/snowfall and snowmelt) have the potential to exacerbate risks. For example, heavy rainfall can increase the flow of water and lead to the destabilization of contaminant containment sites.
- *Interactions with Surface Water*: The connection between groundwater and surface water is complex. The GKMS demonstrates how groundwater is connected to surface water systems and how contamination of groundwater can impact surface water systems and water supplies.
- *Limited Data*: The quality and availability of data on mine conditions and groundwater flow is limited. Considering this missing data, it is nearly impossible to accurately assess risks. For example, what made the GKMS a disaster was the lack of information on the exact connection and conditions of mine tunnels.

- *Liability Ambiguity*: Mining sites often change ownership multiple times in the history of a mine. It can be difficult to identify who is accountable for maintaining a site or mitigating associated risks. This also makes the outcome of liability uncertain, in which determining who is legally or financially responsible for a site is seemingly impossible.
- *Historical Mining Practices*: Mining practices change over time. Previous mining practices have left a legacy of environmental issues (e.g., inadequate or deteriorated containment structures). A combination of old infrastructure and unmanaged waste can exacerbate risk.

Mining operations at Sunnyside continued until 1991, when the mine closed due to depressed gold prices, but Sunnyside's abandoned, unfinished American Tunnel was still a source of continual acid discharges. As a corrective, Sunnyside's owners, Sunnyside Gold Corporation, pulled water from the American Tunnel into a treatment plant designed to remove metals from Cement Creek and improve water quality within the Animas River Watershed. Sunnyside Gold later agreed to a consent decree in 1996 with the state of Colorado that allowed it to shutter the water treatment plant. As part of this agreement, Sunnyside Gold installed a series of bulkheads in the American Tunnel that were designed to plug the mine and stop the acid flow from entering Cement Creek. The bulkheads reduced the flow of toxic mine waste into Cement Creek, which decreased from 1,700 gallons per minute to about 100 gallons per minute (Hannon 2022). However, water drainage from Level 7 increased despite the American Tunnel never being connected to GKM. The increased drainage was peculiar, because GKM had been dry for much of its history due to drainage from the American Tunnel. In 2015, the bulkheads installed at this entry point became the failure point for the mine (Thompson 2016b; EPA 2016). From 2001 to 2015, it was widely believed that Sunnyside's plugged mine was at capacity and spilling into adjacent mines. However, Sunnyside Gold repeatedly denied these claims. According to the Bureau of Reclamation's assessment, the EPA assumed that Level 7 of the GKM was not full of water because of previous excavations and planned for five to six feet of water (Hannon 2022). Previously, the EPA had drilled into the Red and Bonita Mine in 2011 to check water levels but did not do so for GKM.

To address the AMD, EPA sought to inspect the GKM bulkhead and, if necessary, divert water from GKM. Contractors advised the EPA that accessing the mine could result in a blowout; however, the EPA continued anyway. On August 5, 2015 around 10:30 a.m., the contracting crew ruptured the mine, causing the contaminated water to spill out. It is estimated that three million gallons of orange contaminated water poured into Cement Creek and caused the Animas River's pH to drop from 7.8 to 5.8. For eight days the wastewater plume spread throughout the San Juan River Watershed as it coursed through the San Juan and Colorado Rivers and terminated at Lake Powell. The area directly affected encompassed four states (Colorado, New Mexico, Arizona, and Utah) and five American Indian reservations (Southern Ute Indian Tribe, the Navajo Nation, the Ute Mountain Ute Indian Tribe, and the Jicarilla Apache Tribe). Immediate consequences of the disaster included fish kill, increased sediment loading in the Animas and San Juan, pollution of water necessary for caring for livestock on ranches and irrigating farmlands, and exacerbation of the precariousness of water supply in the West.

Box 4.3
Colorado Mining Timeline

This extended timeline presents an expanded view of how the GKMS was not an isolated incident but rather part of a larger legacy of extractive industry in the region to produce multiple risks. The timeline emphasizes spatial-temporal entanglement to show how a network of past industrial actions shapes present and future risks across ecosystems and communities.

1849 | Gold Rush in California: The start of a significant influx of prospectors to the region, leading to widespread mining activity.

1859 | Colorado Gold Rush in the Front Range

1860 | Charles Baker Finds Gold in Eureka: Baker discovers gold but is driven out by the Ute tribe, who had been awarded land in a treaty. Prospectors invade Nez Perce tribal lands. The US government forces the Nez Perce into the "Steal Treaty" of 1863, displacing the tribe for mining purposes.

1871 | Miners Return

1872 | General Mining Law Passed: Congress validates decades of unlawful prospecting on tribal and federal lands.

1873 | Brunot Treaty: The Utes "cede" their lands.

1877 | War Between Nez Perce and US

1878 | Bland-Allison Act: Mandates the purchase of 2–4 million ounces of silver per month, impacting silver value.

1880 | Uranium Discovered in Colorado

1881 | Utes Transferred: The Utes are forcibly moved to Uintah Reservations in northern Utah and the Southern Utes to Four Corners New Mexico.

1889 | Mill and Hydropower Developed in Eureka: Advances in extraction efficiency with new industrial methods.

1890 | Sherman Silver Purchase Act: US government mandates the purchase of 4.5 million ounces of silver per month.

1890s | Industrialization of Mining: Corporate mining practices displace individual prospectors and European immigrants begin to replace Latino/a/x communities historically employed in the mining sector.

1893 | Collapse of Silver Industry: A run on the US Treasury's gold stock due to anxieties over silver dollars leads Congress to repeal the Sherman Silver Purchase Act, causing the collapse of the silver industry.

1896 | Silverton Railroad: Development of infrastructure supporting mining.

1900 | Transition in Mining Focus: Transition from silver and other minerals to coal mining.

1913 | Colorado Fuel and Iron Co. Purchases Holdings: Acquisition of properties in Las Animas County.

1939 | Sunnyside Mill Closes

1953 | US Uranium Mining Boom: The United States was the world's leading producer of uranium from 1953 until 1980.

2020 | Abandoned Mines and Environmental Impact: An estimated 160,000 abandoned hard-rock mines in the American West; 1.1 million hard-rock claims on public domain; 40 percent of Western watersheds impacted by acid mine drainage. Over 600,000 Indigenous people live within 6 miles of abandoned mines.

Respatializing Risk and the Bonita Peak Mining District

This chapter's focus on spatial complexity seeks to enact a methodological commitment to tracing a larger history of risk that encircles the BPMD, rather than working to focus on the disaster as an isolated event, as is the case with many studies of risk communication within disasters (compare box 4.3 and box 4.4). Indeed, following the GKMS, numerous federal, state, tribal, and municipal agencies, including the EPA, the Department of the Interior, the US Army Corps of Engineers, the Colorado Division of Reclamation, Mining, and Safety, the Utah Department of Environmental Quality, the Navajo Nation EPA, the Navajo Nation Department of Public Safety, and the US Congress, sought to mitigate the downstream harm of the spill, understand the causes of the disaster, identify the parties responsible for the disaster, and apply the lessons learned from the disaster to future events. To accomplish this work, agencies undertook investigations, promulgating thousands of pages of transcripts, analytical reviews, technical reports, policy recommendations, and press releases.

Box 4.4
US Environmental Protection Agency's (EPA) Timeline of the Gold King Mine Spill

In contrast to the extended timeline, the EPA timeline represents an institutional framing of risk that reduces scale and complexity. This timeline frames risk as a discrete, manageable accident that can be localized to a single site. Furthermore, spatial definitions reflect how government agencies conceptualize space and prioritize certain scales as proxies for legal boundaries, such as jurisdiction, liability, and response protocols. We ask that you compare both timelines and consider the relationship between narrative power and accountability and note how different actors' assessments of space and time claim authority, assign blame, and ultimately shape public perception.

2014 | EPA releases draft of its Baseline Ecological Risk Assessment (BERA): The EPA determined that metals flowing from Cement Creek present significant risks to the aquatic environment for several miles downstream of the mining area. The aquatic community was expected to experience damage up to thirty miles downstream from Silverton.

August 5, 2015 | Initial Incident: During cleanup efforts a breach occurs in a waste-water retention pond. This breach releases a significant amount of toxic mine waste, including heavy metals like lead, arsenic, and cadmium, into the Animas River.

August 7, 2015 | EPA Response: The EPA publicly acknowledges responsibility for the spill. Officials begin assessing the environmental impact and start efforts to contain and mitigate the contamination.

August 8, 2015 | Emergency Actions: The EPA, along with state and local agencies, initiates emergency response measures to manage the contaminated water and address the concerns of affected communities.

August 9–10, 2015 | Plume arrives at Utah–New Mexico Border

August 11, 2015 | Local Impact: Water quality testing shows elevated levels of pollutants, prompting authorities to issue warnings and advisories for affected areas. The contamination affects agriculture, fisheries, and drinking water supplies.

August 12, 2015 | Federal Response: The federal government begins coordinating with state and local agencies to provide support and resources for the cleanup and recovery efforts.

August 15, 2015 | Plume arrives at Lake Powell

August 15, 2015 | EPA and State Coordination: The EPA works with state agencies to plan for long-term remediation and monitoring of the affected river systems.

August 22, 2015 | Recovery Efforts: The EPA releases a report on the immediate impact and response to the disaster.

October 2015 | Ongoing Impact Assessment: Long-term environmental assessments and health studies begin to evaluate the full impact of the spill on ecosystems and local communities.

January 2016 | Final Report: The EPA's final report outlines the causes of the incident, the response actions taken, and recommendations for preventing future disasters.

2016–2019 | Remediation and Monitoring: Other observed environmental effects prompt the EPA to suggest adding the Bonita Peak Mining District to the National Priorities List (NPL) of hazardous waste sites in the United States eligible for long-term investigation and remedial action financed under the federal Superfund program.

Continued efforts to clean up and monitor the Animas River and surrounding areas.

2020 | Legal and Policy Review: Ongoing legal proceedings and policy reviews related to the spill, including discussions on compensation for affected communities and improvements to mine cleanup practices.

2024 | Continued Monitoring.

While the GKMS, as an event, could warrant a comprehensive, book-length study into what the technical documentation that surrounds this event reveals about risk and communication, and while we, too, began our work by analyzing numerous technical reports, we have decided to purposefully deviate from such a traditional approach. This is because, as we began our analyses of this discourse, we found ourselves asking questions about the spaces and places shaping this riskscape that were conspicuously absent from the reports. Moreover, we began to see that a spectrum of distinct spatial frames was operating tacitly with official statements and discourse about the GKMS that flattened risk in ways that deserved further critical attention. To interrogate those flattened accounts of risk, we have limited our analysis to a single piece of discourse, the opening statements offered during an oversight meeting of the Committee on Environment and Public Works of the US Senate held on September 16, 2015. During the meeting, EPA director Gina McCarthy was called to account for her agency's role in the spill and subsequent disaster response. This piece of discourse was selected because it illustrates how spatial frames tacitly delimit the boundaries of riskscapes such as the BPMD. That is, this example usefully illustrates how accounts of riskscapes, as rhetorical constructions, flatten the spatial (and temporal) complexity of risk and offer productive entry points for considering how to challenge such flattened accounts with spatially and temporally complicated antenarratives like the account we've offered above (Committee on Environment and Public Works, United States Senate, 2015).

When the Senate Committee on Environment and Public Works convened approximately one month following the GKMS, communities such as Durango, Colorado, Farmington, New Mexico, and the Navajo Nation were reeling from the consequences of having lost access to the Animas and San Juan Watersheds. These watersheds underpin recreation and cultural activities, sustain life and ecosystems, and support ranching, tourism, and farming industries in the region. The purpose of the meeting was to identify the root causes of and responsibility for the GKMS, including the role that EPA played in causing, responding to, and mitigating the spill and the specific actions Congress might take to mitigate the risk of future spills. Again, we've selected this piece of discourse because the senators and Director McCarthy of the EPA made statements about risk that illuminate a range of differential spatial frames for understanding this spill.

The first two opening statements of the meeting were issued respectively by Senator Cory Gardner (R-CO) and Senator Michael Bennet (D-CO). In their statements, both senators called attention to the meso-scale of the spill, discussing the economic and environmental impacts shouldered by communities within the region including the Animas River Watershed, the San Juan River Watershed, the City of Durango, the States of Colorado and New Mexico, and the Navajo, Mountain Ute, and Southern Ute Nations and People. However, both senators also considered risk at the micro-scale of the disaster, including the causes of the bulkhead failure within the Gold King Mine, the EPA actions on the day of the spill, and the amount of sediment deposited and resuspended in riverbeds during heavy rains and high flows during spring runoff. Yet, in comparison to Gardner, Bennet's opening statement augmented and extended the spatial frame used to encircle this riskscape. While both senators traced the downstream harm caused by the blowout and release of three millions gallons of AMD from the GKM site into the Animas to the San Juan Watersheds, Bennet specifically sought to contextualize the scope of GKMS as a risk event that illustrated a larger, more comprehensive level of risk faced by the state of Colorado: "There are more than 23,000 abandoned mines in Colorado, Mr. Chairman, including 400 in the San Juan Mountains. We need solutions to address the acid mine drainage coming from all of these old abandoned mines" (Committee on Environment and Public Works 2015, 11). That is, as elected officials representing the interests of the State of Colorado, both shared a concern for this watershed and mentioned the direct impacts of the GKMS on this watershed and its constituents. Yet Bennet offered a perspective toward this riskscape that considered the local effects of this event on this specific watershed *and* considered the broader regional history and impacts of AMD as it related to the tens of thousands of abandoned mines located within Colorado.

Here we want to suggest that the distinctions in the *spatial perspectives* the two senators took toward framing the scale of this risk event appear to illuminate a tacit rhetorical tension that is recurrent across the length of the committee meeting. It appears to be tacit because at no point within the meeting did a speaker overtly draw attention to the different boundaries forwarded to encircle the scope of this riskscape. Despite this direct omission, space nevertheless appeared to be a clear site of tension, as speakers seemed to purposefully delimit the spatial (and temporal) boundaries that influence how risk might be understood within the BPMD. Is this risk event one that is caused by the actions that the EPA took to remediate the Gold King Mine? Is this a risk event that is connected to the complex ways that the various mines in the BPMD have affected the hydrology? Is this a risk event that illustrates the insufficiency of mining regulations? Is it a risk event that illuminates the environmental risks associated with hard-rock mining? Is this a risk event that highlights the environmental impacts of abandoned mines and acid mine drainage? It is a risk event that is, of course, influenced by all of these factors. However, the various speakers appear to be inclined to spatialize risk at differing scales. Why?

The two senators from New Mexico offered their opening statements after the senators from Colorado. First, Senator Tom Udall (D-NM) further expanded the spatial boundaries surrounding the GKM disaster beyond those set earlier by Gardner and Bennet to the meso- and macro-scales. First, he underscored that the affected watersheds are places with rich spiritual significance to Native American Nations and People of this region. Eerily foreshadowing the Standing Rock Sioux protest of the Dakota Access Pipeline, Udall shared that the Navajo have a phrase, water is life (*tó éí íìñá át'é*), that marks the sacred location that water as a relation holds within the Navajo cosmology. Here it appears that Udall recognized that there is a dimension to space, the spiritual value it can hold as a place, that hadn't been acknowledged. Moreover, Udall noted that the risk that encircles this mining location is not unique to Colorado but should be understood "as a big national issue," as the EPA has identified nearly a dozen mines with "similar conditions" that are being considered for the National Priority List or Superfund status (Committee on Environment and Public Works 2015, 16). Similarly, when Senator Martin Heinrich (D-NM) framed the disaster, he also worked from a meso-scale frame, first tracing the flow of the pollution from Cement Creek, through the Animas and San Juan Rivers and into the Four Corners region, before further expanding the spatial frame to add the State of Arizona to the list of regional entities affected. However, he also introduced physical maps of southwestern Colorado and New Mexico that indicate the location of "literally thousands of unreclaimed hard rock mines" (20). His overreaching point: the spatial scale of risk seen in this one disaster is indicative of a more substantial risk that has been widely distributed "across the West" (20).

However, when Senator Jim Inhofe (R-OK) forwarded his statement on the disaster, the frame of risk surrounding the spill was constrained to a much smaller, micro-level scale. His opening statement primarily emphasized discussion of the entrance to the Gold King Mine, the water trapped behind the bulkhead, and the Gold King and Red and Bonita Mines. While Inhofe briefly acknowledged that this mine is located within a region, the BPMD, that has a longer, ongoing history with AMD, his statement largely focused on these more fine-grained spatial locations and dimensions for framing risk. That is, Inhofe expanded the temporal boundaries of risk, while spatially limiting the discussion of risk to this local site in comparison to the frames cast by senators Heinrich, Udall, and Bennet.

When Senator Barbara Boxer (D-CA) offered her opening statement, we see another turn toward expanding the spatial perspective toward risk in the Gold King Mine spill. Boxer made note of the actions of EPA at the site and observed that in California there are nearly fifty thousand abandoned hard-rock mines, before emphasizing that there are half a million abandoned hard-rock mines in the US. In doing so, Boxer acknowledged the micro- (GKM) and meso- (Colorado and California) scales of risk, but framed this as a national exigency that posed risk at a macro-level scale. What is most interesting about Senator Boxer's statement, however, is that she appeared to gesture, indirectly, toward the tension that may underlie the differing spatiotemporal frames contained by the respective senators' risk narratives: "Instead of scoring political points by blaming EPA, Congress could use this and should use this as an opportunity to focus on the longstanding issue of abandoned hard rock mines that pollute our rivers and streams" (Committee on Environment and Public Works 2015, 27). In other words, focusing more narrowly on the spill as a spatially and temporally localized risk event that culminated in the release of pollution into the Animas and San Juan River Watersheds, with direct environmental and economic effects, supports narratives where the EPA is situated as the catalyst for the event. Conversely, focusing more broadly on the national legacy of abandoned hard-rock mines recasts the focus on the macro-scale, systemic risk that these mines pose to communities broadly distributed across the US. In the latter, the actions the EPA took leading up to the spill might be understood as contributing to the risk event but are not framed as the sole cause for the spill.

Yet, when Director McCarthy responded, she largely emphasized the role of the EPA within events that unfolded across the micro- and meso-level scales, offering considerable detail to the constituent components of the watershed, the mining site, EPA actions, and the actions and roles that municipal, state, and tribal entities took on during the planning phases that preceded the spill event as well as their actions and roles during the response phase. In this way, the spatial frame that McCarthy selected also contracted; yet, Director McCarthy in her response offered a richness of detail about the risks at micro- and meso-levels that is ultimately contextualized within a macro-scale frame, as she underscored that these micro- and meso-scale actions must be understood within the larger macro-scale legacy of abandoned hard-rock mines and the jurisdictional mandate that EPA has for administering the Superfund program. This placed EPA with the responsibility of mitigating and solving the risks associated with the most complex and difficult hazardous waste sites across the US.

Relocating Risk: Why Spatializing Risk Matters

In the questioning and responses that followed the opening statements of the committee, we identify similar fluxes in where and how various senators and McCarthy sought to reframe the spatiotemporal perspective toward how risk was or could be understood, communicated, or managed within this event. For instance, Senators Inhofe and Gardner offered the most spatially flattened accounts of risk in their opening statements, suggesting that pollution sealed within a location, released by the actions of a federal agency, adversely impacted downstream communities. Their accounts offered a linear representation of spatiotemporal relations, as the risk-laden waters trapped within the GKM mine rapidly escaped into Cement Creek, before flowing downstream into the larger San Juan and Colorado River Watersheds. Or, even more simply, the risk contained at a micro-scale, local site (GKM) through its travels has meso-scale, regional-level consequences (to the Animas River Watershed and to Colorado–New Mexico–the Navajo Nation–Arizona). Viewed in the broadest spatial frame, their accounts offer a meso-scale perspective that is sensitive to the effects that the risk-laden waters pose to a network of regional stakeholders affected by the disaster (e.g., Colorado, New Mexico, Ute Mountain Ute, Navajo Nation, City of Durango, Four Corners Region, rafting companies operating out of the Durango area, trout). Yet the spatial frame they forwarded also artificially constrains the boundaries of the riskscape within an event-based approach toward disaster.

Conversely, Senators Udall and Boxer offered the most spatially comprehensive accounts of risk in their opening statements, recognizing that this localized event with regional consequences is illustrative of the broader risks that thousands of abandoned hard-rock mines pose across the West and US. Their accounts offered a networked, distributed representation of spatiotemporal relations, reframing the micro-scale, local-origin (risk has been contained in GKM) event that carries meso-scale, regional-level consequences (risk flows and affects downstream locations) as a situated example of the profound scale that mining activity has across the geography of the US. Even still, there are spatial (as well as temporal) dimensions of risk that are still left unconsidered.

Why, then, do we see these senators seeking to spatialize risk in competing ways? We believe these moves, which spatialize risk at a macro-, meso-, or micro-scale, support various senators' rhetorical aims regarding the reality of risk—how risk might be known, who is at risk, who is responsible for risk, and why they are responsible. We understand this rhetorical work as emanating from and activating four key frames of risk in relation to spatiotemporal conditions. Central to our analysis is how we might use the heuristic we've outlined in chapter 3 to help us expand our thinking. Specifically, we can use it to mobilize the realized realities of risk present in this disaster as well as spatiotemporal risk frames that have been overlooked. In what follows, we attend to risks' spatialization in the GKMS.

Spatializing Risk Through a Localized, Event-Driven Frame

A localized-event-driven frame positions risk as the outcomes of a disaster event. One consequence of this frame is that it fails to consider the distributed, system-driven risks that encircle a disaster. Here one narrative is that risk is contained within the GKM: *The EPA caused risk to be dispersed.* From this perspective, the risk is centralized to the mine and its contents. This is largely at the expense of considering risk in relation to the network of abandoned hard-rock mines, which were created when no regulations existed on remediating the harm. If your goal is to promote the growth of extractive industry, or if you benefit from industry having more access to lands, then you're more likely to support antiregulatory stances on the industry's behalf. The master narrative here is that the EPA is the problem and industry is the good guy. This spatial frame advances the argument that too much regulation prohibits industry from accessing sites or remediating sites.

There was never a downstream. In fact, risk in downstream areas never emerged until the EPA caused the spill. This "big government" disposition is an often-recycled argument of scale that points to the size and complexity of bureaucracy in addition to the irony of regulation. "Big government" implies that bureaucracy is too large to respond efficiently to crises. Moreover, it encourages audiences to understand the GKMS as a symptom of this inefficiency, suggesting that government agencies are ill-equipped to manage environmental risks at this scale. It also disallows attending to distal risks and thinking systematically about the risks that surround local choices, which can have consequential effects that range from neglecting distal risks to misguided public perceptions of safety to a limited understanding of how micro-level conditions and choices lead to macro-level risks. Consider how Republican senators emphasized risk and consequence within micro- and meso-level frames (or GKMS as a localized distinct event) and Democratic senators tended to emphasize risk and consequence within meso- and macro-level frames (or the legacy that hard-rock mining, abandoned mines, and AMD have across the BPMD, the American West, and the US). Within the testimony, various entities and officials most commonly spatialized risk at the micro-scale: framing and discussing risk in relation to the GKM, the audit, the bulkhead, or its economic impacts on distinct, local-level entities such as the rafting industry within the city of Durango or farmers in the Navajo Nation; or framing and discussing risk at the meso-scale in relation to the Animas River Watershed, the Bonita Peak Mining District/San Juan Mountains, or the municipalities, states, and tribal nations directly affected by the spill. These statements, we argue, reflect what might be understood as a normative yet flattened disposition toward a spatiality of this riskscape that is especially inflected by the time-bound nature of this disaster as an event.

Spatializing Risk as a Component of Epideictic Rhetoric

In this frame, the rhetorical effects of particular spatial frames become clearer. Here the distinct spatial frames (event driven versus distributed and networked) align with the partisan topoi (commonplaces) that the various senators forwarded within epideictic arguments about causality, accountability, and the responsibility of governments at federal, state, and local levels and the role that industry has played in terms of contributing to the riskscape and the future role they should play in terms of their responsibility for mitigating or resolving pollution. Put more simply, spatial frames enabled speakers to proffer accounts of the riskscape that levy praise and blame on distinct actors. On one hand, Senators Gardner and Inhofe were attuned to risk at the micro-scale, questioning the actions EPA took (or failed to take) at the site in the days preceding the spill, including at (its finest level of resolution) discussion of the EPA's knowledge of conditions behind the adit (an entrance shaft to an underground mine) that sealed the Gold King Mine and influenced the risk of a potential blowout. However, noticeably absent from these accounts were questions about why the EPA was called to the site and the fact that they were seeking to address a risk that existed long before the formation of the agency in 1970. Indeed, Udall's opening statement directly sought to limit the scope of the blame that EPA can or should shoulder for this risk event: "[The] EPA is not the only responsible party. What happened at the Gold King Mine is part of a much, much bigger problem. Abandoned mines in the West are a ticking time bomb, slowly leaking hazardous waste into our streams and rivers" (Committee on Environment and Public Works, United States Senate 2015). Conversely, then, the frames that Senators Udall (D-NM), Boxer (D-CA), and Bennet (D-CO) mobilized not only expanded the spatiotemporal scale of the riskscape but also served as warrants for a distributed perspective toward both risk and responsibility: There are other parties responsible for this event, and the risk associated with this location is one that exists at a massive scale when viewed at both regional and national frames (there are hundreds of thousands of abandoned hard-rock mines in the US). Limiting or expanding the level of spatial acuity in the accounts, then, serves either to open or close attention to structural, root causes of risk in this crisis, and it either attracts or deflects attention toward which groups shoulder the responsibility for various aspects of the crisis.

Spatializing Risk to Obscure the Role of Human Activity Within Crisis and Disasters

As Wijkman and Timberlake (1984) observed, one common disposition toward making sense of disasters is to foreground them as acts of god. They noted that the consequence of such an approach is that it obscures the role of human activity within crisis and disasters. For example, a large-scale flooding event framed as an act of god might neglect mention of the anthropocentric drivers of global climate change that have made severe weather more frequent and intense. Such an approach could also absolve the role of human activity, such as deforesting the landscape and damming watersheds, on a flooding event. Spatializing risk in various frames, then, supports accounts of crises and considerations of risk that may seek to foreground or obscure the role that humans or human activities have within such an account. For instance, with respect to the committee meeting regarding the causes of the Gold King Mine Spill, McCarthy stated that "while excavating above the mine opening, the lower portion of the bedrock crumbled" (Committee on Environment and Public Works 2015, para. 4). The hyperfocused spatialization of risk in this account directed attention to the bedrock below the opening, deflecting attention away from the role that the EPA contractor played as well as the broader history of human activity in the riskscape that has given rise to risk in the first place. What caused the bedrock to crumble? At the sentence level, this representation of risk used a subordinating conjunction to spatially and temporally separate the bedrock crumbling (an act of god) from the excavation work that a contractor was performing above the mine opening (human activity). The story: when we were digging here, this other thing happened there. Yet this move also appears to buttress the EPA from responsibility: the mine entrance collapsed for reasons we cannot be certain of, perhaps this is not connected to the work the EPA was performing but was instead an act of god? In this example, the hyperfocus and hyperlocalization on the mine opening diverted attention from the broader dynamics that encircle this riskscape. For example, when humans installed bulkheads at the American Tunnel it may have impounded AMD within the Sunnyside Mine, which in turn might have caused the water table to rise, eventually backfilling the Gold King Mine. In this account, the bedrock crumbling (the spatial cause proffered by Director McCarthy) does not directly address whether the human activities (excavation or bulkhead installation) contributed to the collapse of the mine entrance.

Spatializing Risk Reveals Dispositions Toward Being-at-Risk Versus Feeling-at-Risk

What compounded these dispositions is a lack of empirical short- and long-term exposure data following mine spills. More than five hundred thousand abandoned mines exist throughout the US. The risk of leaks and spills that could have detrimental impacts on communities and their enveloping ecosystems is largely uncertain. We might consider whose concerns about risks have been amplified or ignored within the space of the hearing—especially given the extensive history of space-related risk we've proffered.

For example, since the early 1990s, Silverton residents have resisted the EPA's efforts to designate part of the local mine network as a Superfund site. Some of this opposition emerged from the indignity of needing federal help; however, most of this opposition emerged from residents' fear that the designation would hurt the local economy and reduce tourism (Olivarius-McAllister 2013). They pointed to existing examples of Superfund sites—Butte, Montana, and Summitville, Colorado—whose cleanup efforts have disrupted local life for years. In this example, we should understand *being-at-risk* and *feeling-at-risk* in two divergent yet linked ways. The distinction between these two states lies between objective conditions and subjective perception. Being-at-risk describes objective conditions in which a person or community is exposed to hazards regardless of their awareness. This state is most recognized because it is based on environmental or medical assessments. Feeling-at-risk describes a subjective perception in which a person or community interprets their vulnerability often when there is no available empirical evidence. We might understand this as a trauma-informed response that is likely the result of personal experience, historical trauma, cultural context, media, and trust or lack of trust in institutions. In the example above, business owners and tourism operators might feel that labeling an area a Superfund site will lead to negative perceptions, harming their livelihoods. Their collective anxiety about potential economic decline reflects a *feeling-at-risk* disposition, as they anticipate loss without experiencing immediate harm. Alternatively, environmental activists or public health professionals might emphasize the likelihood of actual environmental health risks associated with contamination. They might argue that the community is in a state of *feeling-at-risk* due to the unknown and ongoing hazards connected to the mine spill.

The EPA's risk assessment exclusively investigated the environmental impacts of the GKMS, which largely ignored Diné (Navajo)-specific impacts. For example, the assessment did not consider Diné cultural, residential, or dietary needs (Van Horne et al. 2021; Clausen et al. 2023; Navajo 2017). By not considering how the mine spill impacts Diné cultural lifeways around land use or dietary needs, the assessment ignored the tangible ways in which GKMS threatened not only tribal health but also cultural heritage, which extends risk beyond environmental metrics. Simultaneously, the lack of recognition of Diné cultural needs led to feelings of vulnerability because of marginalization, which heightened anxiety about the potential of future risks even if the EPA's environmental assessment suggested otherwise. Additionally, the erosion of trust in federal institutions, specifically the EPA, increased the state of *feeling-at-risk*, because perceptions that one's needs are not being prioritized amplified concerns about the overall state of a community's well-being. We would argue that recognizing both dimensions of risk are essential for understanding the total impact of the GKMS on the Diné.

Quandaries with Localizing Risk: Implications Regarding Spatializing Risk

In this chapter, we have sought to offer scholars, practitioners, and researchers responsible for studying, analyzing, managing, and communicating risk with conceptual tools that might productively complicate how they spatialize risk in their work. Specifically, we have forwarded the concept of the riskscape and sketched a spatialized antenarrative of the BPMD as a riskscape that is sensitive to the ecological, physical, historical, economic, cultural, spiritual, political, and environmental dimensions that encircle it. In this account, we gestured toward a range of spatiotemporal frames that have contributed and given shape to the BPMD as a riskscape; still, there are spatiotemporal frames that our account has not considered. For instance, the choices we have made to localize an account of risk in this geography have not richly considered the Macroscopic-Long-Term Futures spatiotemporal frame within the heuristic we offered in table 3.2. Still, applying the heuristic to carefully attend to the range of spatial scale at play within this riskscape has enabled us to sketch rich aspects of how risk operates within and across the microscopic, mesoscopic, and macroscopic dimensions within the BPMD.

By following this matrix, and creating a case study of this riskscape that accounts for some of the ways risk means and scales across some of these spatiotemporal frames, we were able to construct an antenarrative of the GKMS as a risk event. This not only considers the release of the AMD into the Animas and its downstream regional impacts, but also illustrates the broader array of cultural, social, economic, and environmental risks that have encircled this location, including how those risks have contributed to the movement of populations and species from deep time through the industrial/historical past and into the present and immediate future. We will show in the next two case studies how the risks associated with hard-rock mining, abandoned mines, and AMD might be understood as a component of the cascading risk that affects water access and security in the Colorado River Basin.

In contrast to our antenarrative of risk in the BPMD, we have also provided an analysis of one piece of discourse that illustrates how riskscapes can be spatialized within institutional settings. This analysis, in contrast to the broader account of the riskscape we have sketched of the BPMD, has sought to emphasize how tacit spatial frames functioned as a site of rhetorical tension within the Senate Committee on Environment and Public Works hearing on the GKMS. Within this hearing, the respective senators addressed how this risk event affected their constituents. This analysis highlights moments when the senators spatialized risk in ways that account for ecological risks, economic risks, cultural risks, or spiritual risks. Yet we argue that this piece of discourse also illustrates the way in which the spatial dimensions were uncritically forwarded and engaged by the various parties involved in the hearing. The spatial boundaries undergirding this risk event fluctuated based on the various frames each party brought to the hearing.

Framed broadly, then, one key takeaway from this chapter is the critical importance of transparently defining and delimiting the levels of scope at which an account of a riskscape is bounded. Juxtaposing these accounts, we argue, allows us to illustrate how and whether particular dimensions of risk are considered in relation to a particular riskscape. In both accounts—whether in the Senate hearing or the antenarrative of the BPMD we've forwarded—individuals, groups, and institutions make tacit and overt decisions about which risks are considered, which spatial and temporal scales risk is operating within, and whether (and how) risk interconnects (if at all) across those spatial and temporal scales. Simply put, in localizing risk, we are always deciding to limit, in some way, how risk interconnects across temporal and spatial scales. Consequently, accounts of risk may (at best) inadvertently fail to disclose how they have delimited the boundaries of a riskscape or (at worst) advertently work to obfuscate how they have delimited the boundaries of a riskscape. More simply, parties might consciously or unconsciously ignore how a risk event such as the GKMS can trigger (or be triggered by) cascading risks in nearby areas or systems, such as infrastructural failures or environmental degradations, that exist beyond the immediate sites of the disasters.

In working toward the breadth and depth across spatiotemporal scales and dimensions, we've centered a choice to be inclusive of and critical toward the boundaries that might overlimit how risk spills beyond the immediate site where risk is often named and emplaced in this event: the Gold King Mine. The antenarrative we've presented in this case study seeks to move across spatial and temporal scales to illustrate how risk evolves over time. It challenges an account of this risk event that originates with the actions the EPA took on a day that led to a crisis for species, populations, and communities downstream of the mine. Instead of simply localizing risk, it reveals the tensions that clearly exist within the competing spatial frames offered by parties during the Senate committee hearing on the GKMS and to identify antecedent factors, and possible consequences in the immediate and long-term future, that will continue to shape how risk means within and across this geography. We believe that antenarratives of risk such as this are important to reframe risk for two reasons. First, it enables us to resist rhetorics of disaster exceptionalism that obscure the role of human activity as contributors to events such as the GKMS. Second, by embracing an apparent decolonial feminist approach to risk, we have sought to account directly for the role of coloniality in and upon this riskscape. This is critical because if technical and professional communicators are involved in the analysis, management, and communication of risk in order to do their work critically and with a mind toward justice (Jones, Moore, and Walton 2016; Haas and Eble 2018), they must ensure that their work is sensitive to the ways risk means for vulnerable populations, cultures, places, and populations. It invites TPC researchers doing such work to consider events such as the GKMS not in isolation but as emplaced events that might function as an insult to more systemic forms of injury.

Chapter Five

Timescapes amid a Water Crisis

The Enduring Legacy of the Law of the River Within the Colorado River Basin

> Environmental communication scholars necessarily investigate issues of time when we analyze environmental rhetoric whether we do so directly and explicitly or not. The scale, urgency, and care needed to address environmental degradation warrant thoughtful engagement with time as an abstract concept and a functional—and possibly multiple—reality of the crises we currently face.
>
> —Samantha Senda-Cook, Danielle Endres, Stacey Sowards, and Bridie McGreavy, "Engaging Complex Temporalities in Environmental Rhetoric"

A broad range of scholarship in technical and professional communication (TPC) falls under the banner of risk communication, including studies surrounding industries (e.g., medicine; mining; engineering), organizations (e.g., corporations; nonprofits; federal, state, and local government agencies), and events (e.g., natural disasters; public relations crises; environmental crises). "In technical and professional communication," Elizabeth Angeli (2023) observed, "scholars have tended more fully to *risk communication* than crisis communication" (75, emphasis in original). Further, Angeli expounded, "our contributions to crisis communication subsume 'crisis' under 'risk' . . . in part because [TPC] has not yet parsed through the symbiotic relationship of risk and crisis" (77). We posit that time, specifically, allows us to conceptualize risk and crisis at finer levels of granularity. Risk precedes crisis, as the latter often stems from unrecognized or latent risks that either were not properly addressed or anticipated. A risk is identified and quantifiably measured over time (*chronos*), but if not managed effectively or acted upon at the right moment (*kairos*), risk can become a crisis. Understanding how a risk escalates over time, and how the unfolding of time affects the intensity and urgency of crisis, is crucial in developing a temporal awareness in decision-making.

In this chapter, we interrogate the relationship between these concepts by focusing on the persistent megadrought that has been affecting the North American Southwest (NASW) for the past two decades. That is, we trace how risk has been conceived within the Colorado River Basin (CRB) and the role that conceptions of risk within this geography have on the ongoing climate crisis, threatening water access for humans and nonhumans within the watershed. Following Senda-Cook et al. (2023), we focus on the role of time as a salient factor that inflects how risk and crisis are materially experienced. Indeed, temporal orientation is a key variable that demarcates the fields of crisis communication and risk communication: whereas crisis communication focuses on rapidly unfolding exigencies in present-day contexts, risk communication focuses on the potentiality of exigencies in future contexts (Walaski 2011). Yet communication traverses these temporal frames when what were once represented as future risks manifest as hazards that must be mitigated during present and ongoing crises. Consider wildfire in relation to climate collapse as an example of how temporal orientation plays a role in both risk and crisis communication. Climate change is often framed as a long-term risk that will become increasingly more severe in the future. Thus, risk communication about wildfire focuses on the increased frequency and severity of wildfire (e.g., public awareness campaigns) and preventative management to mitigate wildfire (e.g., increased forest management, revised land development policies). When future risks associated with wildfire materialize into a crisis (e.g., a major wildfire that rapidly escalates due to usually dry conditions and high winds), crisis communication focuses on real-time updates about a fire's locations, containment efforts, and evacuation routes. What was once a future projection now becomes an immediate threat. The relationship between risk and crisis emphasizes the extent to which temporal orientation matters and how technical communicators should pay attention to time *mattering*. This is because the materiality of the world and our embodied experiences within it shape our perceptions and experiences of time. Consequently, the temporal framing of climate change and correlative wildfires redirects resources, messaging, and relationships.

TPC has a robust strand of inquiry that examines environmental risk in relation to bodies of water and watersheds, including scholarship focused on disasters such as hurricanes, floods, and oil spills (e.g., Frost 2013; Haas and Frost 2017; Potts 2013; Richards 2015, 2023; Richards and Jacobsen 2022; Richards and Stephens 2022), watershed management and policy (e.g., Baake 2017; Druschke 2019; Druschke et al. 2024; Walwema 2023), and climate change (Cagle 2018; Itchuaqiyaq 2023; Pflugfelder et al. 2023). Similar to the studies of risk within the mining industry discussed in chapter 4, much of this scholarship has been spatially or temporally bounded to offer a detailed, contextualized analysis of phenomena surrounding the construction of risk in a particular site, event, or organization. In keeping with the tensions surrounding time, crisis, and risk sketched above, many of these studies defy easy categorization, as scholars engage with and complicate tensions between these concepts. For example, in their respective studies, Richards and Stephens (2020) and Richards and Jacobson (2022) described the tensions associated with designing maps and data visualizations that depict for present-day audiences the risk of future coastal flooding disasters. Similarly, Druschke et al. (2024), McGreavy et al. (2021), Itchuaqiyaq (2023), and Lundberg et al. (2017) have documented tensions between Western and Indigenous orientations to time in the context of environmental management decisions surrounding watersheds in North America and the Arctic. These examples demonstrate the importance of examining the diverse range of temporal topoi that influence how distinct populations know, orient to, and communicate about environmental risk, including the timescales through which material consequences and differential exposures manifest for various populations living alongside an ongoing climate crisis.

Indeed, as Druschke (2023) argued in her epilogue to Williams's edited collection *Technical Communication for Environmental Action*, attending to "scalar connections seem[s] centrally important in the current moment—when globally pervasive degradation has the potential to overwhelm" (474–75). Describing contributions to the collection, Druschke underscored the paramount importance of a perspective—what Itchuaqiyaq termed "whole world" and Cagle and Burnes (2023) referred to as "polyvocal"—that is sensitive to the knowledges that "human and more-than-human relations" possess about environments and risk, and how those knowledges may challenge the kinds of knowledge too often privileged by technical and scientific communities.

Such perspectives "deman[d] the recognition, incorporation, and amplification of many human and nonhuman actors and many ways of knowing the issue at hand" (296). These perspectives, in other words, require scholars working in TPC to attend to the diverse range of epistemological and ontological orientations that encircle environments. Moreover, by embracing and affirming the expertise and value of multiple ways of knowing, scholars might work to *reveal*, *reject*, and *replace* (Walton, Moore, and Jones 2019) insular, Western scientific approaches toward environments, risk, disaster, and crises. Specifically, "whole world," "polyvocal," and "scalar" perspectives spotlight "how some stakeholders in networks of risk who attempt to navigate systems of institutions and organizations of environmental power have historically been silenced, ignored, put disproportionately at risk (or otherwise disenfranchised)" (Haas and Frost 2017, 171). That is, these orientations align with Haas and Frost's apparent decolonial feminist approach to risk, another approach that informs our methodological orientation to risk within this book (see chapter 3).

For instance, Druschke and colleagues (2024) recently argued for a revised approach for incorporating the North American beaver in watershed restoration. Rejecting "Western river restoration as a predominantly white settler modality of science" (2–3), the authors instead recentered ways of knowing possessed by Indigenous groups native to the Great Lakes region that "insist on the importance of long-term, place-based knowledge and on the significance of intentionality, time, and relation" (5). Similarly, in the context of a set of sustainability science projects connected to a watershed within the ancestral lands of the Penobscot Nation, McGreavy et al. (2021) also *rejected* the "dominant colonial power in research" by *replacing* such approaches with Wabanaki diplomacy and Indigenous Research Methods. Bridie McGreavy and her collaborators underscored how doing so illustrates the influential role that time plays within Western science: "[Western] science as a discourse creates tensions through the simultaneous production of knowledge and power and how practices of naming and social-material constructions of time shape and reinforce tensions" (945).

The authors expanded on this insight detailing how embracing Indigenous practices for dialogue, place, and relationality within the sustainability studies in the watershed enabled the team to alter "research timescapes" by "orienting to river time" (McGreavy et al. 2021, 942) and "letting the flow of a river set the pace" (944). Ultimately, they emphasized that Indigenous orientations toward the "multiplicity of time" can impact the practice of sustainability science. Across these studies, scholars have illustrated that temporal perspectives influence the semiotic and material dimensions of risk, as particular orientations to deep time, the industrial/historical past, present, immediate future, or long-term futures have a consequential influence on the ontological and epistemological possibilities encircling places and how risks resonate for human and nonhuman relations.

To advance our ideas about time and risk, this chapter attends to a set of interrelated questions:

- How does attention to time either reveal or flatten the complexity of risk?
- How does attention to time help us understand how risk flows within a network?
- How does attention to time allow us to see the ways in which risk is embodied?

In responding to these questions, we extend the previous chapter's spatial analysis by offering a case study of the ongoing water crisis affecting the Colorado River Basin watershed in relation to the Law of the River (LoR), a corpus of legal documents that have governed water rights and watershed management decisions for the last century. We begin the chapter by discussing how time has been considered in technical and professional communication scholarship before introducing three critical concepts that are useful for interrogating dominant orientations to temporality within the field. Thereafter, we identify temporal logics operating within the LoR, interrogating how these documents instantiated industrial timescapes that have posed risks for human and nonhuman relations across the watershed. This case study not only outlines how the LoR has contributed to the water crisis in the CRB, but also sketches how certain species, ecosystems, and vulnerable populations endemic to the watershed have been harmed by the watershed management decisions promulgated within the LoR. As we outline, the temporal logics surrounding management of the Colorado River present within the LoR exemplify how narrow orientations to time can problematically flatten conceptions of risk, which have ripple effects that perpetuate marginalization of the Majority World. They demonstrate how temporal issues of scope and scale can create disproportionate material risks—ranging from ecological degradation, species extinction, and habitat loss to threats to water access, economic development opportunities, and public health—that distinct human and nonhuman populations residing within this watershed have shouldered as a result of management decisions within the LoR. Most broadly, this chapter considers how working in and across temporal perspectives might complicate ontological and epistemological perspectives toward a set of ongoing ecological disasters occasioned by anthropogenic climate change.

Time, Scope, and Risk

TPC (and writing studies more broadly) has long attended to temporality. For example, Leff (1988), Lake (1991), Ridolfo (2005), Ridolfo and DeVoss (2009), and Sackey, Ridolfo, and DeVoss (2018) have shown that rhetorical performances and texts generate their own temporalities with respect to urgency, delivery, velocity, and circulation. However, much of TPC's understanding of time has emerged via chronos and kairos, two distinct yet interconnected concepts that refer to different aspects of time and its relation to rhetorical situations and decision-making. Chronos is a quantitative measure that frames time as linear and sequential. Chronos has been a marginalized concept within rhetorical studies because it is often equated with Newtonian physics, which treats time, space, and motion as absolute and universal (Smith, 1969, 1986). However, some scholars have pointed to the ways in which Newtonian time flattens and naturalizes an understanding of time and fails to account for other temporalities that predate Newtonian physics (Wilcox 1987). In fact, Allen (2018) revived an interest in chronos by calling attention to the ways in which the Newtonian domination of the term suppresses the diversity of ways in which the ancient Greeks understood its flexibility. On the other hand, kairos has been framed as a point of rhetorical invention and intervention. Kairos emphasizes experience in that it is not what rhetoric looks like but rather when it takes place. It requires rhetors to be attuned to rhetorical situations in ways that address cultural, social, and temporal factors that influence an audience's receptiveness to a message. Chronos and kairos, as rhetorical concepts, provide divergent orientations toward how time influences decision-making, particularly in the context of risk management. Chronos underpins risk management frameworks with respect to historical analysis (e.g., data patterns), establishing time-bound goals (e.g., benchmarks), and systemic preparedness (e.g., routine risk assessments), while the emphasis of kairos on timeliness of action necessitates that risk management involve adaptive decision-making (e.g., when is it necessary to issue an air alert?) and strategic communication (e.g., when is the best time to deliver a message about air quality so that an audience not only understands the urgency but also will act?). Although we have isolated kairos and chronos to understand their distinct differences within rhetorical theory, risk management (Walaski 2011) has often required technical communicators to balance both concepts to navigate short- and long-term risks.

Recently, Senda-Cook et al. (2023) observed that "scholars have started to attend to time as a particularly important feature of environmental rhetoric" (1). Pointing to the work of Cox (2007), Killingsworth (2007), and Pezzullo (2017), the authors elaborated that "scholars routinely adhere to the notion that environmental communication as a field of research, teaching, and advocacy is a crisis discipline" (2). Moreover, tracing the influence that time has had upon the field of environmental rhetoric, they identified three thematic strands that are in tension within this body of scholarship: "practical considerations," "epistemological concerns," and "ontological commitments" (1). The authors explained that while urgency is often mobilized within pragmatic arguments about the ways that environmental crises should be managed, urgency often serves to limit how risk might be known, related to, and mitigated, and, further, perpetuates "a colonial temporal formation that centers linear time" (3). Instead, the authors called for "slowness as both a strategy and a tactic" for "resisting dominant temporalities and imagining alternate presents and futures" (4). Similarly, Clark's (2023) focus on efficiency and expediency emphasizes how the rearticulation of time has often been based on the assumption that audiences generally agree with the term's definition. Yet such a definition fails to account for the domination of male perspectives within the discipline. Efficiency often emphasizes speed, precision, and optimization; expediency emphasizes immediate results and pragmatism, sometimes at the cost of long-term consequences. Rethinking efficiency and expediency beyond traditional male-centric perspectives introduces the possibility of exploring time-sensitive risk frameworks to account for collective well-being and sustainability that are more deliberative and participatory.

In this section we follow Clark as well as Senda-Cook and collaborators, taking seriously the question of how conceptions of and orientations to time might enable humans to productively complicate our relationships with climate risk. To do so, we introduce Barbara Adam's (1998) concept of *timescapes*, before turning toward Indigenous ontologies of time such as Whyte's (2020) *kinship time* and Itchuaqiyaq's (2023) *kinship relations*, as these concepts open up a multifaceted orientation toward the ways that time inflects human and nonhuman experiences of risk and crisis. These concepts serve as helpful tools for identifying material and semiotic connections between time and risk within the context of the ongoing water crisis affecting the Colorado River Basin. This watershed has been shaped by a myriad of human and nonhuman forces across various timespaces; beginning to account for the various timescapes, including kinship time and relations, helps to illustrate the conceptual and methodological linkages between time and space—and consequently how time and space mean with and for risk in this ecosystem. While we emphasized the spatial dimensions of risk encircling the Bonita Peak Mining District in the previous chapter, our analysis indirectly traced how the mining district's riskscape has evolved across time. Similarly, here we emphasize the temporal dimensions of risk encircling the CRB, while indirectly tracing the ways that the CRB riskscape unfolds across space and place.

Timescapes

In *Timescapes of Modernity: The Environment and Invisible Hazards*, Barbara Adam examined the role that time plays within the environmental challenges society has been navigating following the Industrial Revolution. Existing approaches to time, Adam posited, offered inadequate tools for addressing the intergenerational scale of environmental disasters such as the pollution of marine and coastal habitats caused by the 1996 *Sea Empress* oil tanker spill in Wales, the nuclear fallout from the reactor failure at Chernobyl's Vladimir Ilyich Lenin Nuclear Power Plant, or endocrine disrupting chemicals often used in food packaging, upholstery and carpets, and cosmetics. Indeed, Adam expounded that "a timescape perspective [which] conceives of the conflictual interpenetration of industrial and natural temporalities" was necessary for developing, appreciating, and managing the true scale of risk associated with postindustrialism:

> Traditional scientific knowledge and environmental safety regulations tend always to be past oriented. They are based on previous poisons and hazards, on that which is by then known and understood. . . . By the time . . . a new hazard is understood, therefore, it is no longer suitable as a basis for preventing the next generation of consequences of technological innovation and the industrial way of life. . . . The difference to earlier

> historical periods is one of scale, degree, and reach of culturally constituted environmental hazards. That is to say, the impact of the industrial way of life is global in its reach and of a temporal scale previously unknown; as such it narrows choices and affects life chances of future being from the next generation and from thousands of years hence. (56)

From a methodological perspective, Adam's timescape is particularly useful for considering risk, as it privileged time while also acknowledging the inseparability of time and space. Adam's timescape was concerned with the tension between the social and physical theories of time and space. She treated the relationship between time and space as co-constitutive and attended to the complex interplay between social, cultural, and material practices and time and space. Furthermore, Adam was interested in tracing the influence of Western capitalism and industrialization and society's shift from a cyclical to a linear to an industrial practice of time. This work shares a similar orientation to Theodore Schatzki's conception of *timespace* (2010). However, Adam's project differed as it specifically sought to develop an approach for addressing environmental crises. Another useful aspect of Adam's timescape is that it highlights how our bodies, shaped by the world around us, temporally respond to crisis. Indeed, Adam explained that "timescapes are . . . the embodiment of practiced approaches to time" (10). The relationship between time and embodiment reminds us that the environment is not an abstract concept, but something we live in and with, and that time shapes our awareness and responses to risk. As risk scales across spatiotemporal boundaries, our bodies respond in divergent ways (e.g., physiological, emotional, social) and our bodily responses become ways of controlling the present and the future. It is, perhaps, then, unsurprising that Adam's concept is well suited for tracing the applied, ethical, and political implications of particular temporal orientations associated with agrarian, industrial, and anthropogenic timescapes. Most notably, Adam argued, "The future created through those technologies [of the industrial era] is not a future managed and controlled, not the future of insurance and computer simulation, not the future of prediction and certitude. It is the future of manufactured risk and uncertainty, of time bombs threatening to go off. It is a world of blank cheques that have to be honoured by cultures at the receiving end of this 'development' and by their already implicated successor generations" (58).

Kinship Time

In addition to *timescapes*, we have also found Indigenous conceptualizations of *kinship time* helpful for thinking toward a more expansive orientation toward the ontological and epistemic relationships between risk and time. In particular, kinship time is useful for tracing interconnections between risk and time that illustrate in/justice. Kinship time offers an ontological and epistemological orientation to time that is distinct from timespace or timescape, as it draws on the notion of kinship, "an ethic of shared responsibility" (Whyte 2021, 40). As Kyle Whyte, an Indigenous scholar, explained, "responsibility refers to bonds of mutual caretaking and mutual guardianship" (42):

> It's not just enough to believe one has a responsibility. For each responsibility we may have, the responsibility matters mainly if certain qualities adhere to it. A quality of the relationship refers to what features of the bond make it achievable in practice to greater or lesser degrees. Qualities include reciprocity, consent, trust, transparency, and confidentiality, among others. It's important to note again that—here—kinship is not the same thing as close family relationships or shared biological descent. Rather, kinship is a category of relationality that can connect anyone together within a society and can even be extended to diplomatic relationships across societies. (48)

To illustrate kinship time, Whyte turned toward an account of climate change articulated by Indigenous ecologist Melissa Nelson (Anishinaabe). Within her account, Nelson described how Anishinaabeg groups have recognized changes to climate through the dwindling availability of wild rice for harvest within lakes, the adapted migration habits of animals venturing further northward to avoid heat, and the expanding prevalence of insects that carry disease to deer and moose. As Whyte explained, the "Anishinaabe intellectual and scientific traditions" that Nelson drew from in her account make sense of "change according to shifts in kinship relationship" rather than "units of linear time" (Whyte 2021, 41–42). Similarly, Itchuaqiyaq (2023), an Iñupiaq scholar from Alaska, described embodied practices such as "white caps visible on waves in particular locations" or "water on top of ice" that members of their family have used to construct knowledge about environmental risks such as unsafe sea conditions or unstable ice (24). As Itchuaqiyaq explained, the types of knowledge Inuit people possess have been cultivated "from our communities observing, interacting, surviving together, and depending on the same lands and waters where our ancestors existed" (32). They expounded, "Indigenous knowledges are at once intuitive, intergenerational, individual, communal, contextual, and complex" (32).

Yet, as scholars like Whyte, Itchuaqiyaq, and others have warned, concepts such as *linear time* continue to operate as limiting frames within Western scientific and scholarly communities. For example, Curley and Smith (2023) observed that the Anthropocene provides an account of climate change that centers a Eurocentric worldview. Narratives about the Anthropocene, the authors explained, center human activity, and in particular, Western civilization, within an account that "bound[s] time and space while generating *linear* narratives about the past and present" (169). Moreover, epistemological orientations such as linear time can be leveraged to delegitimize non-Western, Indigenous, and Black expertise. As Itchuaqiyaq asserted, "Indigenous knowledges are not typically considered 'scientific' but are instead considered 'cultural,' or 'primitive,' basic observations" (33). Itchuaqiyaq rightfully rebuked Western science for discounting the value of Inuit knowledge that has been cultivated across generations through relationships with the Arctic: "It is traditional for my people to have a kincentric worldview in their approach to understanding the 'whole world,' which is in direct contrast to approaches taken by western scientific method" (32–33). Indeed, as Whyte asserted, kinship is a useful approach toward understanding the risk associated with climate change, as "kinship does not obscure responsibility in the way that linear time telling can" (48).

We find the emphasis that *kinship time* places on responsibility particularly valuable for methodologically complicating interrelationships between temporal scale and risk. Foremost, kinship time epistemologically centers an orientation to a relationship that embraces multiplicity and complexity. Within a "kincentric perspective," Itchuaqiyaq explained, "human agency is tempered by, and in concert with, the agency of the world in which humans participate" (30). In other words, kinship time acknowledges that humans and nonhumans experience, know, and exist within different timescapes. Within the context of climate change, time means differently for species such as the greenback cutthroat trout, cottonwood trees, and American white pelicans endemic to the Colorado River Basin. It follows, similarly, that distinctive human populations orient to time within a multitude of timescapes. Geographers Tiki, Oba, and Tvedt (2013), for example, recently described "a time-recall system" that the Borana Oromo people of southern Ethiopia have used to take stock of the "impact of environmentally induced disasters" such as flood, famine, and drought (34). Kinship time, then, also functions as a methodological tool for embracing this complexity and decentering linear time as a dominant orientation for representing the passage of climate events. It is a reminder that there isn't a singular way to know, exist, or practice time, but rather an array of orientations that have different ontological and epistemological commitments. Most importantly, kinship time attunes toward concerns about social and environmental justice through the emphasis it places on shared responsibility. As Whyte underscored, "Kinship relationships serve to facilitate a society's responsiveness to changes that affect its members' safety, well-being, and self-determination" (48).

For us, then, kinship time productively complicates Adam's concept of a timescape. Specifically, a kinship orientation toward timescape emphasizes the emplaced dimensions between distinct hazards and the risks they pose to species, human populations, and ecologies over time. Applied within the context of the ongoing water crisis affecting the Colorado River Basin, a kinship orientation to timescape foregrounds the three critical dimensions between risk and time:

1. *Timescapes* account for risk as a temporally emplaced or embodied phenomena, or both;
2. *Timescapes* reveal networks of risk by tracing the embedded complexity of human, natural, social, and material activity over time;
3. *Timescapes* identify shifts in how risk is situated within or flows across these complex networks over time.

Our case study sketches the evolution of an industrial timescape within the CRB over the past two centuries, focusing attention on the rhetorics of expediency that were operationalized to establish a system of dams, canals, reservoirs, irrigation ditches, and tunnels, at the expense of those most vulnerable to the hazards posed by diverting water at a scale and scope previously unknown within this geography.

A Short History of the Colorado River Basin

The Colorado River Basin watershed spans the US states of Wyoming, Colorado, New Mexico, Utah, Arizona, Nevada, and California and the states of Baja California and Sonora in Mexico. According to the US Bureau of Reclamation (2024), nearly forty million people within the US rely upon the watershed. The watershed generates over $1.4 trillion in annual economic activity across the basin states (James et al. 2014). In no uncertain terms, the watershed "is the lifeblood of the American Southwest" (United States Bureau of Reclamation 2024).

The headwaters of the Colorado River form west of Fort Collins, Colorado, as a thawing alpine snowpack nestled within Rocky Mountain National Park trickles down small brooks forming La Poudre Pass Creek. From this point, the Colorado meanders through the Rocky Mountains toward Colorado's western slope, passing through Glenwood Springs where the Roaring Fork, Eagle, and Blue River tributaries join the Colorado River before continuing toward Grand Junction where the Lake Fork and Uncompahgre tributaries connect through the Gunnison River. As the Colorado continues into Utah, the San Miguel and Dolores tributaries join the river just before Moab; shortly thereafter, the mighty Green River connects a robust network of tributaries, which originate in or pass through western Wyoming, northwestern Colorado, and eastern Utah. As it continues to flow southwest through Utah, it connects with the Dirty Devil River, before meeting the Escalante River and another major tributary, the San Juan River, at Lake Powell. The San Juan tributary comprises a network of rivers, including the Animas, Chaco, and Chinle Rivers. The Colorado River, then, meets Lake Mead, where the White, Meadow Valley Wash, and Muddy tributaries from Nevada converge with the Virgin River, passing through northwest Arizona and southern Nevada. Exiting Lake Mead via the Hoover Dam southeast of Las Vegas, the Colorado travels through Lake Havasu before meeting the Bill Williams River and continuing south to Yuma. Here, in Yuma, the Gila joins, connecting another major network of tributaries, all of which originate in or pass through Arizona or New Mexico. It then flows through the All-American Canal across the US-Mexico border into San Luis, Mexico, forming the Colorado River Delta where water *occasionally* flows into the Gulf of Mexico (and the entire region has been in a state of drought for some time; see box 5.1).

Box 5.1
A Resilient Colorado River Delta Ecosystem: Pulse Flows Briefly Reconnect the Colorado River to the Sea of Cortez

In 2014, an international group of conservationists worked to successfully restore the flow of water through the Colorado River Delta and into the Sea of Cortez. It was the first time in almost two decades that the Colorado River had flowed into the Sea of Cortez.

Over the early twentieth century, the US developed an extensive infrastructure system consisting of dams, reservoirs, canals, pipelines, and irrigation to divert water from the Colorado River toward ranches, farms, and cities. By the mid-twentieth century, more and more of the river was diverted, until very little reached the Delta. By the 1960s, a very small portion, approximately 10 percent, of the Colorado River flowed across the international border with the majority of this being diverted to agricultural or urban uses in Mexico. In turn, the Colorado River Delta (CRD) began to dry up, and the species and people who inhabited the area were displaced, including the lifeways of the Indigenous Cucapá whose ancestors have lived in relation to the CRD for hundreds of years. It dealt the Cucapá another grievous injury, as a century ago the tribe had been divided when, following the Mexican-US war, the international border was drawn through the ancestral lands of the Cucapá—geopolitically severing ties between the Cocopah who were granted a reservation adjacent to the Mexican border within the US, and the Cucapá who subsisted within their ancestral lands surrounding the Colorado River Delta.

In the 1980s and early 1990s, following years of abnormally high snowpack, the reservoir system within the US that stored water reached peak capacity, and the US Department of Interior released additional water downstream. Water flowed into the Delta, which briefly revived and restored portions of the wetlands habitat. However, by the turn of the twenty-first century, drought returned to the NASW and there was no excess supply of water available to flow to the Delta and into the Sea of Cortez. For nearly two decades the Delta remained dry, until a coalition that included conservationists, the Cucapá People, and nongovernmental organizations targeted a limited section of the Delta for restoration. Specifically, in 2012 the coalition successfully negotiated with the

Mexican and US governments to create Minute 319 amending the "1944 US-Mexico Water Treaty: Treaty Relating to the Utilization of Water of the Colorado and Tijuana Rivers and of the Rio Grande." Minute 319 coordinated agreement between the governments to allot a one-time *pulse flow* of water that simulates the flooding that naturally occurs within the Delta in order to restore the habitat. In 2014, the first *pulse flow* was diverted to the CRD reconnecting, briefly, the Colorado River to the Sea of Cortez. Thereafter, Minute 323 (2017) included provisions between the US and Mexico to allot a set quantity of water for both a *base flow*, the more consistent flow of lower amounts of water to the delta, and occasional *pulse flows*. In 2021, a second *pulse flow* again connected the Colorado River to the Sea of Cortez. The coalition has been increasingly focused on purchasing water rights necessary for diverting water back into the CRD (Bergman 2002; Gerlak, Zamora-Arroyo, and Kahler 2013; Pitt et al. 2000; Kendy et al. 2017; US Department of Interior 2019; US Geological Survey 2016; Cocopah Indian Tribe n.d.; Valencia 2024).

However, this is not just a story about location, a narrative of the CRB as a culturally and geographically emplaced riskscape—although place and space is inextricable from a telling of how risk means across these lands and the water that flows through them. Rather, this is also a story about how the flow of the river has evolved over time, a narrative of a shifting timescape that has altered how water flows through and across these locations and how that shifting timescape has altered how people, animals, and plants residing within these lands experience risk. In this way, it is also a story about kinship relations and time.

Once, the Colorado River flowed freely through the Colorado River Delta into the Sea of Cortez in Mexico. Just a century ago, the river sustained a thriving Colorado River Delta ecosystem, but the wetland has since withered, endangering species such as the vaquita porpoise and the totoaba fish (Pitt et al. 2000). Similarly, upstream a number of species are currently endangered or under threat due to habitat loss and changes to the ecosystems from pollution, increased sedimentation and salinity, the rise of nonnative species, and changing temperatures within habitats associated with altering the flow of the river and the advance of anthropogenic climate change. In particular, populations of fish such as the pikeminnow and bonytail (United States National Park Service 2023a), reptiles and amphibians such as the relict leopard frog and the Mojave Desert tortoise (Arizona Game and Fish

2024), birds such as the as the snowy plover and the Yuma clapper rail (Hinojosa-Huerta et al. 2013), and plants such as the Fremont cottonwood (Posch et al. 2024) and the sentry milk-vetch (United States National Park Service 2023b) are struggling to survive as dwindling river levels have adversely impacted their habitats.

The Colorado River Delta, then, serves as a situated example of the broader stress that ecosystems within the NASW have faced as a result of the ongoing, historic megadrought that began at the turn of the twenty-first century. As a distinct crisis event, it is important to emphasize that this megadrought has been the most severe within the region for twelve hundred years (Williams, Cook, and Smerdon 2022). Indeed, the megadrought reached an inflection point in the summer of 2021, when the National Drought Mitigation Center classified most of the NASW within severe, extreme, or exceptional levels of drought categories (see fig. 5.1), compounding the impacts of a water shortage that had reduced Lakes Mead and Powell to "their lowest levels on record" (United States Bureau of Reclamation 2022; Williams, Cook, and Smerdon 2022, 232). And, while ecologies across

Figure 5.1. Visualization of drought affecting the US on July 19, 2022 (National Drought Mitigation Center). *Source:* Public domain.

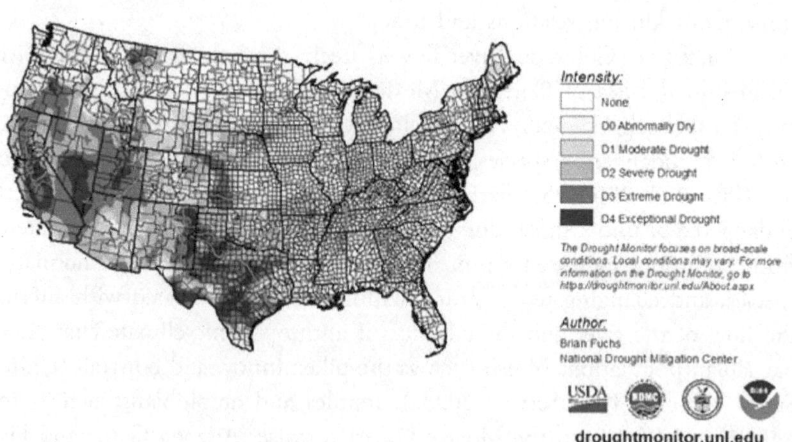

the region have been suffering profound impacts from this drought, as an ecosystem located on the Mexican side of the US-Mexico border, the Colorado River Delta highlights the inequitable burden of risk shouldered by the Majority World as climate warms.

Why is the Colorado River Delta drying up? To address this question, it is important to identify key events over the course of the industrial/historical past that have shifted the timescape of risk within the CRB. In other words, to understand why and how risk has evolved across the CRB as a riskscape, it's important to account for *when* the Colorado River began drying up—to address events that have unfolded during the industrial/historical past, or the present, that have resulted in the current risk profile that people, animals, and plants residing in relation to the CRB must negotiate.

According to Udall and Overpeck (2017), one key factor contributing to the drought is anthropogenic climate change: "previous comparable droughts were caused by a lack of precipitation," whereas the current drought is due to "high temperatures now common in the basin, a result of human caused climate change" (2404). Consequently, the warming temperatures have led to increased evaporation within the watershed, as the river is converted to atmospheric gas as it flows through the CRB (2414). Moreover, as Overpeck and Udall (2020) asserted, the use of hydrocarbons for energy has been driving the process of aridification of the NASW, resulting in "drier soils, widespread tree death, and more severe wildfires" (11856). That is, the global crisis associated with anthropogenic climate change drives cascading risk at local levels, amplifying the effects of the megadrought affecting the NASW by exacerbating water and food insecurity, ecological and environmental harm, and wildfire disasters. Still, the increasing presence of carbon gases within the atmosphere and changing climate processes aren't solely to blame for shortages of water plaguing the region. Indeed, there is a broader set of historical events temporally distant from this crisis moment that also contribute to the network of risks that dwindling levels of water pose for the communities, people, industries, animals, and plants located across the CRB today.

Known as Aha Kwatwat to the Mohave and Hakwata to the Yavapai, the Colorado River carved the Grand Canyon, and for millennia nourished human and nonhuman life in this arid region. Moreover, many of the people and cultures who have resided within this region have developed technologies for managing the water that are thousands of years old. For instance, the Quechan (Olson and Lang 2021), the Mohave (Colorado River Indian Tribes 2022), the Hohokam (Tianduowa, Woodson, and Ertsen 2018), and the

Ancestral Puebloans used practices including floodplain farming, damming, irrigation, and storage to support agriculture (Damp, Hall, and Smith 2002; Wilshusen, Churchill, and Potter 1997). Thereafter, between the sixteenth and nineteenth centuries, irrigation systems were developed further across the NASW by Spanish colonists and Mexican farmers and ranchers who utilized *acequias*, "gravity ditch systems," which were collectively managed as a shared resource by *parcientes*, "a community of irrigators with a shared responsibility in the care, maintenance, and use of the ditch networks" (Peña 1999, 108, 107). Irrigation practices have been in place across the basin for hundreds of years, but were carried out at a scale that didn't fundamentally affect the health of the river. Indeed, when wildlife ecologist Aldo Leopold explored the Colorado River Delta in 1922, he observed a verdant ecosystem rich with thriving plant and animal life supplied by the abundance of water flowing into the Sea of Cortez through the Colorado Delta (Leopold 1949).

By the end of the nineteenth century, a series of events began to unfold that would alter the scale and scope of risk across the Colorado River Basin. It was this moment that marked a shift to an industrial timescape. Perhaps the most significant event was when the US government, which had already become accustomed to auctioning or selling public lands that they wanted to settle, turned its gaze toward westward expansion. President Buchanan, for example, made over ten million acres in California available for auction in 1857, and shortly thereafter, in 1862, Congress passed both the Morrill Land-Grant Act and the Homestead Act, which opened up additional plots of land for settlement for the purposes of ranching and farming (Allen 1991, 15). According to Douglas Allen, the Land-Grant Act awarded California "special advantages . . . to convert 150,000 acres of agricultural land grants to private sales" (15). Thereafter, the Desert Land Act (1877) opened up an additional "thirty-two million acres" in Arizona, California, Nevada, and New Mexico, but in practice this land was predominately utilized "by cattlemen to acquire valuable water rights" (11). As white settlers moved westward, an increased need for water access arose in order to support the homesteads, ranches, and farms that were emerging across the Southwest. According to Bradsher (2012), early homesteaders largely procured water by gathering it from nearby sources such as lakes and streams, storing rainwater in barrels, and where it was feasible, digging wells, "until the 1880s [when] . . . well-drilling machinery [became] commonly available to pioneer families" (32). Moreover, as Howe and Hall (1910) noted, prior to the 1890s, in "the great majority of cases the irrigation . . . existing . . . in the country was carried on by means of small gravity systems, wells, or reservoirs fed either by wells or springs, and no [significant] area was, at that time, under canal or ditch systems" (34). Consequently, President Theodore Roosevelt signed the Reclamation Act of 1902, a piece of legislation that established a dedicated fund with the proceeds from the sale of lands in the Western states toward the development of irrigation systems and infrastructure (Bradsher 2012, 35; Congressional Research Service 2020, 2).

Yet the growth of farming in the NASW was slow until a transcontinental railroad system was established there around 1890. Furthermore, in comparison to other states west of the Mississippi, California housed the highest concentration of farms, with most located along the coast or within California's Central Valley (Bradsher 2012, 34). It was around this time that John Beatty, an entrepreneur, became interested in the viability of developing an irrigation project to provide water to California's Imperial Valley and formed the Colorado River Irrigation Company. Following a series of logistical and legal obstacles, the company was later absorbed by the California Development Company (CDC) (Howe and Hall 1910, 41; Stene 1996). However, in 1901, the company successfully diverted water from the Colorado River through Mexico via the Alamo Canal to irrigate the first crops in the Imperial Valley. Settlements grew rapidly, and by 1903 over one hundred thousand acres of farmlands had been developed (Howe and Hall 1910, 95). Soon thereafter, numerous political events and natural disasters unfolded that adversely impacted the CDC.

First, a series of floods affected the irrigation system that the CDC had developed. In 1904, a flood carried silt downstream and clogged the headgates, which interrupted delivery of water to farmers. The irrigators filed a petition with the federal Reclamation Service (RS) to purchase CDC's infrastructure and address the issue, but the federal government declined, citing the high cost of purchasing the CDC's canal and irrigation system as well as the international difficulties associated with much of the infrastructure being located in Mexico (see box 5.2 for more on US-Mexico water rights conflicts) (Stene 1996; Howe and Hall 1910). In order to resupply the irrigators, the CDC carved a temporary diversion canal through Mexico that ended up causing even more difficulty, as a subsequent series of floods overwhelmed the bypass, allowing the Colorado River to flow, unimpeded, into the valley, flooding much of the farmlands and destroying crops (Stene 1996; Simonds 2015).

Box 5.2
The All-American Canal: The Alamo Canal, the Mexican Revolution, and the Fall-Davis Report

The Colorado River became a site of tension within international relations between the US and Mexico.

The California Development Company secured water for the Imperial Valley through processes that were both legally and politically precarious. First, to divert water to the Imperial Valley the CDC had to purchase the land to build the Alamo Canal, which was primarily located in Mexico. Mexico's General Guillermo Andrade owned the land, and as a condition of the sale, he reserved the future right to enough water to irrigate over half-a-million acres of additional land in Mexico. Second, the CDC had created a shell company in Mexico, Sociedad de Irrigación de la Baja California, to illegally purchase the land, because Mexico had a constitutional provision that foreign nationals were not able to own land near the international border. When the Mexican government learned of the sale, they forwarded a complaint to the US government that the sale was a treaty violation. Third, the CDC had forwarded claims to water rights under California law, but the Reclamation Service considered the diversions to be illegal; consequently, when the CDC sought approval in 1904, the federal government and Congress denied the CDC's requests for recognition of their claims. In turn, the CDC told the US government that they would go to Mexico instead for recognition of their water rights. Fourth, when the floods occurred, they damaged the gate in the US that supplied water to the Alamo Canal from the Colorado River. The CDC then had to negotiate with the Mexican government to build a new gate, but in order to garner those permissions, the CDC had to agree to provide Mexico with half of the amount diverted.

Consequently, in 1904 California politicians brought a subsequent proposal to Congress, requesting that it purchase the CDC's holdings outright and build an All-American Canal that diverted water from the Colorado to the Imperial Valley, traveling exclusively through US territory. They argued that the construction of the All-American Canal could address a number of problems associated with the Imperial Valley at once: reduce the risk of flooding the Imperial Valley, enable the US to exert control over the flow of water, and solidify the financial instability that threatened the CDC following the floods. However, the Reclamation Service, and its director Arthur Powell Davis, had been convinced that a more comprehensive system was needed and had already invested in significant infrastructural development in Yuma, Arizona. Reclamation believed that the price CDC had forwarded for the purchase of its property was unrealistic. However, in 1907, President Roosevelt weighed in directly, appealing to Congress about the need for the federal government to intervene in order to control the Colorado River.

In 1910, tensions about the control of the Colorado River came to a head when Mexican revolutionaries began a war to address widening socioeconomic inequality and government corruption. This was significant for the Imperial Valley, as concerns surfaced that political turmoil or revolutionary forces could disrupt the flow of water that passed through Mexico via the Alamo Canal into the Imperial Valley. Reclamation Service director Davis argued for a study investigating how to manage the Colorado River within the lower basin. While California's focus was on mitigating the risks that threatened Imperial Valley's access to water, Davis was focused on a broader development project that would promote agricultural growth across the Southwest region and ensure that the Reclamation Service could successfully recover its expenditures. A central feature of Davis's vision for the region included the development of a massive hydropower dam for generating electricity to offset the cost of the project. In 1922, the Fall-Davis Report was delivered to Congress. The report not only included a recommendation to create the All-American Canal but also argued for constructing a large dam and reservoir. Moreover, the report emphasized the significant acreage available to Mexico to develop fertile lands, as a means to illustrate the time sensitivity of the project to Congress. In sum, the document established an exigency and a blueprint for the Boulder Canyon Project Act of 1928, legislation that authorized the construction of the Hoover Dam, the All-American Canal, and the Imperial Dam and fundamentally reshaped the scale and magnitude of water management within the CRB for future generations (Hartshorn 1977; Stene 1995; Kishel 1993; Hundley 1973; Howe and Hall 1910; Fall and Davis 1922; Sperry 1975; Imperial Irrigation District 1994; Billington, Jackson, and Melosi 2005; Summit 2013; Andrés 2014).

Second, the Imperial Valley was facing growing political headwinds, as Howe and Hall detail, associated with supporting the CDC's privately developed irrigation system. The RS, which had recently been formed and possessed limited resources, had developed its own plans to supply the valley. Specifically, RS had already committed resources to the Yuma Project, upstream in Arizona, that relied on recouping costs from irrigators downstream (Howe and Hall 1910; Pfaff, Queen, and Clark 1992). Moreover, California had recently advanced federal legislation to solidify its claims to water rights in the Colorado River, which, under state law apportioned ten thousand cubic feet per second to individuals. But challenges were growing about the CDC's claims to secure water from the Colorado River (Howe and Hall 1910).

The flooding situation proved to be economically disastrous for the CDC. The CDC lacked the resources necessary to repair the breach it had caused, and the Southern Pacific Railroad was compelled to address the situation to salvage its own infrastructure. Indeed, the cost of resolving the disaster proved to be so significant that a congressional bill was forwarded to reimburse the Southern Pacific for the cost it had incurred to address the disaster (Howe and Hall 1910). Eventually, the CDC would find itself effectively bankrupt, as ownership passed to the Southern Pacific until its assets, held in receivership, were purchased at auction by the newly formed Imperial Irrigation District (Simonds 2015; Howe and Hall 1910).

While these events led to the downfall of the CDC, they held broader significance to regional, national, and international stakeholders who relied on the Colorado River to fulfill their plans for urban, agricultural, and economic development. For example, government representatives in California, recognizing Imperial Valley's reliance on Mexico, which itself was in the midst of a revolution, sought to develop a new canal that would flow entirely through the US and directly connect the Imperial Valley to the Colorado River (Stene 1996; Summitt 2013). Similarly, President Theodore Roosevelt came to appreciate the difficulty that private companies faced settling Western lands and began advocating for the Bureau of Reclamation and the federal government to play a more significant role in developing infrastructure (Howe and Hall 1910). However, most consequential, perhaps, was the realization across the CRB that California's Imperial Valley was rapidly putting the Colorado River to beneficial use. Concerns were growing that if California continued at this rate, it would outpace the ability of upstream states to develop plans for settlements, irrigation projects, or supply their own farmlands. Certainly, as Benny J. Andrés (2014; cited in Wilson and

Lash 2023) suggested, by the time the floods occurred, the Imperial Valley had "claimed the river's entire flow and then some" (n.p.).

These distinct risk events mobilized settlers, farmers, entrepreneurs, investors, and politicians alike to recognize the critical importance of managing the Colorado River. On one hand, the persistent flooding had repeatedly damaged crops in California's Imperial Valley, threatening the prosperity that these fertile lands had demonstrated they could produce. This drove a wide array of stakeholders with economic interests in the region to seek solutions for protecting the valley. On the other hand, the Imperial Valley was rapidly developing a need for water, propelling concerns in upstream states that water access could become scarce. These concerns reached a boiling point, however, when another set of closely related events unfolded.

First, under the direction of President Theodore Roosevelt, the RS had turned toward undertaking its first infrastructure projects: the Roosevelt Dam in Arizona, the Gunnison Tunnel in Colorado, and the Yuma Project in Arizona. The latter was an ambitious and comprehensive infrastructure system for managing the flow of the Colorado that included the Laguna Dam, the Yuma Main Canal, the Yuma Siphon, drainages, irrigation ditches, and hydroelectric power.

Second, the US Supreme Court delivered a monumental decision regarding water rights in *Winters v. United States* (1908), wherein the justices held that the federal government established water rights for Native Americans when reservations were formed. This ruling came in response to settlers in Montana who had begun encroaching on the lands adjacent to the Fort Belknap Reservation and diverting flows away from the reservation where members of the Gros Ventre and Assiniboine had been forcibly resettled. Moreover, the ruling established the *Winters* Doctrine, which held that Native Americans possess *prior perfected* water rights that must be treated as senior to those instituted by later statutes.

Third, an interstate conflict emerged when Colorado decided to dam water from the Laramie River, drastically limiting the amount that flowed downstream. Wyoming filed suit in 1911, seeking clarity on whether the unsettled doctrine of prior appropriation, or "first in time, first in right" that was previously established by the California Supreme Court, applied across state lines. (In the eastern US, water rights were established using the riparian doctrine, which holds that landowners have a right to water when their property abuts the water.) In 1922, the Supreme Court upheld the doctrine of prior appropriation in *Wyoming v. Colorado*, ruling that upstream states had to take into consideration the impacts that their diversions would have on downstream users. While *Winters* had broken new ground by establishing federal water law, *Wyoming* had direct implications for interstate water rights in the Colorado River Basin, as the claims that had been established in California's Imperial Valley were likely to be affirmed in future rulings. Consequently, the states upstream from California, particularly those in the upper basin where the headwaters resided, recognized that their window to secure rights to water access in the future was narrowing.

Finally, a major flood overwhelmed Yuma, Arizona in the winter of 1916. While the flood did not cause extensive damage to the infrastructure that RS had built, it demonstrated the need for a more comprehensive infrastructural system for controlling the level of water within the Colorado River when it would rise during periods of high runoff. Even more consequently, the flood caused significant economic losses to the farms in Yuma, causing the lands to become unusable for months.

Ultimately, these events catalyzed the need for a more robust solution to manage the Colorado River. Such a solution would not only need to provide a mechanism for infrastructural development across the Colorado River to ensure that its flow could be effectively managed and flooding disasters could be prevented, but more importantly, it would also need to provide a mechanism for addressing the competing claims to the river that were rapidly proliferating across the CRB. Accordingly, the region's politicians recognized that if they did not work toward an agreement that resolved the competing claims, the federal government would have a significant role in shaping the decisions. State representatives came together to work toward a resolution; however, there was significant disagreement, especially between California and Arizona, regarding how the water should be allocated. To overcome the deadlock, Secretary of Commerce Herbert Hoover proposed that the Colorado River Basin be divided in two, between the upper and lower basin, with each receiving one half that the states within each of the respective basins could later allocate. In November 1922, the state delegates formally signed the Colorado River Compact (CRC), a document that has since served as the "cornerstone" for what would later become known as the Law of the River, an evolving corpus of technical and legal documents. Today that corpus includes the Reclamation Act, *Winters v. United States*, *Wyoming v. Colorado*, the Boulder Canyon Project Act (1928), the US-Mexico Water Treaty of 1944, *Arizona v. California* as well as more recent documents such as Minutes 319 (2012) and 323 (2017) of the US-Mexico Water Treaty, the Colorado River Interim Guidelines for Lower Basin Shortages and Coordinated Operations for Lake Powell and Lake Mead (2007), and

Drought Contingency Plans (United States Congress 2019; United States Bureau of Reclamation 2007, 2008). Together, these documents provide a framework that enables federal, state, municipal, and tribal governments to negotiate conflicts about competing claims to water and build support for large-scale infrastructure projects.

The Law of the River: Shifting Risk in the Colorado River Basin

Why have we offered an account of risk that reaches beyond the megadrought presently affecting the CRB? Foremost, as we analyzed the Law of the River, we found ourselves asking questions about the temporal logics that encircled this corpus of documents. In particular, the corpus usefully illustrates how tensions in scale and scope can problematically flatten risk. Methodologically, we felt it was important to sketch the distributed network of events and documents that have influenced the discursive and material construction of risk in the CRB. As such, this case study functions as an antenarrative of risk, delineating interconnected moments that demonstrate the entanglement of the current water crisis and decisions about the management of risk in the watershed that unfolded during the industrial/historical past. (Put simply, the water crisis is not an isolated event.) However, these moments are also important because they engendered increasing awareness of the complex network of economic, political, and environmental risks associated with farmers, ranchers, and capitalists developing settlements in the arid Southwest. As regional stakeholders and state and federal government officials recognized particular risks—flooding, economic loss from damaged farmlands or transportation infrastructure, interstate competition for control of the river, concerns about national security and dependence on Mexico—political support for a collaborative risk management plan within the watershed grew. While today that plan is understood as the LoR, at *that* moment it was a first step toward building a plan, the Colorado River Compact of 1922. As the cornerstone of that larger framework, the CRC marks a turning point toward the instantiation of an industrial timescape because the document established a commitment between the seven basin states and the US government necessary for funding the physical infrastructure to divert the river. In this section, we build on the case study above by offering an analysis of temporal logics in the CRC. Specifically, we consider how the document flattened the temporal complexity surrounding risk, thereby shifting the distribution of risk within the watershed and precipitating exclusionary, unsustainable, and ecologically harmful immediate and long-term futures.

Colorado River Compact and the Introduction of an Industrial Timescape

As the foundational document within the LoR, the CRC established an initial framework for collectively managing the Colorado River that shifted the temporal logics surrounding the CRB to an industrial timescape. That is, as a rhetorical construction, its framers leveraged the document to flatten the temporal (and spatial) complexity of risk, thereby shifting time and redistributing risk within a larger network. Why and how did this happen?

First, the CRC established upper and lower basins, assigning Colorado, New Mexico, Utah, and Wyoming to the upper basin and California, Arizona, and Nevada to the lower basin, and set apportionments equally to each basin at 7.5 million acre-feet (MAF) annually to each basin. However, there were significant problems with the calculus used within the CRC to set the upper and lower basin apportionments, as the shares allotted to each were based on overinflated flow rates (Kuhn and Fleck 2019, 5). As Kuhn and Fleck (2019) explained, the annual mean level of the river, 15 MAF, was established using a longitudinal period when water was considerably more plentiful than in typical years. In doing so, the CRC flattened the temporal complexity of risk by using a mean that failed to account for the natural dynamicity of peaks and lulls in the river flow.

Second, the CRC bound the states to an agreement about their respective obligations to share rights and access the river. Importantly, to reach agreement the CRC did not resolve the underlying conflicts that had surrounded apportionment. Because California had already developed rights to a significant portion of the apportionment allotted to the lower basin, Arizona was aggrieved that it would carry the burden associated with California's existing calls on the river, especially in relation to the upper basin states that had secured future rights to half of the water that flowed through the CRB annually (Billington et al. 2005; Summit 2013). In this way, the CRC flattened the temporal complexity of risk by deferring to the future the need to revisit those conflicts about the specific share of the basin apportionments that each state would receive in order to reach consensus agreement.

Third, Mexico and Native American Nations that held claims to the Colorado River were not included in the policy deliberations. Moreover, the framers of the compact did not quantify a specific apportionment for Mexico or Native American Nations and planned to fulfill obligations to Mexico "first from the waters, which are surplus over and above the aggregate of the quantities . . . then, [in the event of a] deficiency [the burden of delivering water to Mexico] shall be equally borne by the Upper Basin and the Lower Basin" (CRC 1922). In doing so, the CRC flattened the temporal complexity of risk by not only deferring to the future the need to quantify the apportionment that Mexico had been allotted (later quantified at 1.5 MAF) but also potential conflicts with that level, and failing to anticipate that the CRC was constructing a future rooted in negotiating both shortfalls and overapportionment as well as conflict not just between the upper and lower basins, but also between the US, Mexico, and Native American People and Nations.

Fourth, in failing to anticipate the conflicts associated with temporally flattening risk to reach an expedient resolution and garner support for the CRC from the seven basin states, the CRC established an immediate future wherein stakeholders would need to seek legal remedies to address the unanticipated risks that later emerged. The subsequent documents that today comprise the LoR might be understood as attempts to shift the timescapes surrounding the CRB to de-risk the conflicts that emerged.

Fifth, the CRC provided an architecture that allowed *a privileged set of actors* within the CRB to coalesce—while not unanimous—around a future vision for the watershed. The intent of that vision was to reshape the flow of the river. By privileged, we mean that representatives from the US government and the seven basin states established a framework for apportioning the river to the states located in the upper and lower basins. Reaching an agreement on apportionment was critical for these actors, because Congress wanted to be confident a framework for managing conflicts existed prior to moving forward with legislation that invested in capital projects such as the Hoover Dam or the All-American Canal (Summitt 2013). However, in privileging these actors and their priorities, concerns, and visions for the Colorado River, they set aside those held by Mexico and numerous Native American Nations that also depended on the Colorado to sustain their own communities and lifeways but were uninvited to negotiations regarding the CRC. As a framework for apportioning the river, the CRC flattened risk by seeking to mitigate risks that these privileged stakeholders identified in negotiations, while setting aside meaningful consideration of others.

Taken together, the CRC shifted the distribution of risk within the CRB by *privileging a particular view of timescape* within the watershed, an orientation rooted in industrial logics. This was because the CRC provided the framework that was necessary for diverting the flow or the river at a magnitude of order that had previously been unfathomable. Diverting the river for human uses was not new—for centuries humans had been diverting the Colorado—but the CRC divided apportionments in such a way that little or none would be left to flow into the Colorado River Delta. In this way, the CRC temporarily flattened risk, as it failed to anticipate the adverse environmental impacts that diverting the river would have on ecosystems within the CRB. The CRC is particularly insidious, as it demonstrated a lack of care for the kinship between states, the US, and Mexico, and between humans and numerous species and ecosystems adversely affected by the appropriations.

In the following subsections, then, we expand the analysis of three ways that the concept of timescape illuminates a problematic orientation to risk within the CRC:

1. *Timescapes* reveal networks of risk by tracing the embedded complexity of human, natural, social, and material activity over time.
2. *Timescapes* account for risk as a temporally emplaced or embodied phenomena, or both.
3. *Timescapes* identify shifts in how risk is situated within or flows across these complex networks over time.

Let's take a closer look at the CRC and its relationship to the LoR.

Revealing the Embedded Complexity of Networks of Risk in the CRC and LoR

The Boulder Canyon Project Act of 1928, briefly mentioned earlier (see box 5.2), authorized the construction of the Hoover Dam, Lake Mead, and the All-American Canal. These projects enabled the US to store significant amounts of water upstream, altering the historical rates of flow throughout the lower basin of the Colorado River. The All-American Canal enabled the US to deliver water to the Imperial Valley by *physically bypassing* Mexico. However, this document also enabled the US to *bypass geopolitical and political risk*, as it addressed concerns that had arisen regarding US dependency on Mexico and the Alamo Canal. In doing so, the US engendered a political future with unknown, future conflicts between the US and Mexico regarding the governance of the international body of water. Indeed, the US-Mexico Water Treaty of 1944 grew from the necessity of establishing a bilateral entity, the International Boundary and Water Commission, to negotiate a shared approach to managing international rivers, including the Rio Grande, Colorado, and Tijuana. And, as briefly introduced earlier (see box 5.1), a series of successive minutes have since been authored that amended the treaty to address specific tensions and risks. (The Congressional Research Service [2017] has a comprehensive background on the IBWC, the 1944 Treaty, and the Minute Process.)

For instance, "Minute 242: Permanent and Definitive Solution to the International Problem of the Salinity of the Colorado River" (1973) was authorized by the IBWC to address the issue of water salinity that had arisen as the infrastructure and diversions of the Colorado River upstream within the US led to increased salinity levels in the water delivered to Mexico. In the early 1960s, the problem of salinity evolved into a crisis when it adversely affected agricultural production in the Mexicali Valley in Mexico. At this time, geopolitical tensions between the US and the Soviet Union were at their peak, as Fidel Castro had recently toppled the Cuban government and began receiving support from the Soviets. Consequently, when protests emerged south of the border over the harmful impacts increased salinity was having on Mexicali farmlands, US diplomats became concerned that the "salinity crisis" was being used to facilitate anti-American, pro-communist politicization of agricultural workers in the region (Ward 2001; Doyle 2004). However, Item Five within Minute 242 established a shared recognition of the importance of the governments working together in the future to reach a "comprehensive agreement on groundwater in the border areas" (3). This provision has been a site of more recent conflict between the two nations. In 2004, the US began planning work to line a portion of the All-American Canal with concrete. This was significant because the All-American Canal was originally an earthen canal, which had allowed for seepage that recharged a transnational aquifer that spans the international border. In turn, a coalition of international parties filed suit articulating environmental justice concerns and challenging the project under both the National Environmental Policy Act and the Endangered Species Act (*Consejo v. US*). However, work began in 2007, following an appeal to the 9th Circuit that rejected the challenges and upheld an early ruling that maintained the legal right of the US to undertake the project (Cortez-Lara, Donovan, and Whiteford 2009). By lining the canal with concrete, the US limited access to future groundwater that ranchers and farmers in Mexicali have historically relied upon (Cortez-Lara and García-Acevedo 2000). Consequently, as Rosario Sanchez (2021) and an international team of scientists concluded, the rate of groundwater extracted is outpacing the rate at which the aquifer recharges and that has effects that are felt more acutely on the Mexican side of the international border: "Less water leaked into the Mexicali Valley, which put farmers in Mexico under pressure to extract more groundwater more quickly, thereby overexploiting the aquifer, deteriorating water quality and inducing saltwater intrusion from the Mar de Cortés (Gulf of California). This case provides an example of the magnitude of the interlinkages of a shared surface–groundwater system and how they can be impacted at different scales by a unilateral measure on one side of the border" (1022). This example demonstrates the embedded temporal complexity encircling risk, in particular how environmental justice relates to the redistribution of risk, as Sanchez and colleagues emphasized that the unilateral decision to line the canal has placed a disproportionate burden on communities and species located in the Majority World to shoulder the burden associated with this infrastructural change. In this case, future generations of citizens and agricultural workers in Mexicali, as well as the Yuma clapper rail, a bird that resides within the impacted Andrade Mesa Wetlands, will be threatened with less access to water as a result of the decision to line the canal.

Accounting for Risk as Temporally Emplaced and Embodied: Intergenerational Harm and the CRC

In a similar fashion, when the CRC problematically disregarded meaningful consideration of Native American water rights, it initiated a future of intergenerational risk for Native American People and Nations. While the CRC (1922) stated that "nothing in this compact shall be construed as affecting the obligations of the United States of America to Indian tribes," no water was directly set aside or apportioned for this purpose during the negotiations. Subsequently, the CRC created future rhetorical conditions whereby Native American Nations and People have had to pursue legal remedies for recognition of their water rights from US states and the federal government over the past century. For instance, in *Arizona v. California* (1963) the US Supreme Court observed that the United States reserved the water rights for the Indians, effective as of the time the Indian reservations were created, and these water rights, having vested before the act became effective in 1929, are *present perfected rights* that are entitled to priority under the act (598–600).

Despite such priority rights, the *Colorado River Basin Ten Tribes Partnership Tribal Water Study* (2018) recently underscored the drastic inequity that Native Americans have shouldered in terms of accessing the "reserved water rights, including unresolved claims, to . . . 2.8 million acre-feet" of water that flows through the Colorado, as a result of having to litigate rightful access for the past century:

> The Tribal Water Study revealed disparities among the Partnership Tribes, and between the Partnership Tribes and other water users in the Basin. These disparities have created barriers to the full development of federal Indian reserved water rights that include access to funding and capital markets for development, the lack of—and poor condition of—existing infrastructure, the number of tribal members and reservation residents without access to clean drinking water and adequate sanitation, and legal restrictions. (2018, 1)

In creating a moment *when* the US federal government and the upper and lower basin states set apportionments that excluded Native American People and Nations, the CRC delayed to the immediate future a moment where Native Americans would contribute their own priorities, concerns, and visions for the watershed. Holding the discussion in abeyance was detrimental to future generations of Native Americans, as climate change has exacerbated the risks that Native Americans shoulder within the CRB. Over the past century, generations of Native Americans have simultaneously (1) held the most senior water rights within the basin, (2) been required to repeatedly seek recognition of those senior rights from legal courts, and (3) lacked access to the federal funding mechanisms available to states for secure capital investments for establishing water system infrastructure.

Moreover, the *Tribal Water Study* illuminated the unsustainability of water management practices within the Colorado River, as Native American Nations, Mexico, and the US collectively claim rights to 19.3 million acre-feet. However, data from the US Geological Survey revealed that in 2021 the Colorado River produced an annual mean of 11.4 MAF and had a longitudinal mean of 14.5 MAF between 1922 and 2020 (USGS 2022). There are, quite simply, more claims to the river than the river can support.

Identifying How the CRC Shifted Risk over Time: The Pacific Flyway

Finally, the CRC created the conditions that enabled the US government to construct physical infrastructure that altered the temporal relationships between humans, plants, animals, and ecosystems within the CRB. By creating massive dams and diversion systems within the CRB, the US government was able to both reduce the risk of flooding and guard against shortfalls by storing water for use in the future when it would otherwise be unavailable. However, as we've detailed in this case study, this also prevented the water that was now being held upstream from reaching the Colorado River Delta. The development of this infrastructure altered the natural variability of the river, the flux associated with dry and wet seasons that aligns with high and low snowpack years. And, as we discussed above, it altered the embodied dimensions of risk by generating risks that have cascaded into relationships between humans, animals, and ecosystems. For instance, a recent study of the migratory patterns of birds conducted by DeLuca et al. (2021) noted that the Colorado River Delta (CRD) not only serves as critical habitat for birds migrating in North America, but also that the delta functions as a migratory bottleneck within the Pacific Flyway, "constrain[ing] migration, leading to significant concentrations of populations that could elevate threats or risks" (Bayly et al. 2018, qtd. in DeLuca et al. 2021, 11). Indeed, the CRD has historically served as a critical stopping point along the migratory highway for birds going north and south to rest and locate food sources, and prior studies have revealed that there have been significant reductions of the overall avian populations in recent years (Rosenberg et al. 2019) as birds struggle to locate habitat along a migratory route where water is sparse (Kelly and Hutto 2005; Azpiroz et al. 2012).

This example illustrates how climate risk could potentially impact migratory disruptions (Immediate Futures-Regional) or lead to species extinction (Long Term Futures-Global) based on the particular transnational and trophic relations that human and nonhuman actors share as a result of the past century of water management practices (Industrial/Historical Past and Present-Regional). Moreover, it demonstrates the networked complexity of risk between the three analytical categories that we've discussed. For instance, the complex, inter-networked dimensions of risk challenge isolated spatial perspectives of risk, as both local species endemic to the habitat of the CRD as well as migratory species of land, water, and shorebirds depend on the ecosystem to sustain their populations. Moreover, the anthropogenic risks that humans have introduced to the CRD over the past century, through the large-scale diversion of water, the development of global climate change, and increasing aridification of the NASW, represent both population-level risks to human and nonhuman populations for both immediate and long-term futures. Yet we also can trace the disproportionate levels of risk exposure that distinct populations face, as those populations that are already more susceptible to risk and carry a greater burden of risk exposure take on additional risk when the ecosystems and lifeways they depend upon are threatened. In this case, the loss of wetland and riparian habitats affects the ability of migrating species to identify locations necessary for resting along their migratory route that places additional stress on these species. Because the CRD serves as a critical bottleneck for species migrating along the Pacific Flyway, it illustrates the interlinkage of immediate and long-term risk futures for migratory bird populations and restoration work seeking to nourish the CRD through pulse flows in the present and immediate future. That is, this example illustrates how decisions about risk taken nearly a century ago have resulted in a present day where they have manifested as ecological harm that is having populational-level effects and disrupting migratory patterns.

Implications with Risk Futures in the CRB

We write these words in 2025. Four key legal agreements that were set in place to regulate water management decisions within the Colorado River Basin will soon expire. The documents, which include the Colorado River Interim Guidelines for Lower Basin Shortages (2007), the Drought Contingency Plan (2019), and Minutes 323 (2017) and Minutes 330 (2024) of the US-Mexico Water Treaty (1944), were designed as short-term solutions to manage conflicts between water users and rights holders within the basin amid historic shortfalls associated with an extended period of drought. To establish a long-term plan for governing apportionments, stakeholders from seven US states, thirty Native American nations and tribes, two Mexican states, and federal agencies from both Mexico and the US have participated in a multiyear planning and deliberation process, following the National Environmental Policy Act, referred to as the Post-2026 Operations for the Colorado River. This process provides water to rights' holders for consumptive use, while also ensuring that environmental impacts of proposed decisions have been evaluated and that water levels are maintained within reservoirs, which are critical for water storage, hydroelectric production, and recreation within the basin. The result of these negotiations will once again redistribute risk across the CRB. Will a revised approach address the historical inequities that have surrounded the promulgation of the LoR?

This brief case study of the LoR illustrates the complexity surrounding climate risk, as anthropogenic behaviors associated with diverting water for farming and burning fossil fuels for transportation have resulted in significant harm to humans, animals, and natural ecosystems in the CRB. Today, the Post-2026 Operations for the Colorado River process aligns with rules that require federal agencies to create Environmental Impact Statements (EISs) to evaluate and manage risk in decision-making processes. As genres, EISs function as social practices that guide federal decision-making about projects that might pose an environmental risk. Moreover, as social practices located within a timescape that is historically, politically, and culturally distinctive, EISs reflect a recent concern with constructing and communicating risk in a time-bound, systematic process that provides moments for democratic deliberation and participation (e.g., forty-five-day public comment periods). Ultimately, social and rhetorical practices such as EISs create particular ontological and epistemological orientations to risk, limiting when risk can be known, how risk can be communicated, who can participate within the social practice, on what terms and timelines participation can occur, where risk exists (or does not), why particular types of risk matter (or not), and, *ultimately, define what risk is*. Yet we wonder whether this process will alter the industrial timescape established by the CRC (1922). And we wonder to what extent this process will be sensitive to the kinship responsibilities that humans across the geopolitical locations have to animals and ecosystems that aren't able to directly engage with the risks they have shouldered within such genres.

Following Haas and Frost (2017), we recognize the "common topics of *human rights* and *human regulations*" operationalized within the rhetorics that encircle risk management in the LoR (172). Specifically, these rhetorics prioritize the regulatory agency of basin states to exploit the water flowing through the Colorado River to promote agriculture, commerce, and economic growth, while attending less meaningfully to the transnational, environmental, and sociocultural risks directly connected to overconsuming water. Moreover, we observe parallels between our case study and Haas and Frost's studies of the Oahe dam project and the Yucca Mountain nuclear waste repository in terms like *environmental equity*, which we consider to be the differential harms that specific humans, nonhumans, and ecosystems shoulder within networks of practice.

In this case, the primary aim of the LoR was to create the regulatory and legal agency needed for federal and state governments to develop infrastructure to "divi[de] and apportio[n] . . . the waters of the Colorado River System" (CRC 1922). Absent within these documents have been meaningful consideration of how developing this natural resource for agriculture and commerce reifies existing inequities and adversely impacts the health of the river, the ecosystems and species it supports, and the human populations that depend on it for sustenance. For example, the ancestral land of the Sovereign Nation of the Cocopahs is not only fractured by the US-Mexico border, but also includes the Colorado River Delta, which has been starved due to damming upriver. That is, our case study also gestures toward the injustice that flows from inequitable rhetorical agency that various actors have within legal and political deliberations about water access and climate risk. Resultantly, groups like the Cocopah Indian Tribe, species like the totoaba fish, and ecosystems like the Colorado River Delta have shouldered a disproportionate burden for a network of risks—such as species endangerment and extinction, habitat destruction, and social, economic, and health disparities—that are directly connected to legal and sociotechnical practices that have enabled basin states within the US to overdraw the river (e.g., Power et al. 2020).

Thus, we want to recognize that the limited scope of our case study reflects the methodological limitations common in studies of risk in TPC, while also opening space for a perspective that advances Haas and Frost's apparent decolonial feminist approach to risk communication. This approach "recognizes and works to identify and redress how some stakeholders in networks of risk who attempt to navigate systems of institutions and organizations of environmental power have historically been silenced, ignored, put disproportionately at risk (or otherwise disenfranchised)" (Haas and Frost 2017, 171). The case study of the water crisis currently affecting the CRB offered here, then, has sought to emphasize both those silences and the disproportionate risks introduced as a result of decisions about water management practices that have been largely unilateral. Our hope is that the inclusion of a wider set of constituents in the Post-2026 Operations for the Colorado River negotiating process (United States Bureau of Reclamation 2025) might engender immediate and long-term futures of water management in the region that address the inequitable distributions of risk we've sketched as well as invest purposefully in healing and caring for those most harmed by past decisions. Through this approach, we've applied the concept of *timescape* to productively consider the temporal dimensions of risk and to do so with a specific concern for how timescapes and risk affect climate justice by

1. Promoting a deeper understanding of the interdependencies between local, global, and international risks and across

economic, environmental, geopolitical, cultural, and technological risks.

2. Making connections between historical, contemporary, and future risks.
3. Requiring responsible and ethical engagement of underrepresented rhetorics and realities of risks. (Haas and Frost 2017, 169)

Moreover, our approach has privileged a diachronic and trans-spatial perspective on climate risk, as this case study illustrates how risk decisions ultimately affect people, animals, and environments across generations and geopolitical borders. When a cascading risk manifests in local crisis, it threatens to inflame the existing inequities between the Majority World and the Minority World—in this case, as the economic and ecological value of water grows, access to the resource becomes increasingly fraught and limited. In the next chapter, we turn more fully toward a case that considers the flux of risk within these networks.

Chapter Six

Contradictory Risk Flows

The Uinta Basin Railway Project and the East Palestine Train Derailment

> The "cumulative" effects within the Uinta Basin of a major expansion of oil drilling there, on Gulf Coast communities of refining the oil, and the climate effects of the combustion of the fuel intended to be extracted are foreseeable environmental effects of the project. These are effects the Board ultimately has the authority to prevent.
>
> —The US Court of Appeals, responding to the Uinta Basin railway environmental impact statement (Eagle County, Colorado v. Surface Transportation Board, No. 22-1019 [D.C. Cir. 2023])

In *Ducks: Two Years in the Oil Sands* (2022), comic artist Kate Beaton grapples with several forms of violence within the span of just a few weeks. Beaton had been working for petroleum and petrochemical extractors in Alberta's oil sands in the hopes of paying off her student loans. Moving from her home in Cape Breton to entry-level supply positions at plants owned by the Syncrude corporation, then an Opti-Nexen site, and finally at Albian Sands, Beaton worked alongside men and women who faced heightened bodily and psychological risks in their day-to-day jobs extracting bitumen. In the space of a few dozen pages, Beaton recalls her experience of sexual assaults at the camps, the death of a coworker on one of the many dangerous highways, the discovery of fresh, pollution-related welts on her back, and the death of over five hundred migrating ducks who landed in a tailings pond. All of these experiences are then framed by a safety briefing Beaton attends, in which a manager points to a "safety pyramid" and in a few sentences cautions a room of disinterested workers to pay attention to "at-risk behaviors" before they turn into "near-miss incidents" (366). Their boredom at the presentation belies the disregard that the management has for the workers and the regularity in which such abstract invocations to workplace safety are made. The juxtaposition of the mundanity by which the companies she worked for addressed risk, versus the risks she witnessed and experienced, drive a central takeaway from *Ducks*. Beaton's work showcases how immediate workplace hazards were given lip service, all while the staggering forms of structural violence and risk that accompany the transportation of energy were either ignored or accepted. These energy pipelines, both literal and figurative, dominate her memoir, and illustrate how scores of vulnerable people and ecosystems have been made to bear an increased likelihood of harm, all while resource extraction is lauded.

While her experience in the oil sands was temporary, the experience gave Beaton an insight into the workplace conditions experienced by people and the environmental impacts wrought by the labor they provided to national petroleum and petrochemical companies. Risk, in the context of her graphic novel, operates on several different scalar levels—that much is clear—but risk also functions in inverse proportion to the directional flow of energy. While work in the Alberta oil sands means a larger-than-average paycheck, it also represents riskier labor; the closer workers are to the literal extraction points, the greater the likelihood of harm. Similarly, the tar sands themselves have become environmental wastelands: open pit mining razes forests, in situ extraction techniques divert rivers, fluid from tailings ponds escape into the watershed, ecosystems are destroyed or severely degraded, and greenhouse gas emissions increase. The pipelines that transport this oil to refineries—the Keystone Pipeline, Trans Mountain Pipeline, and the Enbridge Mainline among them—also create increased risks from ruptures and spills, which can lead to soil and water pollution. These pipelines are often constructed in increasingly key wildlife areas, and just as frequently, the lands of the rural poor, minorities, and Indigenous groups. Pipelines, by their very nature, transport energy from within the earth to refineries and eventually to high-energy users—and as they do so, produce risk in inverse proportion to their direction of travel (the further the energy travels, the less risky it becomes for its surroundings—a light switch being less dangerous than an oil rig, for example). Risk impacts those along that trajectory and often isn't present to those who benefit from that same system of energy production. In this chapter, we consider what TPC may learn from grappling with these *contradictory risk flows.*

Risk within the petroleum industry has been addressed by some scholars in TPC (see Graves and Beard 2019; Katz-Rosene 2016; Piotrowski 2013; Plec and Pettenger 2012; Thomlison 2019), where researchers have also studied oil technologies, though most notably for pipelines in the northern plains states and the protests concerning their expansion. The Keystone XL Pipeline, a proposed extension of the Keystone Pipeline system, along with the Dakota Access Pipeline, which begins in the shale fields of North Dakota, became the loci for numerous protests. These pipelines move bitumen, oil, and natural gas from Alberta, North Dakota, and other energy-rich geologies to refinery locations, often on the North American coast. Others have focused on protest events and discourse surrounding the Keystone XL pipeline and considered how opportunities for rural opposition were developed (Moscato 2019, 2022). For instance, Wagnon and Baniya (2024) analyzed the Mountain Valley Pipeline protests and community messaging, Welch and Scott (2019) considered rhetorical ethics in the context of the North Dakota Access Pipeline, Smith and van Ierland (2018) and Falc (2020) studied influential framing strategies and representations of Indigenous women in the #NoDAPL hashtag, and Deem (2018) probed the disruptive potential of social media. Still other research has considered the extent of persuasive messages surrounding the petrochemical industry. These studies include a Burkean analysis of "failed" protests against the Trans Mountain Pipeline in Burnaby, Canada (Zwagerman 2019) and attention to distributed symbolic action at pipeline protests (Schandorf and Karatzogianni 2018).

Of greater significance to our study of pipelines and risk is Erin Frost's work, specifically her study (2013) of transcultural risk communication activities after the Deepwater Horizon oil spill. The Deepwater Horizon was a BP-owned offshore oil rig in the Gulf of Mexico that exploded into a fireball on April 20, 2010, killing eleven crew members and expelling four million barrels of oil in the following months (United States Environmental Protection Agency 2024). Frost studied the risk messaging that occurred after the event around Dauphin Island, a small community impacted by the oil spill. Frost addressed the incongruity between both the government- and BP-sponsored materials, which focused on the economic risks, and the materials local to Dauphin Island, which highlighted "more nuanced constructions of combined and interdependent economic and ecologic risk"

(Frost 2013, 51). Calling these disparities "ironic," Frost considered the flux and flow of risk communication materials, noting that they emphasized different formations of risk. "International and national entities utilized local spaces," Frost argued, "whereas regional and local communicators turned to globalized digital sites to narrate the disaster and engaged in more nuanced constructions of combined and interdependent economic and ecologic risk" (51). Key lessons for TPC professionals include our obligation to "pay attention to complex transcultural flows of communication that move between local and global cultural spaces as they participate in constructing both the risks and the histories of particular events" (51). Expanding Frost's claims here, we argue that these contradictions of risk and how they flow are at the heart of any extraction, movement, and transportation of energy. A transcultural approach like Frost's can illuminate these historical and global flows of energy, and a transcultural approach is aligned with the exploration that we engage in this chapter—the analysis of contradictory flows of risk in systems of energy extraction and transportation. We address the following interrelated questions:

- How can our expansion of scope and scale be leveraged to critique the risks that result from energy extraction, transportation, and refinement?
- How have other theorists conceptualized Western forms of "on-demand" energy and what forms of risk do these cultural conceptions of energy permit?
- What arguments does the energy industry forward to justify continued extraction of carbon fuels?
- How does risk to people and ecosystems increase in contradiction to the directional flow of energy? How does the plan for the Uinta Basin Railway exemplify contradictory risk flows?
- How can more geographically and time-distant harms be included as part of an analysis of, and case study approach to, risk? How can TPC use time-limited case studies, not to predict risk, but to advocate against unnecessary risk?
- How can TPC address contradictory risk flows in case studies that move beyond postmortem analyses, and where can TPC documentation also function in/as a deliberative rhetoric?

This chapter provides a case study that showcases *contradictory risk flows* for energy extraction and refinement trajectories. We explain this concept as the process by which energy is pulled from the earth and turned into usable fuel, in a system of energy extraction and use, but one that leaves an increased likelihood of harm in its wake. These energy flows are "contradictory" because extractive energy companies claim to transport energy for the public good, but those closest to systems of extraction, transportation, and refinement bear the burden of harm and receive few benefits. Our approach to contradictory risk flows is to highlight Western assumptions about energy that underlie an expectation that more energy is always better and that energy should be made available on demand. These assumptions have roots in twentieth-century anthropology, which linked a culture's increased energy availability to the (beneficial) complexity of their civilization. However, these arguments are not limited to anthropological theory, but often parroted by energy industries and transformed into a rationale that links, and sometimes equates, human rights and energy extraction. Potential development and human rights move in one location, harm moves in a contradictory direction. As a focal point to the chapter, we offer a case study of the Uinta Basin Railway, a proposed rail line intended to ship crude oil from Utah through the Colorado River Basin to processing facilities along the Gulf coast. This case study showcases both these contradictory risk flows and Western energy rationales. Moreover, we highlight these flows across time and space, from the deep time geologic events that deposited layers of waxy crude to the long-term future atmospheric release of those hydrocarbons, and from the logics of energy extraction to an environmental impact statement that ignores future risks.

We also interrupt this larger case study to emphasize additional, more time-compressed industrial/historical past and present-day harms that arrive within contradictory risk flows. Here, we highlight the 2013 Lac-Mégantic rail disaster and the 2023 East Palestine train derailment. The way these various diachronic events coalesce into one "case" is itself a methodological argument. This chapter makes use of an expansive sense of scope and scale to provide a different form of case study—one that pushes back against more typical technical communication case studies of risk where risk is limited to a time-compressed, after-the-fact diagnosis of a mesoscopic, or regional, disaster. We imagine that many in TPC could envision what a postmortem case study of the East Palestine train derailment could be—an analysis of the accident that identifies a precipitating element of miscommunication that a rhetorically trained technical writer could have helped avoid. Here, we use train disasters not to justify the value and importance of our work but to locate similar cases where actions can still be reasonably taken. Traditional case studies can be useful, but they have limits. They fail to close the cycle of disaster; the more immediate causal relationships between communication and disaster aren't the only dimensions of risk to which TPC must attend. Here, we consider the long history and long future of the Uinta Basin Railway and include the Lac-Mégantic rail disaster and the East Palestine derailment case as time-limited examples of what could happen and as a deliberative argument concerning what we should expect to happen. This shift toward combining cases is intentional, not only in expanding our field's notion of a risk/disaster case study, but in choosing to focus on a site where a disaster, or disasters, *will happen*. More immediate cause-and-effect relationships are always part of the riskscape, even as we focus on both long-term and distant impacts. Indeed, the movement of energy provides for an especially generative site to study how risk travels within and through space and time.

Energy and Contradictory Risk Flows

Part of the difficulty in understanding how risk changes and mutates in contradiction to energy flows comes in simply being able to see how energy changes people—not just literal reactions to an increase or decrease of energy in relation to the worldwide supply, but the cultural changes that accompany energy extraction, transportation, and production. Humanities scholars have been exploring this concept for some time, mostly recently in the form of "energy humanities" and "petrocultures" research. Energy humanities is a rather broad term for critical attention toward both the environmental and humanitarian consequences of industrial energy and the difficulties in addressing global warming (Szeman and Boyer 2017, 1). Any critical study of energy must necessarily grapple with how the West created a narrative of (industrial/historical) modernity that requires science, industry, capitalism, and democracy, though this narrative is entirely dependent upon how new forms of energy are able to hold "these very different spheres of social life together under the sign of 'progress' in a powerful way" (Szeman and Boyer 2017, 1). Energy, then, can be read as an inextricable component to modernity. Scholars in the energy humanities have been attentive to the affordances this work has for providing nuance and guidance to the coming energy challenges, though it must be said that the future of energy is deeply connected to the current state of energy and the cultures that have developed alongside our current energy sources. Another name for the critical analysis of our most dominant energy formation is the study of "petroculture."

Research on how petroleum products have shaped culture can be used to point to how oil wealth changes the cultural values in so-called petrostates like Venezuela or Kuwait, but it can also be used to address the deep interplay between all petrochemicals (though primarily oil used for energy) and postindustrial society writ large. The Petrocultures Research Group explained that the term "petroculture" is necessary because we are "shaped by oil in physical and material ways, from the automobiles and highways we use to the plastics that permeate our food supply and built environments" (2016, 9). The production and use of oil, waxy crude, bitumen, natural gas, naphtha, gasoline, kerosene, polyethylene, polypropylene, nylon, polyester, epoxy, and a range of other hydrocarbons make up the materials of everyday life for many—and not just the materials we interact with, but the "social imaginaries constituted by the knowledge, practices, and discourses resulting from the consumption of and subsequent dependence on oil" (Baptista 2017, n.p.). As Wilson, Szeman, and Carlson argued, petrochemical products "are folded into every aspect of our lives, linking our deepest hopes and desires to the spaces of energy extraction and to the measure of watts used per person per year" (2017, 4). The scale and reach of the extraction, transportation, refinement, and use of hydrocarbon-based energy invades almost all aspects of global society. However, not only has every culture been molded by and shaped by the energy systems it uses, but energy is also shaped by culture. We know that cultures are shaped by the dominant forms of energy production, but energy itself is likewise culturally and discursively constructed.

While we might more easily agree that the forms of energy we use shape our cultural life, the claim that energy is likewise altered by rhetorical and discursive pressures may not be as easily recognizable. Much of the insight that we have on the relationship between culture, energy, and power comes from the field of anthropology, and anthropological insights into energy and technology have driven what are called "substantivist" and "formalist" models of energy. "Substantivist models of energy are reflections on energy as a qualitative force that is socially embedded and mediated by people's relationships with each other and with the conditions of their daily lives," as opposed to "formalist" models, which "refer to quantifiable energy systems that provide the technical infrastructure on which high-energy, high-technology, information-saturated city residents depend" (Rupp 2013,

80). Energy justice researcher Larry Lohmann explained that the concept of "energy" is one that many people take for granted as existing in a stable, on-demand, at-hand resource. Lohmann has called this orientation to energy, *E*nergy with a capital "E," the Western energy of modernity and the energy of fossil-fueled industrial capitalism (Rupp 2013, 26). This energy can be "accumulated and deployed in unprecedented quantities anywhere regardless of the particularities of the local environment, allowing for the concentration of workers and, through mechanisation, expanding the surplus that can be extracted from them" (Rupp 2013, 26). The energy of Western industrial modernity is also often culturally abstracted, as fossil fuels become electromechanical energy in rural power plants via infrastructure that remains hidden. Such abstract conceptions of "always available" substantivist energy forms allow for capital *E*nergy to remain fluid and adaptable, quietly supportive of modernity (until it isn't). Further, these energy infrastructures can be said to legitimate and reify the discourse of market capitalism (Özden-Schilling 2015). Critics have explained how Western energy and political support are identifiable via "energopower," something Boyer described as "a genealogy of modern power that rethinks political power through the twin analytics of electricity and fuel" (Boyer 2014, 325). For Boyer, the idea of energopower extends Foucault's concept of biopower by emphasizing the relationships between energy, "discourse, materiality, and history" (325). Increasingly, the forms of politics that propel energy extraction, refining, and delivery systems are classifiable through energopower.

While the concept of energopower can be used to articulate connections between the modern industrial state and energy regimes, there exist alternate formations of energy and power—formations that proliferated long before Western extractive capitalism. Lohmann described the alternative to Western *E*nergy as lower-case "*e*nergies," energies that "remain entangled with particular times—seasons, the daily cycle of light, the months it takes to grow crops or the years it takes to grow trees—and particular places—rivers where mills can be built, forests from which wood can be cut, latitudes where trade winds blow" (2013, 26). These energies are not easily absorbed into industrial modernity, less transportable, and unable to be stored in vast, abstract, on-demand quantities. In this way, energies align with the preindustrial timescapes (Adam 1998) and kinship time (Whyte 2021) discussed in chapter 5, as both operate as foils to naturalized hegemonic forms of time and energy, respectively. Access to, and control over, on-demand *E*nergy and *e*nergies are often, as Myles Lennon explained, divided along lines of race, class, ability, geography, and gender. Locating this energopower, Lennon argued that "highly educated white male 'energy experts' overwhelmingly shape capital-E Energy conceptually [and] produce knowledge grounded in simplistic understandings of energy based on statistical abstractions" (Lennon 2017, 19). Consequently, the dominant narratives of energy are those where Western, industrial, on-demand energy have been defined as socially and economically beneficial and aspirational, while cultures that emphasize lowercase energies have been ghettoized and cast as sites of anthropological interest or future economic development. "People tend to think about changes in the quantity and quality of energy in positive terms," because for many in the West, "the economic intensification and enhanced potential for social prestige that are hallmarks of modernity have, over the unprecedented development of the past century, come to seem not only desirable but almost magical (the American Dream) and unstoppable (the Industrial Revolution)" (Lennon 2017, 13). For many implicated in Western petroleum and petrochemical companies, energy is aligned with success in present-day or immediate futures, where additional energy, as an available resource, brings access to other cultural benefits. This belief runs deep—and has been supported by specific claims within Western anthropology.

Connections between culture and energy have long been present in anthropology research, but the work of Leslie White, specifically in *The Science of Culture* (1949) and later in *The Evolution of Culture* (1959), precisely located the relationship between a culture's "evolution" and its energy use. White was a Marxist anthropologist who believed that "cultural evolution," the advancement of a particular culture, was tied to the amount of energy that same culture was able to harness. He argued that "other things being equal, the degree of [a society's] cultural development varies directly as the amount of energy per capita per year harnessed and put to work" (1943, 346). Key to White's argument was his claim that the disparity in technological and cultural advancement around the world was due to access to and containment of energy—and not inherent cultural or biological differences. At the time, White's argument was more radical than it appears today, and his rejection of race-based explanations for economic disparity aligned with his Marxism. In his history of cultural evolutionism and cultural relativism, Kevin Fernlund explained that "White removed race from the table and focused instead on the purity of energy" and came to describe all civilizations and cultures as "thermodynamic systems" (2020, 16). So strong was White's belief in the value of harnessing energy to cultural advancement (also described as "cultural evolution") that he devised mathematical-sounding formulas for determining their relationship.

While we recognize limitations to White's theories of energy-based cultural evolution, his work was both prescient of modern capitalist petroculture and is still often used to rationalize energy extraction today. White created a "master narrative" that classified different cultures by their capacity to harness energy, and therefore compared cultures in terms of their development in a reframing of bias. Even though his concept of cultural evolution was stripped of the biological racism of social Darwinism, he grounded a new form of cultural bias out of a comparison of different culture's level of technology and energy use. Fernlund also explained that White "accepted, unapologetically, that the industrial and capitalist West, propelled by what he called the 'Fuels Revolution,' was the world's most advanced society" (2020, 17). White could be said to support the idea that the only energy forms that matter are those that have advanced culture in the industrial/historical past, and the only energy that matters is the aforementioned uppercase *E*nergy synonymous with the industrialized West—because lowercase energies fail (in his formulation) to support cultural evolution. White's ideas for comparing cultures should now strike us as both circular and deeply prejudiced, not only for their overreliance on one cultural definition of energy, but also for their willingness to compare cultures based on a flawed assumption about "evolution." Still, White's ideas persist within the arguments that energy companies forward to rationalize their continued extraction of fossil fuels.

This anthropological theory remains important today because White's assumptions about the supremacy of Western industrial *E*nergy form the basis for how the carbon energy industry has argued for the continued exploration of fossil-fuel energy resources. While White nuanced his claims about energy by noting that, because of their close relationship, dominant cultures tend to resist progressive transformations in energy regimes, such nuance is lost on those who make use of his broader logics. Specifically, modern petroleum and petrochemical industries have argued that continued exploration and exploitation of fossil fuels are necessary because the world's cultures are not all equitably powered by a Western conception of Energy. Often, this argument is placed within the frame of "human rights," where the denial of access to on-demand Energy is harmful, and where the intensive extraction techniques of fossil fuels are the only realistic option to relieve global Energy poverty. ExxonMobil has argued that "more oil and gas production is necessary to maintain and raise global living standards" and its CEO has contended that "the societal benefits of oil and gas are unmatched in human history. . . . No country has ever joined the developed world without access to oil and gas" (Domonoske and Simon 2023). Sultan al-Jaber, the CEO of the United Arab Emirate's state-run oil company, echoed this sentiment and challenged others to show him "a roadmap for a phase-out of fossil fuels that will allow for sustainable socioeconomic development, unless you want to take the world back into caves" (Domonoske and Simon 2023). Often, this argument is bolstered by insincere claims to reduce "energy poverty"; appeals to the United Nations' Sustainable Development Goal #7, which addresses affordable and clean energy (even though fossil fuels do not fit the category; see box 6.1); and comparisons between how cultures use energy (Drilling Matters n.d.). Arguments for carbon Energy-as-a-human-right are promoted by pundits such as Alex Epstein, a global warming denier who has argued that increasing fossil fuel production is a moral imperative.

Box 6.1
Manipulation of the UN's Sustainable Development Goals

The UN's *2030 Agenda for Sustainable Development* can be used by energy companies to support their agendas, regardless of whether their energy production fits the goals of sustainable development.

In 2015, the United Nations adopted a document called the *2030 Agenda for Sustainable Development*, a declaration that covered numerous topics, but focused on sustainable development to eradicate poverty while preserving global ecosystems (UN General Assembly 2015). The declaration included seventeen sustainable development goals, and these are often interpreted as expanding Western logics of "green" capitalist production while excluding voices that have historically not been invited to the conversation about future development. Some critics have argued that the goals frame the environment as an instrumental feature that must be managed only insofar as it supports economic growth. Others have argued that the Agenda 2030 is too focused on goals and less concerned with rights (Belda-Miquel and Calabuig 2019), and still additional critiques have found that these goals do not significantly challenge historical inequalities (Clements and Sweetman 2020).

Despite the critiques, petroleum energy companies have used one particular goal in the 2030 Agenda for Sustainable Development: Goal #7, to "Ensure access to affordable, reliable, sustainable and modern energy for all." While the goal emphasizes locating clean and renewable energy, increasing energy efficiency, and lowering costs, it also assumes on-demand "formalist" formations of capital-E Energy. Industries can utilize Goal #7 to rationalize their continued extraction of hydrocarbons, because such extraction could play a role in expanding energy access and lowering costs as we continue to transition to clean and sustainable energy sources. Industries have also frequently argued that extractive work is part of a larger moral obligation, because to not expand fossil fuel production would be to fail to support those without access to on-demand energy. The logics of this argument are specious at best, and constitute a form of "social washing," where social obligations are used as a shield for continued, profitable energy extraction techniques.

Continued fossil fuel energy extraction is often supported by claims about its necessity and role in greater humanitarian action; it is also rationalized as necessary to reduce the harms of lowercase energy production. Yet fossil fuel extraction, refinement, and transportation systems bring their own risks. Laborers at extraction sites face some of the highest incidents of workplace accidents, tailings ponds poison the watershed, refineries produce carcinogenic air pollution, and waste contaminates soil. Pipelines, rail networks, offshore oil rigs, supertanker ships, and tanker trucks leak, rupture, spill, or crash. Those who live and work near these extraction points, along their transportation corridors, and around their refinement sites face disproportionate levels of risk, as do the ecosystems these infrastructural systems are built upon. This is the central contradiction operating in the relationship between Western Energy and risk, in the unequal distribution of harm. *Risk flows in contradiction to energy.* Multinational corporations that benefit from the extraction and production of energy have argued that their actions are an ethical commitment to support human development, though their profit margins suggest otherwise. Those who live in locations far from sites of extraction, transportation, and refinement tend to benefit from increasing energy resources and the safeguards that energy will be available on demand. Their risks are long term, as increased fossil fuel extraction leads to greater atmospheric CO_2, which drives global warming, but the more immediate forms of risk are shouldered by those people and ecosystems that are already vulnerable. Energy flows away from people and ecosystems that have been made more vulnerable, is transported alongside similar vulnerabilities, and then refined in sites often referred to as "sacrifice zones" (Juskus 2023). In the following case study focused on the Uinta Basin Railway, we show where these contradictory risk flows operate across time and geographic space.

We expand both scope and scale in this case study, but also allow for how time- and space-collapsed events emphasize where risks will manifest into crises. Including these disasters will, we hope, provide case study approaches with explicit opportunities for deliberative exposition.

Uinta Basin Energy Flows

The Uinta Basin is a broad section of high desert and forest located in the northeast corner of Utah, situated between the Wasatch Mountains to the west and the taller Uinta Mountains to the north (see fig. 6.1). The

Figure 6.1. Geology and fuel resources of the Green River formation in the Southeastern Uinta Basin, Utah and Colorado (W. B. Cashion 1967). *Source:* Public domain.

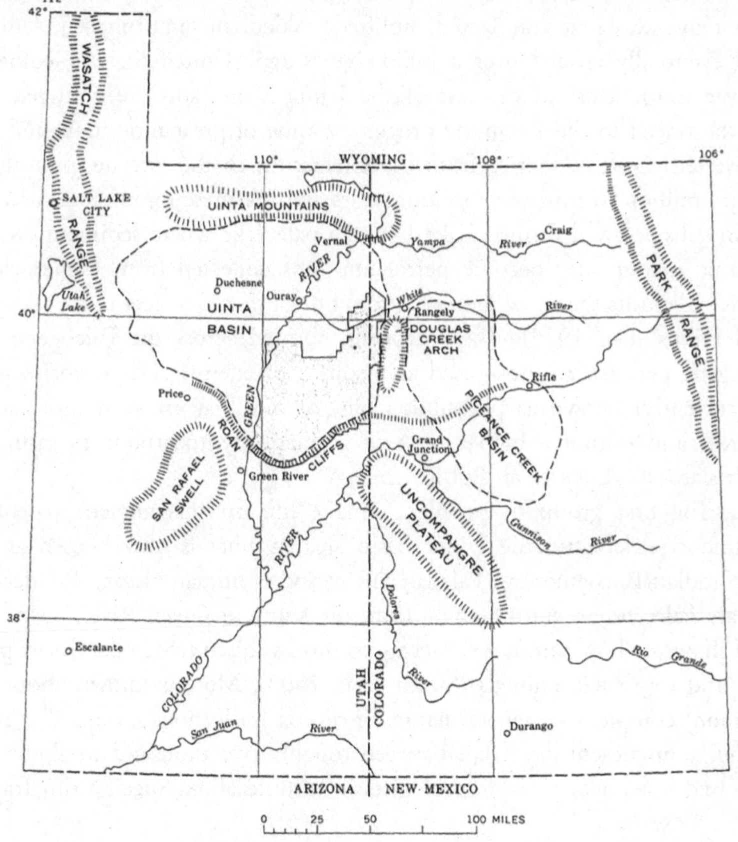

name Uinta derives from a Ute word "Yoov-we-teuh," which means "pine forest," a name more applicable to the slopes of the Uinta Mountains than to the basin below. Much of the basin is five thousand to ten thousand feet above sea level and is (currently) classified as "steppe" in the Koppen climate classification, as a semiarid intermediate zone between deserts and more humid climates (US Forest Service n.d.). Much of the basin is covered by water-thrifty species of trees such as piñon and juniper and shrubs like sagebrush, greasewood, shadscale, horsebrush, and winterfat. While locations throughout the Uinta Basin (currently) receive less than ten inches of rainfall a year, the basin benefits from greater precipitation in the Uinta Mountains and hosts several major tributaries of the Colorado River, including the Duchesne River, which feeds into the Green River, which in turn is the main tributary for the Colorado (for more detail on Colorado River Basin tributaries, see chapter 5). In terms of deep time, the Uinta Mountains that collect much of the snowmelt (which flows into the basin) are over two billion years old, when the precambrian Red Creek Quartzite mountain range was first compacted, uplifted, folded, metamorphosed, faulted, and eventually eroded over a billion years ago (United States Geological Survey n.d.). Most of the rest of the Uinta Mountains are younger, and can be traced to the Laramide orogeny, a time of great mountain building in western North America from the Cretaceous to the Eocene, or roughly eighty million to thirty-five million years ago. As these mountains rose, the basin subsided and formed Lake Uinta, a paleolake where sediment (whose organic matter later become petroleum) was collected from higher elevations—deposits that now measure up to fifteen thousand feet thick (Keighin and Hibpshman 1975). These deposits, formed across the Paleogene and Neogene periods, are now used as a source of energy, and comprise what is (currently) known as phosphoria oils, or oils that are from nonmarine sources and exhibit a higher ratio of aromatic hydrocarbons to saturated hydrocarbons (Lillis et al. 2003).

The first group of people to make life on this ancient paleolake sediment settled into the Uinta Basin area in what is now known as the Paleoindian/Paleoamerican/Paleoarchaic period of human history. Renderings of late Paleoindian culture come from the study of Green River basin sites and showcase how camps were set up to process biscuitroot (aka desert parsley) and trap small animals (Smith et al. 2003). More is known about the Fremont complex—a general name for several Indigenous groups that lived throughout present-day Utah between roughly two thousand to about five hundred years ago, with archeologists in dispute about specific timeframes

(Spangler 2000). The Uinta Fremont, a name given by anthropologists to the people living in the basin during this climactic and agricultural transition, took advantage of a warmer, wetter period and farmed maize, hunted via bow and arrow, and developed unique methods for pottery (US Forest Service, Ashley National Forest n.d.). What drove the close of the Uinta Fremont period of habitation is unknown, but climatic change apparently played a role as inhabitants moved settlements and possibly merged with the Ute people, who would come to settle in the area or merge with other Numic-speaking people in the southwest. As of 1300 AD, the Uinta-ats (Uinta), a band of Utes (the Ute today distinguish themselves into Northern Ute, Southern Ute, and Mountain Ute tribes), were the area's dominant group, though the basin was also occupied by the Northern and Northwestern Shoshones (Fuller n.d.). The Ute's origin is to Sinauf, a half-man, half-wolf god, brother of both Coyote and Wolf. One day, while getting ready for a journey, Sinauf put many sticks into a bag, sticks that became people with a wide range of languages and cultures. Curious as to what these people were like, Coyote cut a hole in the bag to see. As Sinauf ventured to the mountain Una-u-quich, the people spilled out and populated the land. Later, upon looking into the bag, Sinauf saw that only a few people were left and named them the Utikas (Utah Indians).

Along with early quasi-paleontological exploration, and some anthropological research, the early white colonists were interested in energy extraction. The first written descriptions of paleontological findings were Spanish, from around the time of the American Revolutionary War, though later, more formal descriptions of Utah's fossil record were made in *The Report of the Exploring Expedition to the Rocky Mountains* by John C. Frémont—the same man whose name also is used for the Fremont complex (1845). Further expedition reports of vertebrate dinosaurs and more substantial, government-funded geological surveys were accomplished in the 1860s, kicking off an intense period of paleontological excavation that lasted well into the twentieth century. These explorations, and the competition surrounding them, were not limited to the discovery of animal and plant fossils, but occurred alongside intense energy exploration. The first governmental discovery of petroleum in Utah came in an Army Corps of Topographical Engineers survey of the Great Salt Lake in 1850. Many paleontologists of the age were also oil surveyors, and the first railroad in the area, the Uintah Railway (see box 6.2), was designed to haul gilsonite (a hydrocarbon resin), but also hauled people, library books, and dinosaur fossils, before being dismantled in 1939 (W. Jones n.d.).

Box 6.2
Extraction and a Brief History of Uinta/Uintah Railways

There exists a substantial industrial history of petroleum transportation from the Uinta Basin, and wherever there is extraction, there are companies willing to create additional harms for commercial profit.

The predecessor to the Uinta Basin Railway project was the Uintah Railway, a smaller-gauge rail line that carried Gilsonite, a solid, black shiny hydrocarbon, from Mack, Colorado, to Watson, Utah, from 1904 until World War II. Gilsonite was named after Samuel H. Gilson, who didn't discover the material, but financially supported mining via the Gilson Asphaltum Company (later purchased by Anheuser-Busch, who used Gilsonite to line their beer barrels) (American Gilsonite n.d.). When Gilsonite was identified within the Uintah Reservation, Gilson petitioned Congress to strip the reservation of those lands, which it did in 1888, removing seven thousand acres from the eastern side of the reservation to allow mining to proceed "legally" (Lewis n.d.). Mining and financial interests have long held influence in rural Utah, and have enthusiastically displaced or marginalized those with less political power.

In a more modern context, DHIP, one the companies tapped to run the current Uinta Basin Railway, was also behind plans to build the Plaquemines Liquids Terminal, an oil export terminal and pipeline intended for a Louisiana parish often known as the center of the sacrifice zone called "cancer alley." The terminal was to be built on top of a burial ground for enslaved people, would have contributed to the area's air pollution, and could have further slowed coastal recovery efforts (Rubiano 2022). The Rio Grande Pacific corporation, the other company connected to the Uinta Basin Railway, has previously tried to operate a passenger service with "limited freight" along the Tennessee Pass Line, a rail line between Parkdale, Colorado, an unincorporated community, to Dotsero, Colorado, another unincorporated community—a rail line that would not connect to the nation's active rail network. Critics have been skeptical that these plans for a passenger train are simply a front to transport waxy crude once the line has been built (Webb 2023).

Amid this era of energy exploration, the Ute tribes were largely seen by white colonizers as a hindrance to the acquisition of natural resources and economic expansion in the state. In 1868, desire for mining and mineral rights led to the so-called Kit Carson Treaty, in which the US government forcibly removed many Northern Ute people out of Colorado's Central Rockies (see chapter 4 for additional detail). This treaty was essentially invalidated by the Indian Appropriations Act in 1871, and by 1882, the US government removed additional Ute families onto the least hospitable, least energy-resource rich location in the state—what became the Uintah and Ouray Reservations, which comprise much of the Uinta Basin (Utah Division of Indian Affairs). Compared to Ute traditional lands, these reservations were tiny, and made traditional Ute farming practices unsustainable, forcing families into poverty, and removing them from ancestral and spiritual lands (Summers 2020).

Jump ahead to 1949, and yellow waxy crude oil, which was deposited in the Uinta Basin during the Paleogene and Neogene periods, was identified in the Altamont field in Duchesne County, Utah. A black waxy crude was located in the Red Wash field in Uinta County soon after. Chevron constructed pipelines to refineries near Salt Lake City to remove the crude, though the pipelines could only carry a certain percentage of the material, and needed to be heated, as waxy crude contains paraffin and is solid at room temperature (it apparently resembles shoe polish). The pipeline had to be heated with electricity, and eventually natural gas, actions that increase the temperature of the crude to near 180°F and keep it above 120°F (Utah Energy 2015, 36). Numerous failures and ruptures plagued these lines, which are currently inoperable as waxy crude pipelines, including the 2010 Red Butte Creek spill, which released eight hundred barrels of oil into the Red Butte Creek and received an aggressive cleanup response (possibly because of the recent BP Deepwater Horizon spill earlier in the same year). With no major pipelines available to move waxy crude from the Uinta Basin, this transportation is currently accomplished by heated tanker trucks, though a proposal to construct a new railway line would allow for increased volume of waxy crude to be transported to major refinery sites elsewhere in the US.

Contradictory Risk Flows and the Uinta Railway

One proposed solution to increase waxy crude exports from the Uinta Basin has been to increase the modern rail transport links, as waxy crude is currently transported via heated tractor trailers. A rail line designed to carry heated waxy crude from the Uinta Basin to refineries has been in development at least since 2001, when the Utah Department of Community and Economic Development studied the feasibility of constructing a freight line (Utah Department of Transportation 2021, 1). Later, the Utah Department of Transportation, and eventually a private firm named HDR Engineering, conducted more specific studies of waxy crude rail transport. Funding for the proposed railroad has been dispersed by a coalition of seven Utah counties (known as the Seven County Infrastructure Coalition) through a $27.9 million grant of public funds made available from the Utah Permanent Community Impact Fund Board (Stop Uinta Basin Railway n.d.). The legality of using this funding source for a petroleum rail line was contested by the Center for Biological Diversity (Center for Biological Diversity 2019) and other environmental groups, but upheld by court decision (Maffly 2022). The rail line, and the most recent proposal named the "Whitmore Park alternative route," would begin at Leland Bench (a "bench" is a small level piece of land on a slope) roughly near Randlett, Utah, a small town with a predominantly Indigenous population. The tracks would continue southwest, through land (currently) controlled by tribal trust, the US Forest Service, the Bureau of Land Management, the state of Utah, and private ownership, until reaching an existing rail line, one controlled by Union Pacific and BNSF.

The most vocal advocate of the proposed railway has been the Seven County Infrastructure Coalition, a group comprising Carbon, Daggett, Dushense, Emery, San Juan, Sevier, and Uintah Counties. They claim to "promote cooperative regional planning, increase economic opportunity and public services, and implement sustainable infrastructure projects," though ten of their current twelve projects involve energy transportation and infrastructure (Seven County Infrastructure Coalition n.d.). The Seven County Infrastructure Coalition has engaged two companies to run the proposed rail line, DHIP, which will develop, finance, and build the railway, and the Texas-based Rio Grande Pacific Corporation, which will operate and maintain the railway (Center 2019). These companies are used to creating financial resources out of energy infrastructure, and also passing on an increased likelihood of harm to those who live near or along the locations where the energy is extracted, transported, or refined.

Four other companies are heavily invested in the Uinta Basin and (at present) produce ~127,000 barrels of oil equivalent per day, measured in Mb/d, which accounts for roughly 70 percent of the production from the Uinta Basin (East Daley Analytics 2024). These four are Ovintiv Inc., SM Energy, Crescent Energy, and Uinta Wax Operating (owned by Finley Resources, Inc.). Each of these companies has claimed to be invested in generating clean(er), more sustainable forms of energy—and doing so for a range of reasons, from assisting local economies and providing the essentials for modern life to supporting an inevitable global energy transition. Ovintiv argued that their work is essential, as they support basic human needs, from healthcare and education to food and clothing (Ovintiv Inc. n.d.); SM Energy has similarly claimed they are invested in making "people's lives better by responsibly producing energy supplies" (SM Energy n.d.); Crescent Energy emphasized that their role in providing conventional energy sources "is critical to maintaining quality of life" (Crescent Energy 2022); and Finley Resources perceived their efforts as necessary to the current energy transition, contradictorily, away from the actual energy forms they create (Finley Resources n. d.). Of course, these companies have emphasized their extraction work as necessary, but each has also argued for the inherent value of their "products" as essential, in what we recognize as a formalist mode of energopower. Their petroleum extraction exists within a system of quantifiable energy extraction and infrastructure that overwhelmingly benefits those who live elsewhere from the sites of extraction. This is capital-E Energy as a stable, on-demand, at-hand resource that is provided to those living under Western industrial modernity—a modernity that is supposedly beneficial to all. Anthropologist Leslie White's assumptions about the equivalence of energy use and cultural evolution support the fundamental rationales for this continued extraction. Further, the risks from this energy generation are not distributed equally, as those who live near the sites of extraction, transportation, and refinement bear an unequal burden of the harms they generate.

In general, when there are new sites of energy extraction, transportation, and refinement, those that live and work alongside the trajectories of energy bear an unequal burden of harm. Under a petroculture, energy is often unearthed and moved away from rural locations and distributed toward population-intensive locations, while providing wealth for those who invested capital in that particular industry. Energy flows away from those (predominantly rural, predominantly minority populated) sites toward (predominantly Western, predominantly capital-intensive) locations, and harm is distributed to those who live near mines, pipelines, or refineries, not those who demand energy from their household outlets or gas stations. This contradictory energy flow, as we have described above, distributes a Western form of capital Energy in one direction and risk in reverse.

The rapid ascension of an extraction economy for predominantly rural locations can bring increases in a variety of harms. As Terry Karl argued in *The Paradox of Plenty* (2017), petrostates can experience some immediate financial benefit from petroleum discovery, extraction, and export, but increased oil revenues also produce some unpleasant side effects. Economically and politically, oil wealth can absolve a government of a need to raise taxes, which can create strong voter opposition to taxes, leaving tax collection underdeveloped and the government dependent upon powerful interest groups—often connected to the same extraction companies. For example, in rural North Dakota, specifically in counties that have benefited from connection to the Bakken Formation/Three Forks (a large area of shale source rock for unconventional oil extraction), researchers have found that oil boom periods place stress on social services, hospitals, and educational facilities; bring increases in crime, especially violence against Indigenous women and children (Colorado Law 2020); and cause food insecurity and inflation more generally (see Bohnenkamp et al. 2011; Bushnell et al. 2022; Fernando and Cooley 2016; Weber et al. 2014). Increased extraction also impacts air quality and increases the parts per million of numerous harmful particulates (see Colorado State n.d.; Evanoski-Cole et al. 2017; Gadhamshetty et al. 2015). Ecosystems connected to sites of energy extraction and transportation likewise experience elevated water pollution (Shrestha et al. 2017), negative impacts on wildlife habitat and increased habitat fragmentation (Howden et al. 2019), and the potential impact of accidents, pipeline spills, and derailments. While it hardly needs to be emphasized, here we see contradictory risk flows yet again; those benefiting from the extracted energy are not those who are spatially adjacent to the sites of extraction, transportation, and refinement.

East Palestine, Ohio and Contradictory Risk Flows

People and ecosystems made vulnerable by their proximity to sites of energy removal suffer the burden of increased likelihood of harm—in inverse proportion to the trajectories that energy flows. Some of these harms arrive in the sense of *slow violence*, where increased rates of cancer, diminishing wildlife habitat, or groundwater contamination can take decades to fully arrive. Of course, there are other more immediate and more catastrophic forms of industrial/historical and present violence happening as a result of contradictory risk flow. For risks stemming from extraction sites within the Bakken Formation, we need look no further than the Lac-Mégantic rail disaster, or, as we will explore in more depth, the 2023 East Palestine, Ohio train derailment. The Lac-Mégantic rail disaster occurred in 2013, when a train carrying crude oil extracted from the Bakken Formation was left unattended outside of the town of Lac-Mégantic, Quebec. A train engine failed, due to a faulty repair, and caught fire, at which point the hand brakes released, and the train, carrying over 6.7 million liters of crude oil, rolled downhill into Lac-Mégantic, derailed, and then exploded, killing forty-seven people and destroying dozens of buildings (Transportation Safety Board of Canada 2014). Oil from the explosion leaked into the nearby Chaudière River, and the soil was contaminated by benzene and hydrocarbons. The explosion resulted from several more immediately causal forms of negligence, but the broader cause can easily be seen within the scope of structural violence where trains running on outdated technology, functioning within a system of crumbling infrastructure maintained by for-profit corporations, and carrying dangerous cargo were allowed to pass through numerous towns, and alongside important waterways, on the way toward refineries, ports, or other destinations. While large-scale rail-based hazardous chemical leaks are relatively infrequent, the scale of their cargo, combined with rail line locations, puts many people and ecosystems at continual risk of immediate crises like that which occurred in Lac-Mégantic.

The train derailment and subsequent intentional burnoff of vinyl chloride in East Palestine, Ohio in 2023, by contrast, offers us perhaps more recent and immediate evidence of the danger presented by hazardous petrochemical transportation—and another representation of contradictory risk flows. However, we should make clear our goals in exploring the East Palestine vinyl chloride derailment within our larger focus on the Uinta Basin Railway: We are not overly concerned with the rhetorical contexts that led to the derailment, the rupture of eleven tanker cars, which released vinyl chloride, butyl acrylate, ethylhexyl acrylate, and ethylene glycol monobutyl ether, or the rhetorical choices made by decision-makers as they created a "controlled" release and burn of vinyl chloride (US EPA 2023b). Instead, we are concerned with establishing how a contradictory risk flow of energy led to the increased likelihood of harm to certain groups, and how the slow violence more easily witnessed in the Uinta Basin Railway case can magnify into a time-constrained disaster. In brief, we're interested in stretching both time and space around the disaster, in order to expand the scale and scope of risk, specifically as it relates to the transportation of risk.

The vinyl chloride transported by the Norfolk Southern train passing through the Ohio-Pennsylvania border initially came from the Permian Basin, a sedimentary basin in west Texas and southern New Mexico. Occidental Petroleum, and their parent company, OxyVinyls, manufactures vinyl chloride, a key building block for making polyvinyl chloride, or PVC plastic, by reacting chlorine gas with ethylene to produce ethylene dichloride, which is further processed to create vinyl chloride monomer. Vinyl chloride is listed by OSHA as a class IA flammable liquid, but a liquid that can form a dense, highly explosive cloud if leaked (NOAA n.d.). The chemical plants that produce vinyl chloride and PVC produce a significant amount of air pollution, and in 2022 "OxyVinyls and its joint venture partner, Orbia, ranked as the country's third and fifth leading sources of vinyl chloride air pollution" (Toxic-Free Future 2024). Vinyl chloride is a human carcinogen and associated with hepatic angiosarcoma (a rare form of liver cancer) along with hepatocellular carcinoma (primary liver cancer), lymphoma, and leukemia (National Cancer Institute 2024). Roughly thirty-six million pounds of vinyl chloride are transported by rail in the US and Canada at any given moment (Toxic-Free Future 2024), a portion of the larger 4.5 million tons of toxic chemicals that are shipped in the US by rail each year, with an average of twelve thousand rail cars carrying hazardous materials passing through cities and towns each day (Lartey 2023).

Toxic-Free Future, an antipollution advocacy group, along with Materials Research, a low-profit LLC that provides environmental justice-oriented open access data, created a map describing where the vinyl chloride involved in the East Palestine derailment came from and which communities bore the unequal distribution of harm in that transportation. Unsurprisingly, on route between the Texas ports of Ingleside and La Porte and the New Jersey port of Pedricktown, the train traveled through cities where "more than three million people live, and [where] about 670,000 children attend more than 1,500 schools" within one mile of the main train station for the rail line. That vinyl chloride shipment, and many others, passed through cities like Philadelphia, San Antonio, and Houston, and rail lines are located close to large population centers, though primarily through low-income communities of color. In Philadelphia, 95 percent of the people within a one-mile radius of the North Philadelphia Train Station are people of color, in San Antonio, 85 percent, and in Houston, 97 percent (Toxic-Free Future 2024).

After the train derailment of thirty-eight cars, which was initially caused by overheating wheel bearings that forced an axle to separate, three tank cars breached and burst into flames (National Transportation Safety Board n.d.). The fire then consumed additional derailed train cars, at which point Norfolk Southern and their employed contractors advocated for and then chose to "vent and burn" five additional rail cars that contained vinyl chloride (National Transportation Safety Board n.d.). Their fear, later determined to be unfounded, was that the fire could have breached the cars carrying vinyl chloride, which was stored under pressure, causing it to polymerize and the tank cars to explode (Runwal 2024). Certainly, there was a technical communication failure present, as Norfolk Southern did not communicate the "relevant expertise and dissenting opinions to the incident commander," and they gave an "inaccurate representation . . . that the tank cars were at risk of catastrophic failure" (National Transportation Safety Board n.d.). The vent and burn of vinyl chloride accompanied an evacuation order for roughly two thousand people. Analysis of rain and snow samples in the following weeks, from Wisconsin to Maine, resulted in elevated pH levels and "exceptionally elevated levels of base cations exceeding 99th percentiles versus the historic record" (Gay et al. 2024). The pollution had spread so far in part because the fire and controlled vinyl chloride burn was so hot and concentrated that "it sent a towering plume into the Earth's free troposphere, where winds often blow between 50 and 100 mph" (Perkins 2024). The Ohio Department of Natural Resources estimated that more than forty-two thousand animals, including minnows, crayfish, amphibians, macroinvertebrates, were potentially directly killed as a result of the derailment (ODNR 2023), and some residents reported their chickens also died as a direct result of the vent and burn (Grimley 2023).

Before being vented into the troposphere, the vinyl chloride was headed to an Oxyvinyls/Occidental Petroleum plant in Pedricktown, New Jersey. The plant produces and distributes numerous products, many of which are used in the production of plastics in general and polyvinyl chloride (PVC) in particular. Most of the PVC produced goes into building materials, including water pipes and electric insulation sheathing, but also vinyl siding, flooring, cabinetry, gutters, and windows. Roughly forty-four million metric tons of PVC resin were produced in 2018, and almost sixty million metric tons were estimated to be produced in 2023 (Alsabri et al. 2020). The primary production stage of synthetic resins like PVC involves the largest proportion of carbon emissions (69–86%) of the total carbon emission of their life cycle, and, to give some sense of the scope of the production, "if the production and use of plastics continue to grow according to current plans, these emissions could reach 1.34 billion tons CO_2 per year by 2030—equivalent to over 295 new 500 MW coal-fired power plants" (Liang and Yu 2023, 2). Those most impacted by the additional CO_2 released through the manufacture of PVC, as well as those impacted by the plastics in our waterways and garbage dumps, are not often those who benefit from the production of PVC, nor those who benefit from the new housing where PVC products are predominantly used; they are instead unjustly impacted by the extraction of natural gas and oil, the "cracking" of those carbons to create ethylene, the further transportation of vinyl chloride, and then the manufacture of polyvinyl chloride.

The Uinta Basin and Preventing Contradictory Risk Flows

The dangers manifested in both the Lac-Mégantic rail disaster and the East Palestine derailment are of course present in plans for the Uinta Basin Railway project; they represent future conditions that could also give rise to more dramatic and immediate events like derailments, chemical spills, and explosions. However, the industrial/historical past of the Uinta Basin Railway, like any and all extractive transportation projects, also includes the slow violences inherit in the systematic exploitation of limited resources for markets that do not involve, and often explicitly or implicitly disregard, many more people and ecosystems than will be impacted by the manufacture of energy. Certainly, any rail line that carries waxy crude from the Uinta Basin will increase the immediate future ecological risk to the Colorado River watershed and the risk of derailment/spill in the communities it passes through, but it would also distribute risk to those living in the shadow of refineries in "cancer alley" Louisiana and those living in the Maldives, as sea levels rise due to global warming, due to increasing atmospheric CO_2. The Uinta Basin Railway is estimated to facilitate the production of fifty-three million metric tons of atmospheric carbon a year. Such is the case despite the claims of energy companies to have the Majority World and those without access to on-demand energy or energy-rich products at the forefront of their rationale for continued extraction. Such companies have denied the contradictory risk flows of their energy extraction practices, and, conversely, argued that their extraction, transportation, refinement, and production goals have been to reduce global risk and increase access to Western conceptions of energy and related services.

We see arguments for the denial of contradictory risk flows in many locations, and most often these denials are founded upon claims about a lack of knowledge or ability to predict future states of risk; these claims are often combined with a greater certainty about how immediate economic benefits outweigh that indeterminate immediate future and long-term future risk. The broader argument for the Uinta Basin Railway neatly matches this scenario, and while railway plans were halted for a time, the court case about the railway exposes the logics used by those seeking to maximize the economic benefit of mining activities and the counterlogics used by judges. These counterlogics showcase how a revaluation of the scope and scale of risk beyond present human economic benefit, and beyond Western conceptions of energy, can be located and promoted. Specifically, in the case of the Uinta Basin Railway, the US Court of Appeals rendered a verdict that expanded what risk can mean and provided an opportunity to consider the contradictory risk flows so inherent in much present-day energy extraction, transportation, and refinement activities. This consideration of environmental documentation is also where TPC practitioners can more assertively contribute to exposing contradictory risk flows and offering pathways that push back against Western conceptions of continued energy extraction and highlight the cause-and-effect chains that generate future risk. Here, we'll consider the environmental impact statement (EIS) in some depth.

First, some background. In May 2020, the Seven County Coalition, in seeking to develop the Uinta Basin Railway project, sought an exemption from formal application requirements to develop the railway from the Surface Transportation Board (STB). Congress granted the Surface Transportation Board jurisdiction and governance over the construction and operation of rail carriers in the Interstate Commerce Commission Termination Act of 1995. Arguing that the COVID-19 pandemic had impacted the economy of the Uinta Basin, the coalition asked for conditional approval, which was granted, pending a more complete environmental impact statement. The National Environmental Protection Agency requires all federal agencies to examine the environmental effects of proposed federal actions and consider impacts to the quality of the human environment, endangered species and their environments, and historical property, offering an investigation into these aspects in an EIS (US Government Publishing Office n.d.). TPC practitioners are often involved in the production of an EIS, and TPC researchers, since the field emerged as an academic discipline, have consistently focused on the EIS as a rhetorically complex document (see, e.g., Dayton 2002; Killingsworth and Steffens 1989; Miller 1980; Moore 2016; Ryan 1993). In October 2020, the STB published a draft EIS for review, had six public online meetings, and collected over nineteen hundred comments before formally submitting the document in August 2021 (US Department of the Interior 2021, 1). The STB approved the Uinta Basin railway project, specifying the "Whitmore Park Alternative" route, which would take the railway through tribal trust lands in the Uintah and Ouray Reservation, in December 2021 (Eagle County 2023, 10). In response, Eagle County,

Colorado and the Center for Biological Diversity filed separate petitions opposing the exemption and the US Fish and Wildlife Service's Biological Opinion, which was used in developing the EIS. The two petitions were consolidated by a United States Court of Appeals in February 2022.

The final EIS proposed by the Seven County Coalition made the case for the proposed rail line and considered some of the effects. In brief, it explained that the Uinta Basin Railway's purpose would be to transport crude oil from the Basin to markets, which would result in 3.68 to 9.92 trains per day, on average, with each loaded train consisting of roughly 110 oil tanker cars, including locomotives and additional rail cars (US Department of the Interior 2021, 1–4). The reason for building the rail line is simply presented—to create jobs for construction, operations, and maintenance workers, and increase tax revenue (2021, S–9). They estimated that the Uinta Basin Railway would create three thousand jobs (either directly or indirectly), create labor income of $209.7 million, and create $311.8 million in "value-added" (aka profit) (2021, 3.13–26). The EIS also considered the environmental impacts of this job creation, though it did so by omitting some potentially valuable information. To understand "downline" impacts, or impacts to locations and people that are literally further down a rail line or downstream for water quality, for example, the STB's Office of Environmental Analysis defined a downline study area that extended to the edge of the Denver Metro/North Front Range. They found that increased locomotive exhaust, wayside noise, and the risk of accidents at crossings would not be significant—but also found that the new rail line and increased rail traffic "could result in cumulative adverse impacts on water resources, biological resources, paleontological resources, land use and recreation, visual resources, and socioeconomics" (2021, S–13). Further risks include the likelihood that an accident "involving a loaded oil train would occur approximately once every 3 to 10 years" but the EIS also explained that "these accidents would not all be serious—some might involve derailments of a few rail cars and no release of crude oil, while others could involve more derailed cars and could release crude oil into the environment" (2021, 3.2–4). In a brief discussion of long-term global impacts, the EIS noted that high-production scenarios of waxy crude on the rail line would account for "approximately 0.8 percent of nationwide GHG and 0.1 percent of global GHG emissions," but the EIS ultimately argued that any major impacts would be insignificant or otherwise mitigated (2021, 3.15–36).

Following approval of the EIS by the STB, both Eagle County, Colorado and the Center for Biological Diversity appealed the case to the US

Court of Appeals, arguing that the STB failed to scrutinize future global environmental impacts sufficiently and that the STB should not have granted an exemption to the full application process (Eagle County 2023, 13). The US Court of Appeals disagreed with several of the objections raised by the petitioners, but ultimately found "that the EIS failed to demonstrate that the [STB] took the requisite 'hard look' at all of the environmental impacts of the Railway" (25). Most notably, the Center for Biological Diversity argued that oil spills, derailments, air pollution, river pollution, harms to wildlife, and ecosystem damage risks do not end when the Uinta Basin railway connects to the national rail network in Denver, especially because these trains will run on lines parallel to the Colorado River for 233 miles (19). The Court of Appeals ruling specifically called out the EIS for limiting the environmental impacts of the rail line to, as the Center for Biological Diversity described it, the area adjacent to and "within several hundred feet of the [proposed] rail line"—a relatively local level of immediate future risk (28). The EIS further limited the scope of their examination of accident risk from increased waxy crude rail traffic, using national data for rail accidents and not data that considered the challenging terrain and the cargo (38). Nor did the EIS appropriately evaluate wildfire risk, arguing that the trains would not constitute a "new ignition source" and only considered additional drips of fuel or lubricant on the ground (US Department of the Interior 2021, 3.4–43), an argument that the court found "utterly unreasoned" (Eagle County 2023, 42). However, the largest flaw in the EIS, and the most significant argument as to why the exemption should have failed, had to do with an even broader scope and scale and points to the significance of contradictory risk flows in energy transportation infrastructure.

The Center for Biological Diversity put forth the claim that the EIS ignored the upstream and downstream impacts of the proposed rail line—impacts beyond those posed to Denver or to the Colorado River as it runs alongside the national rail network. The Center argued, and the Court of Appeals agreed, that the EIS "failed to disclose the downstream environmental impacts of increased crude oil refining along the Gulf Coast," especially because the EIS acknowledged that the petroleum products extracted from the Uinta Basin "would be delivered to Houston and/or Port Arthur, Texas, and another 35 percent to the Louisiana Gulf Coast" (Eagle County 2023, 28). Further, they faulted the EIS for not analyzing "the potential for tens of thousands of additional barrels of oil shipments daily and their processing in these locales to further worsen pollution burdens" in "locales with known, disproportionate exposure to pollution already" (28). The STB acknowledged that the railway could result in nearly 1 percent of total US greenhouse gas emissions, but failed to adequately consider both the immediate and long-term future impact of those emissions and the impact upon the communities that would bear the burden of harm. In short, the EIS did not appropriately account for the contradictory flows of risk when energy is extracted, transported, and refined. The US Court of Appeals found that the STB and the EIS

> did not adequately consider the incredibly significant environmental effects identified in the EIS in weighing those impacts against the uncertain transportation benefits of the Railway. The "cumulative" effects within the Uinta Basin of a major expansion of oil drilling there, on Gulf Coast communities of refining the oil, and the climate effects of the combustion of the fuel intended to be extracted are foreseeable environmental effects of the project. These are effects the Board ultimately has the authority to prevent. The Board was required not only to identify those effects under NEPA, as discussed above, but also to weigh them in its ICCT [Interstate Commerce Commission Termination] Act analysis. Its failure to do so contributes to our conclusion that the [Surface Transportation] Board's order is arbitrary and capricious. (62)

Ultimately, the Court of Appeals ruled that the STB was "required to compare both sides of the ledger, not just acknowledge that both sides exist" and was incorrect in its approval of an exemption, largely because of the deficiencies of the EIS to consider downstream impacts (55).

The STB's response to these petitions reflected an intentional unwillingness to consider cause and effect beyond immediate and local impacts to geography abutting the rail line. The STB argued that "upstream and downstream impacts from oil development in the Uinta Basin are not reasonably foreseeable impacts" and that it is not reasonable to "consider the environmental effects of downline oil refining on Gulf Coast communities or on greenhouse gases from oil combustion because the board "cannot regulate or mitigate impacts caused by [downline train] operations" (Eagle County 2023, 29). The STB argued that these impacts are essentially beyond the scope of risk for an EIS. They argued that any estimates about the amount of petroleum products to be transported by the Uinta Railway, and therefore with the potential to impact other ecosystems and communities, "are merely estimates and otherwise the actual numbers are 'simply unknown and unknowable'" (29). The Court of Appeals did not agree and found that the STB "cannot avoid its responsibility under NEPA to identify and describe the environmental effects of increased oil drilling and refining on the ground that it lacks authority to prevent, control, or mitigate those developments" (33). While these intentional omissions of scope, in the Court of Appeal's words, "renders arbitrary the Board's consideration of the relevant Rail Policies and the final order's exemption of the Railway," the court also found that the STB failed to "weigh the Project's uncertain financial viability and the full potential for environmental harm against the transportation benefits it identified" (66).

The US Supreme Court ruled 8–0 in *Seven County Infrastructure Coalition et al. v. Eagle County, Colorado, et al.* (2025) against the Court of Appeals, finding that it is not the responsibility of the Surface Transportation Board to consider additional risks. The court found the EIS to be sufficient—in terms of scope—in part because in 2023 Congress passed an amendment to NEPA (as part of the Fiscal Responsibility Act of 2023) that clarified that "environmental impact statements should include discussion of reasonably foreseeable effects of a proposed action, reasonably foreseeable effects that cannot be avoided, and a reasonable range of alternatives to the proposed action" (Council on Environmental Quality 2023). "Reasonable impacts," in this reading, do not include impacts that will, by all accounts, happen to people and ecosystems downwind and downstream of an immense increase of extraction. In effect, this amendment—and a Supreme Court ruling on the Uinta Basin Railway case—will likely authorize future EIS statements to limit the scope of their risk analysis and limit the scope of NEPA in the future. That said, the Seven County Coalition will still need to address other deficiencies in their EIS, including violations of the Interstate Commerce Commission Termination Act and the Endangered Species Act.

Implications Regarding Risk Flow Futures

In this chapter, we have attempted to answer a number of questions concerning what happens to risk when we expand both the scale and the scope of our analysis, and what happens to our case studies when expanded similarly. The explicit extraction, transportation, and refining of energy has been the locus of our case study, as we have posited that when energy is in these states, it accompanies a supposed contradiction—that the energy benefits those at the receiving end of such infrastructure while generating harms to the communities or ecosystems that haunt those sites. Unlike the promises of many petrochemical and hydrocarbon industries, the benefits of continued energy extraction, while supposedly meant for those without access to Western, on-demand forms of energy, rarely reach their intended destination. Instead, we see risk flowing in contradiction to those claims. We have also tried to show how these contradictory risk flows can be highlighted, and potentially halted, when the TPC of environmental impact statements emphasizes the expanded scope and scale of risk to "downstream" communities and ecosystems that can (and should) be taken into account by any large-scale infrastructure development. To some extent, we have tried to position this case study as deliberative—to emphasize how the known cause-and-effect relationships so central to good risk communication can be marshaled to identify the future unequal distribution of harm as well as more closely located harms. In part, this chapter has been an attempt to create a case study that explicitly advocates for an extended scope and scale that can highlight structural violences before they happen.

One approach TPC practitioners and scholars can engage in to identify and address future risks occurs through the documentation that we've highlighted here—the environmental impact statement. The US Court of Appeals created a brief window of opportunity to advocate for those impacted by any large infrastructural project, but especially through the contradictory risk flows of energy extraction, transportation, and refinement. Unfortunately, because of the trajectory of the Uinta Basin Railway case, we may soon see that opportunity curtailed. The US Supreme Court, minus Justice Gorsuch, who has a long-standing friendship with Phil Anschutz, owner of an oil and gas company, ruled that downstream impacts, like the ones the Appeals Court found to be valid, do not need to be considered in future environmental impact statements. The Uinta Basin Railway proposal still has additional work to do before it can be built, but such a judgment means that future EISs would be justified in limiting their scope and scale to much more immediate causes and effects. Of course, such a judgment does not mean that TPC researchers have to accept newly imposed limitations on scope and scale in environmental impact statements, but we can advocate for the inclusion of clear, causal impacts to people and ecosystems whenever possible.

Essentially, the arguments we have made for expanding the scope and scale of risk, and adjusting risk communication accordingly, can be found in the legal issues over how extensively an EIS should consider "downstream" impacts. EIS documents are always in part deliberative, insofar as they help make a case for a future plan of action, and weigh complex causal relationships between development projects and who and what could be harmed by those projects. An EIS that considers downstream impacts of a new rail line that vastly expands waxy crude extraction, transportation, and refinement should consider future risks to air quality in the Uinta Basin, water quality along the Colorado River system, ecosystem degradation, rail accidents, pollution in Louisiana, and an increase in nationwide greenhouse gas emissions of approximately 0.8 percent. Including immediate and long-term impacts that *will happen* as we follow the relationships of structural violence extending out from the decision to facilitate the extraction of more petroleum products is a responsibility of an EIS and the deep concern of all TPC and risk researchers. We have attempted to show how case studies, while also accounting for an expansion in scope and scale, can be situated toward future potential action.

Conclusion

Implications and Polyvocality

Put simply, we think there are (at least) four implications for our work throughout the past six chapters. First, we think the field of TPC ought to continue in more depth with exploring, unpacking, and ultimately reckoning with the ethical entanglements our field has had with extractive industries. The success of the field has been for too long positively correlated with the harm done to humans, animals, and the environment, and existing case studies proving our value are often devoid of ethical considerations concerning our participation in extraction. Some of these missing ethical commitments have been revealed over time, as they were simply a product of their era, while other work has intentionally eschewed ethical complications in favor of other theoretical or methodological commitments. Our work in this book does not cover all possible approaches or topics for ethical concerns in TPC, of course, but we feel that our approach can be expanded, intensified, and improved upon in order to more fully engage the many times our field has crossed paths with, and sometimes held hands with, extractive and exploitative industries.

How we rectify this void in historical work leads us to a second implication: an expansion of our case study methodology. To be clear, we are not arguing that case studies of industrial-era or present-day disasters are not important, nor are we arguing that technical writers should quit their jobs if they are working on specifications for naval shipbuilding or safety protocols for oil rig workers. Those are still important locations for TPC. We are also not arguing that the case study as a methodology is harmful for the field. In fact, many of the pieces that we ourselves have published argue for the importance of case studies in TPC and it could be said that this book makes an argument for the value of case studies more generally. However, we are arguing that when we draft an idea for a case study we should also be thinking of the scope and scale of risk being investigated and "locate" our work accordingly. Not all risks are the same and so not all risk case studies should be the same. However, in our estimation, we have reached a critical mass of scholars researching risk in TPC contexts where we might find use value in organizing our risk-based case study work by scope and scale.

Our third implication is that more accurately differentiating between types of risks and their industry-specific constraints might be accomplished by a deeper engagement with the industrial/historical past and present and the current models of risk communication used by industry professionals. The criticisms of TPC's engagement with the field of risk communication, from within TPC, remain valid. In chapter 1, we explained how Mirel (1994) and Reamer (2015) both found TPC's consideration and incorporation of risk communication to be lacking. Unsurprisingly, more than ten years later, we still find this coordination missing. Some of this gap comes from TPC's rhetorical and theoretical emphasis, but there is not one universal "industrial" approach to risk communication, and not everything done outside of academic work falls under the information-deficit model of risk communication. Many organizations, governmental and otherwise, utilize dialogic, participatory, and even user-centered models of risk analysis, assessment, and communication. Familiarizing ourselves with these existing models can help bridge a lot of our work to existing practices outside of our field and perhaps even lend some more empirical credence to the work we do.

The fourth and final implication doesn't pertain to rewriting our past or expanding our methodological or practical engagement with the present—it has to do with anticipating our immediate and long-term risk and disaster futures. In many poignant ways, the script of our future has already been written. We are past the point of no return with our climate crisis, that is, at the time of writing, the world is on track to exceed the 1.5 °C threshold. The microplastics in our bodies aren't decreasing, nor are the water levels along our coasts. We are and have been for a long time on the precipice of a disaster. Often, we wait until the train derails, the oil spills, the shuttle explodes, or the water is contaminated to write up a postmortem that deciphers the role communication played in each tragedy and how it might be avoided next time. David Harvey (1999) has described this as the "standard view" of a Western approach to environmental problems, where we deal with events on a case-by-case basis after they have occurred. What would risk work look like if we instead selected as case studies or rhetorical analyses sites of disaster futures? When a train carrying crude oil derails, might we use the exigence to connect the case to other railways on the verge of being built? Would this see more value assigned to the work we do as risk scholars in TPC?

We'd like to end this book with a bit more explicit polyvocality. All four of us have been involved in the writing of these chapters but—despite our alignment—we all assign different values of this book to our own work and its position within TPC and adjacent fields. Here are the individual ways we position ourselves with this book.

Dan

I'll go first since my perspective is the most rudimentary. The amount of work TPC and rhetoric have done in the areas of risk communication and disaster studies since the mid-1990s has been impressive. (On a personal note, this work is what brought me into the field of TPC in the first place.) As my research in these areas progressed over time, I have always wanted to "bring together" in some way the multitude of case studies the field has done to provide newcomers an overview of risk in TPC. A meta-analysis of sorts. In my mind we had reached a critical mass of work being done to provide a comprehensive overview of all the various case studies and categorize them by type, scope, or theory being used. What is a distinct TPC approach to studying risk and risk communication (is there one? should there be one?) and what is its story?

On a pedagogical level, I am excited that this book offers itself as an option to be included in graduate level courses on TPC and risk—and all the various intersections therein. When we started this project, one of our first tasks was to develop a comprehensive list of all the work done on risk and disasters in TPC from its inception as an academic field. (As you read in chapter 2, we also did this for nonacademic work as well, afterwards.) Every article, every case study, every chapter in edited collections published by defunct presses. Everything. We wanted to ensure that all of these pieces were woven into the book so that our readers felt confident that our narrativizing and categorizing were as inclusive as possible. While we invariably focus more on some articles than others, and read some books as being more pivotal than others, we feel confident that graduate student readers of this book will walk away with a fairly comprehensive sense of the risk and TPC scene as it has evolved over the years.

And, finally, I have always felt a bit unsure how to feel about how much disaster and harm have played a role in the legitimizing of our field. Given the plain ubiquity of technical communication in industrial settings, it makes sense that we as a field are drawn to moments of failure that can be traced back to miscommunication or faulty communicative structures. It makes sense that we care deeply about moments of environmental harm and seek to rectify them. Disasters and moments or trajectories of harm *do* highlight the vital function of TPC in organizational and public settings. But to what extent do we use these cases to further justify our presence? Or to point to our field as a remedy for such ills? I'm genuinely not sure and am looking forward to seeing the role this book might play in facilitating such conversations.

Donnie

Risk work in TPC, especially concerning extractive industries and climate change, must navigate the complexities of temporal and spatial scales to convey the true magnitude of risks. Extractive industries—such as oil, gas, and mining—often frame their operations as primarily affecting local communities, emphasizing short-term economic gains (e.g., local employment, infrastructure development, foreign direct investment, cost reductions for energy and raw materials) while downplaying long-term and global risks (e.g., environmental degradation, climate change acceleration). This framing obscures how localized extraction can have ripple effects that contribute to global crises like rising sea levels, extreme weather events, and biodiversity loss. Conversely, large-scale global risks such as climate change may be perceived as abstract or distant, making it challenging to mobilize local action. Perception of risk in relation to environmental problems depends on epistemological distance: "we are epistemologically 'closer' to some environmental 'fact' (e.g., oil spills) than to others (e.g., dioxin)" (Carolan 2004, 498). The question that I have wrestled with in this project is how to manage the spatiotemporal complexity of risk as complexity illuminates social, economic, and cultural impacts that can't all be attended to simultaneously. For me, this problem is all too similar to the fundamental measurement limit as part of Heisenberg's uncertainty principle, which implies that no matter how good our measuring instruments are, we cannot determine both the exact position and exact momentum of a particle simultaneously. The more precisely we know one, the less precisely we can know the other. Risk analyses face fundamental limits in predicting both immediate/local consequences and long-term/global consequences with any certainty.

I am not sure that there is a real way to get beyond scale dependence and the observer effect. However, what this project does emphasize is what we measure and how we frame it can dramatically alter our understanding of risks' severity, urgency, and distribution and how we should be attuned to this fact. This also raises some ethical implications of complexity. Since uncertainty cannot be eliminated, how we communicate and act on risk becomes an even greater ethical concern. Acknowledging uncertainty does not mean inaction—it means designing policies and technologies that reckon with the past, attend to the present, and prioritize resilience in the future.

Finally, our work regarding risk emphasizes the need to advocate for proactive measures, especially amid uncertainty. Perhaps a corrective to the complexity of risk might be to consider the *precautionary principle*, which presents opportunities for speculating and designing alternative futures in response to realized and anticipated risk. The principle asserts that when an activity poses potential risks to human health or the environment, precautionary measures should be implemented even if scientific evidence does not yet fully confirm the cause-and-effect relationship. It includes four key elements: proactively preventing harm despite uncertainty, placing the burden of proof on those advocating for the activity, considering a broad range of alternatives to potentially harmful actions, and fostering greater public involvement in decision-making (Kriebel et al. 2001). Many environmental risks unfold slowly over time (e.g., climate change, groundwater contamination). The precautionary principle encourages action before damage becomes irreversible, recognizing that waiting for full scientific certainty may be too late.

Tim

In many ways, this project grew from conversations we'd been having about risk for years about the ways that spatial and temporal complexity complicates how risk might be known and communicated. For me, Dan's points highlight our shared longing for a history of risk communication in TPC, because first as students and then as scholars and designers of risk communication, or both, it would be helpful to orient our own perspectives and practices to this history. Similarly, Donnie's discussion of complexity gets right toward the difficulty of spatially and temporally focusing a study of risk within TPC. Simply put, some of the approaches that scholars in TPC have used to *bound* their case studies of risk are just ill-suited for engaging with technologies such as microplastics and per- and polyfluoroalkyl substances (PFAS), which present future risks that we're really struggling to consider in the present. Moreover, these technologies also illustrate the unjust economies and distributions of risk that surround the practice of these technologies, as they have been engineered by (and created profits for) corporations located in the Minority World while posing risks that extend much more widely (e.g., Lim 2021; Kurwadkar et al. 2022).

Recently, Gallagher (2019) reflected on the use of the case study within writing studies, including TPC, emphasizing the important role that *defining boundaries* and *bounding* play in "enabl[ing] researchers to *create* and *craft* a system under study" (2). Indeed, the choices that researchers make when establishing the boundaries of a case study have received considerable methodological attention (e.g., Kendall 2009; Merriam 1998; Stake 2005; VanWynsberghe and Khan 2007; Yin 2018). Kendall (2009), as Gallagher explained, not only outlined three frames that researchers might use to bound a case (spatial, temporal, and relational), but also outlined four categories that shape those choices (analytical, ethical, personal, and practical) (6). And Gallagher contended that "it is the job of any case study researcher . . . to be explicit about the methodology that one uses to create a case so that the case can be better understood on both its own terms as well as the reasons researchers present the case in the way that they do" (2).

So, mostly, I'd like to take a bit of space to clarify the approach that we've taken to designing the case studies forwarded within the book. Certainly, we haven't fully articulated our approach, including the boundaries that we've used to construct the cases. And, we've been intentional about being a bit less explicit about this. In Kendall's terms, we've leaned more heavily into the ethical and analytical spheres of influence to inform our approach to bounding the case studies. There are, undoubtedly, ways in which the case(s)—whether the book is received as an extended case study of risk in the Colorado River Basin or as a set of closely related cases that consider risk across the basin (we'd like to think it's both)—we've presented here reflect the kinds of challenges of scope that are common to case study as a method. Yet, as Diem, Good, and Walters (2023) argued, those who have been most influential in articulating the method of case study do not "approach research from a critical perspective" that focuses on "issues of (in)equity and (in)equality" (241).

For us, a key intention of this project has been to critically challenge the spatial and temporal frames operationalized in case studies, as uncritical frames can exacerbate the disproportionate levels of material and epistemic risk that Majority World peoples, species, and ecosystems shoulder (see Hopton and Rajan 2023). In particular, we've turned to the work of Clark (2023), Frost (2013), Haas (2012), and Haas and Frost (2017), especially their articulation of an apparent decolonial feminist approach to risk, because they have advanced a critical perspective toward risk that we believe is vitally important for our field to engage with right now. We've sought to build on their apparent decolonial feminist approach to risk by interrogating how the spatial and temporal frames we employ when studying risk, often through case study, work to instantiate colonial logics. And, we've looked to scholars like Itchiqiyaq (2023), Jones (2021), Druschke (2023), Clary-Lemon (2019), among others, for additional critical guidance, as they have also been productively challenging the spatial and temporal—and ultimately relational—dimensions of our research frames. What we've found particularly helpful is that these scholars have been working to reconcile relationships between Indigenous and posthumanist rhetorics, in which the distinct traditions offer ontological and epistemological orientations that are useful for illuminating the anthropocentric and colonial logics instantiated within technologies.

From this perspective, the Gold King Mine disaster is not an isolated event, but a consequence of systematic extractivism rooted in colonial, white-settler logics of dominion. Indeed, Haas (2012) argued for the importance of "case studies [focused] on certain culturally situated technological practices of a specific race, using a broader, more flexible, and more historically situated definition of technologies" in order to "reflect a larger history of technological design and use by people of color and other underrepresented populations" (291). We've sought to construct case studies that foreground the interplay between federal legislation, industrial development, and the legacies of colonial westward expansion in the US. Technologies such as mills, smelters, dams, reservoirs, irrigation canals, railroads, and intermodal transportation were designed, certainly, to support mining, agricultural, and energy industries, but more importantly those industries have scaffolded and continue to scaffold logics of white-settler colonialism as a primary mode of socio-technical organization in this country.

Consequently, we have purposefully bound the case studies to illustrate the ways in which risk extends across tidy geographic and temporal boundaries and to emphasize the problematic constraints associated with focusing on disasters and risk as isolated events that impact a here and now. In this way, we've foregrounded how many of the technologies introduced to the CRB within our recent industrial past shifted the boundaries surrounding those riskscapes and timescapes in ways that redistributed risk across new economic, racial, and sociocultural lines. The discovery of gold in Colorado not only led to the development of mining in the state, but engendered the systematic expatriation of Native American Nations and People such as the Ute from their traditional and ancestral lifeways and relations to the lands across the CRB. Similarly, the development of water management technologies didn't simply support agriculture and the development of farming in the West. These technologies exacerbated previous colonial violence through a double move that at once further disconnected Indigenous people from their traditional lifeways and relations with rivers and river beings and excluded them from participating in the emerging lifeways and relations with rivers and river beings, as they were uninvited to decisions about developing a water management system that would divert water at a level of scale and scope that fundamentally reshaped ecologies in the region. And, in this particular way, I hope that this book illustrates that while methodological decisions such as bounding in case study tend to be discussed in terms of how they affect the rigor or the validity or the empiricism of a project, more importantly they are also decisions that might uncritically reproduce or critically challenge the legacies of harm and the past, present, and future risks that extend from white-settler colonialism as a socio-technical system.

Ehren

For me, this research project has brought a particular frustration to light, or rather I should say a series of connected frustrations. My initial frustration—sorry, "motivating dissatisfaction," as I try to encourage my students to consider them—has to do with the long-standing discomfort I have had with the history of TPC as often presented. As this history was explained to me, through the historical work done by technical communication researchers, we were an academic discipline that emerged after a long history of practice connected to industry. The problem was that those practical, industry connections were treated as benign when they carried more weight than was often acknowledged. Agricola's mining text is presented as an early example, mining engineers produced the field's first textbooks, wartime accidents provided the exigence for additional teaching, and our curricula was justified via an insistent alignment with industry. Frankly, when first reading about TPC's history, I kept asking myself why so many weren't bothered by these relationships. TPC researchers have now presented antenarratives and counterhistories to this received legacy, but this historicizing has been more recent (see, e.g., Jones, Moore, and Walton 2016; Jones and Williams 2018; Shelton and Warren-Riley 2023; van Winkle 2021; Walwema, Colton, and Holmes 2024; Williams 2010). Our project presents an alternative history in order to recalibrate these industrial origins as anything but benign or inconsequential, and we follow how extractive industries have shaped the field and contributed to the ongoing destruction of the environment while exploiting people through unsafe working and living conditions. In highlighting these connections—connections that were there all along—we try to undermine the field and shape TPC toward an expanded sense of scope and scale in order to reduce risk, which means reducing the unequal likelihood of harm more broadly. For me, the first implication for future work is that it will hopefully prompt TPC toward a greater awareness of how our dominant historical narrative has been (and is) deeply problematic.

Our attempt to reframe TPC's history brings me to another motivating dissatisfaction about the lack of ecological approaches to risk. Even though risk is always a material-discursive formation in a complex set of relations, many of which stem from environmental conditions, we've seen less explicit connection between risk, risk communication, and environmental danger, and instead focused on environmental hazards. The latter approach is a risk communication approach (pick any from chapter 3) to a topic that just happens to be "environmental." I suppose I'm interested in seeing a productive synergy between environmental rhetoric and rhetorics of risk. Ecological concepts in rhetoric now abound, with "rhetorical ecologies" taking over for "rhetorical situations," and with capacity, vulnerability, and resilience emerging as useful concepts to build from (Stormer and McGreavy 2017). Yet, in large part, the connections between ecology and rhetoric have been largely "analogical," by which I mean ecological thinking has been assumed to be "similar to" rhetorical thinking and used in rhetorical analysis. These have been productive connections, but the more abstract nature of ecological thinking, as distinct from ecological science, may not be doing more than advancing ideas within the bubble of discourse known as environmental humanities—and preaching to the already converted.

Perhaps one of my takeaways from this book has been additional motivation to seek out how ecological rhetoric can be productive for risk communication, possibly by blending rhetorics of risk and the lessons from ecological science in more intentional scalar cuts. Caroline Gottschalk Druschke (2019) has called this kind of rhetorical fieldwork a "practice of controlled equivocation across multiple ontologies: a name for various and even divergent kinds of relationality" (n.p.). I see similar attempts in animal rhetorics, namely in Ellen Gorsevski's peacebuilding biotic rhetorics (2017) and Erika Szymanski's work on multispecies rhetorics (2023). But rhetorical fieldwork on risk is difficult, not only because we articulate risk for humans (something TPC has been adept at, with participant action research, user experience studies, and qualitative research more generally), but also because doing so requires connecting with lessons from ecological science at different scales. Scalar issues often disrupt our best intentions. Further, we also run into problems of overreaching the limits of our capacity to advocate as we blend ecological science and an anthropocentric application of values into analysis and solution-oriented problem-solving. This is challenging territory, not the least because in building approaches to risk in TPC with/from ecological science, we also need to contend with ecological science's own problematic history (Jones 2021). That said, some recent explorations have prodded the productive tensions in TPC and the environment. Here I'm thinking of Sean Williams's edited collection *Technical Communication for Environmental Action* (2023), Olman and DeVasto (2020), or a lot of the work that Dan, Tim, and Donnie have accomplished in recent years.

I'm encouraged by the new direction of rhetoric and TPC scholars, especially as we see a blending of ecologic, biotic, and geologic concerns. No singular approach is going to be able to account for all scales at once (nor should it try), but investigations that question previously unexplored rhetorical formations, like Matthew Halm's molten circulation (2023) and my own attempt to articulate a geologic rhetoric (2022), apply a broader sense of geographic scale to scientific and rhetorical world-building. Some of the most exciting work (for me) has been in this confluence of anthropology, social geology, and rhetoric. Many of the projects that tackle social and environmental justice, material-discursive rhetorics and their environmental impacts, or our neoliberal Anthropocene futures may not be explicitly in TPC, nor are they explicitly about risk, but their proliferation can only aid risk researchers and risk communicators in doing their work in more effective and inclusive ways.

References

Adam, B. 1998. *Timescapes of Modernity: The Environment and Invisible Hazards.* Routledge.

Agboka, G. Y. 2013. "Participatory Localization: A Social Justice Approach to Navigating Unenfranchised/Disenfranchised Cultural Sites." *Technical Communication Quarterly* 22 (1): 28–49. https://doi.org/10.1080/10572252.2013.730966.

Agricola, G. 1556. *De re Metallica.* [Translated from the Latin]. Gutenberg. www.gutenberg.org/files/38015/38015-h/38015-h.htm.

Allen, D. W. 1991. "Homesteading and Property Rights; Or, 'How the West Was Really Won.'" *Journal of Law and Economics* 33: 1–23.

Allen, N. T. 2018. "A Reconsidering Chronos: Chronistic Criticism and the First 'Iraqi' National Calendar." *Quarterly Journal of Speech* 104 (4): 361–83. https://doi.org/10.1080/00335630.2018.1519256.

Alsabri, A., and S. Al-Ghamdi. 2020. "Carbon Footprint and Embodied Energy of PVC, PE, and PP Piping: Perspective on Environmental Performance." *Energy Reports* 6 (Supplement 8): 364–70. https://doi.org/10.1016/j.egyr.2020.11.173.

American Gilsonite Company. N.d. "History." American Gilsonite. https://www.americangilsonite.com/about-us/history/.

Amidon, T. R., E. A. Williams, T. Lipsey, R. Callahan, G. Nuckols, and S. Rice. 2018. "Sensors and Gizmos and Data, Oh My: Informating Firefighters' Personal Protective Equipment." *Communication Design Quarterly* 5 (4): 15–30. https://dl.acm.org/doi/10.1145/3188387.3188389.

Anderson, B. 1983. *Imagined Communities: Reflections on the Origins and Spread of Nationalism.* Verso.

Andrés Jr., B. 2014. *Power and Control in the Imperial Valley: Nature, Agribusiness, and Workers on the California Borderland, 1900–1940.* Texas A and M Press.

Angeli, E. 2018. *Rhetorical Work in Emergency Medical Services: Communicating in the Unpredictable Workplace.* Routledge.

Angeli, E. 2023. "Crisis Communication." In *Keywords in Technical and Professional Communication,* edited by H. Yu and J. Buehl. WAC Clearinghouse; University Press of Colorado. https://doi.org/10.37514/TPC-B.2023.1923.

Appadurai, A. 1990. "Disjuncture and Difference in the Global Cultural Economy." *Theory, Culture, and Society* 7 (2–3): 295–310.

Arduser, L. 2017. *Living Chronic: Agency and Expertise in the Rhetoric of Diabetes*. Ohio State University Press.

Arendt, H. 2006. *Eichmann in Jerusalem: A Report on the Banality of Evil*. Penguin.

Arizona Game and Fish. 2024. *Arizona Wildlife Conservation Strategy*. https://awcs.azgfd.com/habitats/mohave-desertscrub.

Arizona v. California, 373 U.S. 546. 1963. https://www.loc.gov/item/usrep373546/.

Azpiroz, A. B., J. P. Isacch, R. A. Dias, A. S. Di Giacomo, C. S. Fontana, and C. M. Palarea. 2012. "Ecology and Conservation of Grassland Birds in Southeastern South America." *Journal of Field* Ornithology 83: 217–46.

Baake, K. 2017. "Remembering the Alamo: Commonplaces in Texas Water Policy Arguments." In *Topic-Driven Environmental Rhetoric*, edited by D. Ross, 125–48. Routledge.

Balog-Way, D., K. McComas, and J. Besley. 2020. "The Evolving Field of Risk Communication." *Risk Analysis* 40 (S1): 2240–62. https://doi.org/10.1111/risa.13615.

Banazek, K., R. Mohammed, K. Sharp-Hoskins, K. Surya, and A. Zouaoui. 2022. "Scalar Transactions and Ethical Actions in TPC." *Reflections* 22 (1): 132–65.

Baniya, S. 2024. *Transnational Assemblages: Social Justice and Crisis Communication During Disaster*. National Council of Teachers of English/WAC Clearinghouse.

Baptista, K. 2017. "Petrocultures." *Global South Studies*, August 17. https://globalsouthstudies.as.virginia.edu/key-concepts/petrocultures.

Barrera-Osorio, A. 2006. "Experiencing Nature: The Science of the Environment in the Spanish Empire." In *Nature and the Spanish Empire*, edited by J. A. Secord, 123–45. University of Chicago Press.

Bartesaghi, M., S. H. Grey, and S. Gibson. 2012. "Defining (the Concept of) Risk." *Poroi* 8 (1): 1–6. https://doi.org/10.13008/2151-2957.1112.

Bartlett, R. A. 1980. *Great Surveys of the American West*. Vol, 38, American Exploration and Travel Series. University of Oklahoma Press.

Bayly, N. J., K. V. Rosenberg, W. E. Easton, C. Goméz, J. Carlisle, N. Ewert, A. Drake, and L. Goodrich. 2018. "Major Stopover Regions and Migratory Bottlenecks for Nearctic-Neotropical Landbirds Within the Neotropics: A Review." *Bird Conservation International* 28: 1–26.

Beaton, K. 2022. *Ducks: Two Years in the Oil Sands*. Drawn and Quarterly.

Beck, U. 1992. *Risk Society: Towards a New Modernity*. Translated by M. Ritter. SAGE.

Beck, U. 2006. *The Cosmopolitan Vision*. Polity Press.

Belda-Miquel, S., A. Boni, and C. Calabuig. 2019. "SDG Localisation and Decentralised Development Aid: Exploring Opposing Discourses and Practices in Valencia's Aid Sector." *Journal of Human Development and Capabilities* 20 (4): 386–402. https://doi.org/10.1080/19452829.2019.1624512.

Bergman, C. 2002. *Red Delta: Fighting for Life at the End of the Colorado River.* Fulcrum Publishing.

Berlant, L. 2007. "Slow Death (Sovereignty, Obesity, Lateral Agency)." *Critical Inquiry* 33 (4): 754–80. https://doi.org/10.1086/521568.

Berlant, L. 2011. *Cruel Optimism.* Duke University Press.

Berlin, J. A. 1984. *Writing Instruction in Nineteenth-Century American Colleges.* Southern Illinois University Press.

Berlin, J. A. 1987. *Rhetoric and Reality: Writing Instruction in American Colleges, 1900–1985.* Southern Illinois University Press.

Bernal, M. 1987. *Black Athena: The Afroasiatic Roots of Classical Civilization.* Vol. 1. Rutgers University Press.

Bernauer, W. 2019. "The Limits to Extraction: Mining and Colonialism in Nunavut." *Canadian Journal of Development Studies / Revue Canadienne d'études du Développement* 40 (3): 404–22. https://doi.org/10.1080/02255189.2019.1629883.

Berwanger, E. H. 2007. *The Rise of the Centennial State: Colorado Territory, 1861–76.* University of Illinois Press.

Bevir, M. 1999. "Foucault, Power, and Institutions." *Political Studies* 47 (2): 345–59. https://doi.org/10.1111/1467-9248.00204.

Bigelow, A. M. 2021. *Mining Language: Racial Thinking, Indigenous Knowledge, and Colonial Metallurgy in the Early Modern Iberian World.* University of North Carolina Press.

Billington, D. P., D. C. Jackson, and M. V. Melosi. 2005. *The History of Large Federal Dams: Planning, Design, and Construction.* U.S. Department of the Interior, Bureau of Reclamation, Government Printing Office. https://www.usbr.gov/lc/phoenix/. AZ100/1920/topstory.html

Bohnenkamp, S., A. Finken, E. McCallum, A. Putz, and G. A. Goreham. 2011. *Concerns of the North Dakota Bakken Oil Counties: Extension Service and Other Organizations' Program Responses to These Concerns.* Center for Community Vitality, North Dakota State University Extension Service. https://www.ag.ndsu.edu/ccv/documents/bakken-oil-concerns.

Bolos of Mendes. c. 200 BCE. *Physica et Mystica.*

Bowie, A. J. 1887. *A Practical Treatise on Hydraulic Mining in California.* D. Van Nostrand.

Boyer, D. 2014. "Energopower: An Introduction." *Anthropological Quarterly* 87 (2) 309–33. https://dx.doi.org/10.1353/anq.2014.0020.

Boyle, Robert 1660. *New Experiments Physico-Mechanical, Touching the Spring of the Air, and Its Effects (Made, for the Most Part, in a New Pneumatical Engine).* H. Hall, Printer to the University, for T. Robinson.

Bradsher, G. 2012. "How the West Was Settled: The 150-Year-Old Homestead Act Lured Americans Looking for a New Life and New Opportunities." *Prologue* 44 (4): 26–35. https://www.archives.gov/files/publications/prologue/2012/winter/homestead.pdf.

Brereton, J. 1989. "The Professional Writing Program and the English Department." In *Writing in the Business Professions*, edited by M. Kogen, 279–96. National Council of Teachers of English and Association for Business Communication.

Brown, K. W. 2001. "Workers' Health and Colonial Mercury Mining at Huancavelica, Peru." *The Americas* 57 (4): 467–96. https://doi.org/10.1353/tam.2001.0030.

Brunot Agreement, between the United States and the Ute Nation, September 13, 1873. U.S. National Archives. https://treaties.okstate.edu/treaties/brunot-agreement-1873-22218.

Burbank, W. S., and R. G. Luedke. 1969. Plate 6 [Image of Cross Section of Gold King and Sunnyside Mines]. Geology and Ore Deposits of the Eureka and Adjoining Districts, San Juan Mountains, Colorado. Geological Survey Professional Paper 535. US Department of the Interior.

Bushnell, J. B, J. E. Hughes, and A. Smith. 2022. "Food Versus Fuel? Impacts of the North Dakota Oil Boom on Agricultural Prices." *Journal of the Association of Environmental and Resource Economists* 9 (1): 79–112. https://doi.org/10.1086/716522.

Butler, J. 2009. "Performativity, Precarity and Sexual Politics." *Revista de Antropología Iberoamericana* 4 (3): 1–13. https://doi.org/10.11156/aibr.040303e.

Cagle, L. E. 2018. "Climate Change and the Virtue of Civility: Cultivating Productive Deliberation Around Public Scientific Controversy." *Rhetoric Review* 37 (4): 370–79.

Cagle, L. E., and R. Burnes. 2023. "Collaborating for Clean Air: Ethics and the Cultivation of Transformational Service-Learning Partnerships." In *Technical Communication for Environmental Action*, edited by S. D. Williams, 121–46. State University of New York Press.

Cagle, L. E., and D. Tillery. 2015. "Climate Change Research Across Disciplines: The Value and Uses of Multidisciplinary Research Reviews for Technical Communication." *Technical Communication Quarterly* 24 (2): 147–63. https://doi.org/10.1080/10572252.2015.1001296.

Carliner, S. 1995. "Finding a Common Ground: What STC Is, and Should Be, Doing to Advance Education and Information in Design and Development." *Technical Communication* 42 (4): 546–54.

Carolan, M. S. 2004. "Ontological Politics: Mapping a Complex Environmental Problem." *Environmental Values* 13 (4): 497–522. https://doi.org/10.3197/0963271042772 5.

Carpenter, C. P., C. S. Weil, and H. F. Smyth. 1953. "Chronic Oral Toxicity of Di(2-ethylhexyl) Phthalate for Rats, Guinea Pigs, and Dogs." *Archives of Industrial Hygiene and Occupational Medicine* 8 (3): 219–26.

Carr, E. S., and M. Lempert, eds. 2016. *Scale: Discourse and Dimensions of Social Life*. University of California Press.

Carradini, S., and J. Swarts. 2023. *Text at Scale: Corpus Analysis in Technical Communication*. University Press of Colorado.

Carter, P. 1996. *The Lie of the Land*. Faber and Faber.

Cashion, W. B. 1967. *Geology and Fuel Resources of the Green River Formation Southeastern Uinta Basin Utah and Colorado*. Geological Survey Professional Paper 548. United States Government Printing Office. https://pubs.usgs.gov/pp/0548/report.pdf.

Castro-Sotomayor, J. 2020. "Territorialidad as Environmental Communication." *Annals of the International Communication Association* 44 (1): 50–66. https://doi.org/10.1080/23808985.2019.1647443.

Center for Biological Diversity. 2019. "Conservation Groups Letter to CIB." Center for Biological Diversity. https://www.biologicaldiversity.org/programs/public_lands/energy/dirty_energy_development/oil_and_gas/pdfs/19-6-12-Conservation-Groups-Letter-to-CIB.pdf.

Chaucer, G. 2002. *A Treatise on the Astrolabe* (1391–1393). Edited by S. Eisner. University of Oklahoma Press.

Chave, J. 2013. "The Problem of Pattern and Scale in Ecology: What Have We Learned in 20 Years?" *Ecology Letters* 16 (Suppl. 1): 4–16. https://doi.org/10.1111/ele.12048.

Chen, C. 2022. "The Communicative and Affective Labor of Public Pandemic Diaries: The Case of Fang Fang's Wuhan Diary." *Journal of Rhetoric, Professional Communication, Globalization* 11 (1): 57–76. https://docs.lib.purdue.edu/rpcg/vol11/iss1/5.

Clark, E. 2023. *Feminist Technical Communication: Apparent Feminisms, Slow Crisis, and the Deepwater Horizon Disaster*. Utah State University Press.

Clark, N. 2011. *Inhuman Nature: Sociable Life on a Dynamic Planet*. SAGE.

Clark, T. 2012. "Scale." In *Telemorphosis: Theory in the Era of Climate Change*, edited by T. Cohen, 148–66. Open Humanities Press.

Clary-Lemon, J. 2019. "Gifts, Ancestors, and Relations: Notes Toward an Indigenous New Materialism." *Enculturation: A Journal of Rhetoric, Writing, and Culture* 30 (1). http://enculturation.net/gifts_ancestors_and_relations.

Clausen, R. J., C. Chief, N. I. Teufel-Shone, M. A. Begay, P. H. Charley, P. I. Beamer, N. Anako, and K. Chief. 2023. "Diné-Centered Research Reframes the Gold King Mine Spill: Understanding Social and Spiritual Impacts Across Space and Time." *Journal of Rural Studies* 97: 449–57. https://doi.org/10.1016/j.jrurstud.2022.12.021.

Clements, M. A., and C. Sweetman. 2020. "Introduction: Reimagining International Development." *Gender and Development* 28 (1): 1–9. https://doi.org/10.1080/13552074.2020.1735800.

Cobos, C., G. Raquel Ríos, D. J. Sackey, J. Sano-Franchini, and A. M. Haas. 2018." Interfacing Cultural Rhetorics: A History and a Call." *Rhetoric Review* 37 (2): 139–54. https://doi.org/10.1080/07350198.2018.1424470.

Cocopah Indian Tribe. N.d. "About Us: Cocopah Indian Tribe of Arizona History." https://www.cocopah.com/about-us.html.

Colorado Law. 2020, January 29. *Violence from Extractive Industry "Man Camps" Endangers Indigenous Women and Children*. University of Colorado, Boulder.

https://www.colorado.edu/program/tallgrass/2020/01/29/violence-extractive-industry-man-camps-endangers-indigenous-women-and-children.

Colorado River Indian Tribes. 2022. "Colorado River Indian Tribes." https://tentribespartnership.org/tribes/colorado-river-indian-tribes/.

Colorado State University. N.d. *Bakken Air Quality Study (BAQS)*. Colorado State University. https://vista.cira.colostate.edu/Improve/bakken-air-quality-study-baqs/.

Committee on Environment and Public Works, United States Senate. 2015. *Oversight of the Cause, Response, and Impacts of EPA's Gold King Mine Spill* (Senate Hearing 114–188). September 16. U.S. Government Publishing Office. https://www.govinfo.gov/content/pkg/CHRG-114shrg98709/html/CHRG-114shrg98709.htm.

Congressional Research Service. 2017. *US-Mexico Water Sharing: Background and Recent Developments*. https://crsreports.congress.gov/product/pdf/R/R43312/8.

Congressional Research Service. 2020. *Bureau of Reclamation: History, Authorities, and Issues for Congress*. CRS Report R46303. https://crsreports.congress.gov/product/pdf/R/R46303.

Connors, R. J. 1981. "Current-Traditional Rhetoric: Thirty Years of Writing with a Purpose." *Rhetoric Society Quarterly* 11 (4): 208–21. http://www.jstor.org/stable/3885599.

Connors, R. J. 1982. "The Rise of Technical Writing Instruction in America." *Journal of Technical Writing and Communication* 12 (4): 329–52. https://doi.org/10.1177/004728168201200406.

Conophagos, C. 1980. *Le Laurium antique et la technique grécque de la production de l'argent*. Athens.

Consejo v. U.S., 482 F.3d 1157. 9th Cir. 2007.

Cortez Lara, A. A., M. K. Donovan, and S. Whiteford. 2009. "The All-American Canal Lining Dispute: An American Resolution over Mexican Groundwater Rights?" *Frontera norte* 21 (41): 127–50.

Cortez-Lara, A. A., and M. R. García-Acevado. 2000. "The Lining of the All–American Canal: The Forgotten Voices. "*Natural Resources Journal* 40 (2): 261–79.

Council on Environmental Quality. 2023. *Federal Railroad Administration (FRA) Regulations*. https://ceq.doe.gov/laws-regulations/fra.html.

Counts, J. 2016. "Failures at DEQ in Flint Water Crisis Proved Catastrophic." MLive, May 3. https://www.mlive.com/news/2016/05/department_of_environmental_qu.html.

Covello, V. 2020. "Mental Noise Blocks Communication—and What You Can Do About It." Pathway to Communication. https://pathwaycommunication.com/mental-noise-blocks-communication-and-what-you-can-do-about-it/.

Cox, R. 2007. "Nature's 'Crisis Disciplines': Does Environmental Communication Have an Ethical Duty?" *Environmental Communication* 1 (1): 5–20. https://doi.org/10.1080/17524030701333948.

Crabtree, R., and D. Sapp. 2005. "Technical Communication, Participatory Action Research, and Global Civic Engagement: A Teaching, Research, and Social

Action Collaboration in Kenya." *Reflections: A Journal of Rhetoric, Civic Writing and Service Learning* 4 (2): 9–33.

Cram, E. 2022. *Violent Inheritance: Sexuality, Land, and Energy in Making the North American West.* University of California Press.

Crescent Energy. 2022. "Crescent Energy 2022 Sustainability Report." https://crescentenergy.wpenginepowered.com/wp-content/uploads/2024/04/Crescent-Energy-2022-Sustainability-Report-1.pdf.

Curley, A., and S. Smith. 2023. "The Cene Scene: Who Gets to Theorize Global Time and How Do We Center Indigenous and Black Futurities?" *Environment and Planning E: Nature and Space* 7 (1): 166–88. https://doi.org/10.1177/25148486231173865.

Cvetkovich, G., M. Siegrist, R. Murray, and S. Tragesser. 2008. "New Information and Social Trust: Asymmetry and Perseverance of Attributions About Hazard Managers." *Risk Analysis* 22 (2): 359–67. https://doi.org/10.1111/0272-4332.00030.

Damp, J. E., S. A. Hall, and S. J. Smith. 2002. "Early Irrigation on the Colorado Plateau Near Zuni Pueblo, New Mexico." *American Antiquity* 67 (4): 665–76. https://doi.org/10.2307/1593797.

Davies, J. C., V. T. Covello, and F. W. Allen, eds. 1987. *Risk Communication: Proceedings of the National Conference on Risk Communication, Held in Washington, D.C., January 29–31, 1986.* Conservation Foundation. https://archive.org/details/riskcommunicatio0000nati.

Davies, T. 2022. "Slow Violence and Toxic Geographies: 'Out of Sight' to Whom?" *Environment and Planning C: Politics and Space* 40 (2): 409–27. https://doi.org/10.1177/2399654419841063.

Dayton, D. 2002. "Evaluating Environmental Impact Statements as Communicative Action." *Journal of Business and Technical Communication* 16 (4): 355–405. https://doi.org/10.1177/105065102236524.

Deem, A. 2018. "Mediated Intersections of Environmental and Decolonial Politics in the North Dakota Access Pipeline Movement." *Theory, Culture and Society* 36 (5): 113–31. https://doi.org/10.1177/0263276418807002.

DeLuca, W. V., T. Meehan, N. Seavy, A. Jones, J. Pitt, J. L. Deppe, and C. B. Wilsey. 2021. "The Colorado River Delta and California's Central Valley Are Critical Regions for Many Migrating North American Landbirds." *Ornithological Applications* 123 (1): 1–14. https://10.1093/ornithapp/duaa064.

Denison, B. 2017. *Ute Land Religion in the American West, 1879–2009.* University of Nebraska Press.

de Onís, C. M. 2021. *Energy Islands: Metaphors of Power, Extractivism, and Justice in Puerto Rico.* University of California Press.

DiCaglio, J. 2021. *Scale Theory: A Nondisciplinary Inquiry.* University of Minnesota Press.

Diem, S., M. W. Good, and S. W. Walters. 2023. "Toward Critical Approaches to Case Study Research." In *Handbook of Critical Education Research: Qualitative, Quantitative, and Emerging Approaches*, edited by M. D. Young and S. D. Diem. Routledge.

Ding, H. 2009. "Rhetorics of Alternative Media in an Emerging Epidemic: SARS, Censorship, and Extrainstitutional Risk Communication." *Technical Communication Quarterly* 18 (4): 327–50. https://doi.org/10.1080/1057225090314954 8.

Ding, H. 2014. *Rhetoric of a Global Epidemic: Transcultural Communication About SARS.* Southern Illinois University Press.

Dobrin, D. N. 1987. "Guest Editorial: Writing Without Discipline(s)." *Iowa State Journal of Business and Technical Communication* 1 (1): 5–8. https://doi.org/10.1177/105065198700100102.

Dombrowski, P. M. 1991. "The Lessons of the Challenger Investigations." *IEEE: Transactions on Professional Communication* 34 (4): 211–16.

Dombrowski, P. M. 1994. *Humanistic Aspects of Technical Communication.* Routledge.

Domergue, C. 2008. *Les mines antiques: La production des métaux aux époques grecque et romaine.* Paris.

Domonoske, C., and J. Simon. 2023. "Oil Companies Are Embracing Terms Like 'Lower Carbon.' Here's What They Really Mean." *NPR,* December 5. https://www.npr.org/2023/12/05/1215499778/cop28-uae-climate-talks-oil-exxon-mobil-chevron-climate-change-net-zero-unabated.

Doyle, K. 2004. "After the Revolution: Lázaro Cárdenas and the Movimiento de Liberación Nacional." NSA Electronic Briefing Book No. 124, May 31. https://nsarchive2.gwu.edu/NSAEBB/NSAEBB124/index.htm.

Drilling Matters. N.d. "Energy Poverty." Drillingmatters.org. https://drillingmatters.org/energy-poverty/.

Druschke, C. G. 2013. "Watershed as Common Place: Communicating for Conservation at the Watershed Scale." *Environmental Communication* 7 (1): 80–96. https://doi.org/10.1080/17524032.2012.749295.

Druschke, C. G. 2019. "A Trophic Future for Rhetorical Ecologies." *Enculturation: A Journal of Rhetoric, Writing, and* Culture 28 (1). https://enculturation.net/a-trophic-future.

Druschke, C. G. 2023. "Right Relation with the Whole World: Creating a Richer Polyvocality for Environmental Technical Communication." In *Technical Communication for Environmental Action*, edited by S. D. Williams, 293–306. State University of New York Press.

Druschke, C. G., E. G. Booth, B. Demuth, J. M. Holtgren, R. Lave, E. Lundberg, N. Myhal, B. Sellers, S. Widell, and C. A. Woelfe-Hazard. 2024. "Re-centering Relations: The Trouble with Quick Fix Approaches to Beaver-Based Restoration." *Geoforum* 156: 104121.

Eagle County, Colorado v. Surface Transportation Board, No. 22-1019 (D.C. Cir. 2023). https://media.cadc.uscourts.gov/opinions/docs/2023/08/22-1019-2013122.pdf.

East Daley Analytics. 2024. "New Markets Drive Uinta Production Growth." November 6. https://www.eastdaley.com/crude-oil-edge/new-markets-drive-uinta-production-growth.

Ehrenfeld, D. 2020. "'Sharing a World with Others': Rhetoric's Ecological Turn and the Transformation of the Networked Public Sphere." *Rhetoric Society Quarterly* 50 (5): 305–20.

Ellis, R. N. 1996. "The Utes." In *The Western San Juan Mountains: Their Geology, Ecology, and Human History*, edited by R. Blair. University Press of Colorado.

Endres, D. 2009. "The Rhetoric of Nuclear Colonialism: Rhetorical Exclusion of American Indian Arguments in the Yucca Mountain Nuclear Waste Siting Decision." *Communication and Critical/Cultural Studies* 6 (1): 39–60.

Endres, D. 2023. *Nuclear Decolonization: Indigenous Resistance to High-Level Nuclear Waste Siting*. Ohio State University Press.

Evanoski-Cole, A. R., K. A. Gebhart, B. C. Sive, Y. Zhou, S. L. Capps, D. E. Day, A. J. Prenni, et al. 2017. "Composition and Sources of Winter Haze in the Bakken Oil and Gas Extraction Region." *Atmospheric Environment* 156: 77–87. https://doi.org/10.1016/j.atmosenv.2017.02.019.

Evans, Mark L. 2023. "Environmental Protection Agency. 120036: Draft HRS Documentation Record Reference 13, The Silverton Railroads, Gladstone, Colorado." November 6. https://www.epa.gov/goldkingmine/august-31-2015-documents-related-prior-national-priorities-list-discussions.

Evia, C., and A. Patriarca. 2012. "Beyond Compliance: Participatory Translation of Safety Communication for Latino Construction Workers." *Journal of Business and Technical Communication* 26 (3): 340–67. https://doi.org/10.1177/1050651912439697.

Exchange Project. N.d. "Warren County: Landfill Location." University of North Carolina. https://exchangeproject.unc.edu/real_people/afton_overview/landfill_location.

Falc, E. 2020. "Water Is life: Shared Destinies." In *Water, Rhetoric, and Social Justice: A Critical Confluence*, edited by C. R. Schmitt, C. S. Thomas, and T. R. Castor, 19–42. Lexington Books.

Fall, A., and A. P. Davis. 1922. "US Bureau of Reclamation. Problems of Imperial Valley and Vicinity: Letter from the Secretary of the Interior." 67th Congress. Document no. 142. Government Printing Office. https://www.varuna.io/LOTR/1922/Problems_of_Imperial _Valley_and_Vicinity_1922.pdf.

Fanon, F. 2004. *The Wretched of the Earth*. Translated by R. Philcox. Grove Press.

Farmer, P. E., B. Nizeye, S. Stulac, and S. Keshavjee. 2006. "Structural Violence and Clinical Medicine." *PLOS Medicine* 3 (10): e449. https://doi.org/10.1371/journal.pmed.0030449.

Fell, J. E., and E. Twitty. 2008. *The Mining Industry in Colorado*. NPS Form 10-900-b. US DOI/NPS. National Register of Historic Places: Multiple Property Documentation Form. 1–253. https://www.historycolorado.org/sites/default/files/media/document/2017/651.pdf.

Fernández de Oviedo y Valdés, G. 1526. *De la natural hystoria de las Indias*. Ramón Petras.

Fernando, F. N., and D. R. Cooley. 2016. "Socioeconomic System of the Oil Boom and Rural Community Development in Western North Dakota." *Rural Sociology* 81: 407–44. https://doi.org/10.1111/ruso.12100.

Fernlund, K. J. 2020. "The Great Battle of the Books Between the Cultural Evolutionists and the Cultural Relativists: From the Beginning of Infinity to the End of History." *Journal of Big History* 4 (3): 6–30. https://jbh.journals.villanova.edu/article/view/2612.

Finley Resources. N.d. "Finley Resources." https://finleyresources.com.

Fischer, E. B., F. C. Lawrence, and G. Freund. 1883. *Map of the San Juan Mining Districts, Colorado.* Colorado School of Mines Repository. https://repository.mines.edu/handle/11124/170623.

Fischhoff, B. 1995. "Risk Perception and Communication Unplugged: Twenty Years of Process." *Risk Analysis* 15 (2): 137–45. https://doi.org/10.1111/j.1539-6924.1995.tb00308.x.

Flesch, R. 1949. *The Art of Readable Writing.* Harper & Brothers.

Flower, L. 2002. "Intercultural Inquiry and the Transformation of Service." *College English* 65 (2): 181–201. https://doi.org/10.2307/3250762.

Freire, P. 2000. *Pedagogy of the Oppressed.* 30th anniversary ed. Continuum.

Frémont, J. C. 1845. *Report of the Exploring Expedition to the Rocky Mountains in the Year 1842, and to Oregon and North California in the Years 1843–'44.* Gales and Seaton.

Frost, E. A. 2013. "Transcultural Risk Communication on Dauphin Island: An Analysis of Ironically Located Responses to the Deepwater Horizon Disaster." *Technical Communication Quarterly* 22 (1): 50–66. https://doi.org/10.1080/10572252.2013.

Fuller, C. N.d. "Uinta Basin." *Utah History Encyclopedia.* https://www.uen.org/utah_history_encyclopedia/u/UINTA_BASIN.shtml.

Gadhamshetty, V., N. Shrestha, G. Chilkoor, and J. R. Bathi. 2015. "Emerging Environmental Impacts of Unconventional Oil Development in the Bakken Formation in the Williston Basin of Western North Dakota." In *Hydraulic Fracturing: Environmental Issues,* edited by J. D. Arthur, D. M. Bohm, and M. Layne, 151–80. American Chemical Society. https://doi.org/10.1021/bk-2015-1216.ch007.

Gallagher, J. R. 2019. "A Framework for Internet Case Study Methodology in Writing Studies." *Computers and Composition* 54 (4): 1–14. https://doi.org/10.1016/j.compcom.2019.102509.

Galtung, J. 1969. "Violence, Peace, and Peace Research." *Journal of Peace Research* 6 (3): 167–91. http://www.jstor.org/stable/422690.

Ganning, A. E., U. Brunk, and G. Dallner. 1984. "Phthalate Esters and Their Effect on the Liver." *Hepatology* 4 (3): 541–47. https://doi.org/10.1002/hep.1840040331.

Gay, D. A., K. Blaydes, J. J. Schauer, and M. Shafer. 2024. "Widespread Impacts to Precipitation of the East Palestine Ohio Train Accident." *Environmental Research Letters* 19 (7): 074022. https://doi.org/10.1088/1748-9326/ad52ac.

Gerlak, A. K., F. Zamora-Arroyo, and H. P. Kahler. 2013. "A Delta in Repair: Restoration, Binational Cooperation, and the Future of the Colorado River Delta." *Environment: Science and Policy for Sustainable Development* 55 (3): 29–40.

Giddens, A. 1991. *Modernity and Self-Identity: Self and Society in the Late Modern Age.* Polity Press.

Giles, T. D. 2010. "Communicating the Risk of Scientific Research." *Journal of Technical Writing and Communication* 40 (3): 265–81. https://doi.org/10.2190/TW.40.3.c.

Giulivo, M., M. Lopez de Alda, E. Capri, and D. Barceló. 2016. "Human Exposure to Endocrine Disrupting Compounds: Their Role in Reproductive Systems, Metabolic Syndrome, and Breast Cancer." *Environmental Research* 151: 251–64. https://doi.org/10.1016/j.envres.2016.07.011.

Goldwasser, O. 2010. "How the Alphabet Was Born from Hieroglyphs." *Biblical Archaeology Review* 36 (2): 40–53.

Goldwasser, O. 2011. "The Advantage of Cultural Periphery: The Invention of the Alphabet in Sinai (Circa 1840 B.C.E)." In *Culture Contacts and the Making of Cultures: Papers in Homage to Itamar Even-Zohar*, edited by R. Sela-Sheffy and G. Toury, 251–316. Tel Aviv University.

Gómez-Barris, M. 2017. *The Extractive Zone: Social Ecologies and Decolonial Perspectives.* Duke University Press.

Gorsevski, E. W. 2017. "The Biotic Turn in Rhetoric: Ethical Internatural Communication as Suasory Peacebuilding." In *Rhetorical Animals: Boundaries of the Human in the Study of Persuasion*, edited by K. Bjørkdahl and A. C. Parrish, 123–45. Lexington Books.

Gottlieb, M. S. 1980. "Lung Cancer and the Petroleum Industry in Louisiana." *Journal of Occupational Medicine* 22 (6): 384–88. http://www.jstor.org/stable/45013171.

Government of Western Australia. 1972. Aboriginal Heritage Act, No. 53 of 1972. www.legislation.wa.gov.au.

Government of Western Australia. 2021. Aboriginal Cultural Heritage Act, No. 27 of 2021. www.legislation.wa.gov.au.

Grabill, J. T., and W. M. Simmons. 1998. "Toward a Critical Rhetoric of Risk Communication: Producing Citizens and the Role of Technical Communicators." *Technical Communication Quarterly* 7 (4): 415–41. https://doi.org/10.1080/10572259809364640.

Graeber, D., and D. Wengrow. 2021. *The Dawn of Everything: A New History of Humanity.* Farrar, Straus and Giroux.

Graulau, J. 2019. *The Underground Wealth of Nations: On the Capitalist Origins of Silver Mining, A.D. 1150–1450.* Yale University Press.

Graves, H., and D. Beard, eds. 2019. *The Rhetoric of Oil in the Twenty-First Century: Government, Corporate, and Activist Discourses.* Routledge.

Grimley, N. 2023. "North Lima Woman Finds Chickens Dead Tuesday, Questions Chemical Release from Train." *WKBN*, February 7. https://www.wkbn.com/news/local-news/east-palestine-train-derailment/north-lima-woman-finds-chickens-dead-tuesday-questions-chemical-release-from-train/.

Haas, A. M. 2012. "Race, Rhetoric, and Technology: A Case Study of Decolonial Technical Communication Theory, Methodology, and Pedagogy." *Journal of Business and Technical Communication* 26 (3): 277–310.

Haas, A. M., and M. Eble, eds. 2018. *Key Theoretical Frameworks: Teaching Technical Communication in the Twenty-First Century.* Utah State University Press.

Haas, A. M., and E. A. Frost. 2017. "Toward an Apparent Decolonial Feminist Rhetoric of Risk." In *Topic-Driven Environmental Rhetoric*, edited by D. G. Ross, 168–86. Routledge.

Hadden, S. G. 1989. "Institutional Barriers to Risk Communication." *Risk Analysis* 9: 301–8.

Hager, P. J., and R. J. Nelson. 1993. "Chaucer's 'A Treatise on the Astrolabe': A 600-Year-Old Model for Humanizing Technical Documents." *IEEE Transactions on Professional Communication* 36 (2): 87–94. https://doi.org/10.1109/47.222687.

Hagge, J. 1990. "The First Technical Writer in English: A Challenge to the Hegemony of Chaucer." *Journal of Technical Writing and Communication* 20 (3): 269–89. https://doi.org/10.2190/VWCW-XKMV-949F-VLF7.

Hall, S. 2015. "Exxon Knew About Climate Change Almost 40 Years Ago." *Scientific American*, October 27. www.scientificamerican.com/article/exxon-knew-about-climate-change-almost-40-years-ago/.

Halm, M. 2023. "Molten Circulation: The Geologic Turn in Rhetoric and Composition." *Enculturation: A Journal of Rhetoric, Writing, and Culture* (August 9). https://enculturation.net/molten_circulation.

Hamilton, G. J. 2006. *The Origins of the West Semitic Alphabet in Egyptian Scripts.* Catholic Biblical Association of America.

Hamlett, R. T. 1956. "Technical Writing—Good or Bad." *TWE Journal* 2 (2): 9–11.

Hammond, H. 1940. *The Hammond Report.* Society for the Promotion of Engineering Education. Report of the Committee on Aims and Scope of Engineering Curricula. http://web.mit.edu/~jwk/www/docs/Hammond%20Report%201940.pdf.

Hammond, H. 1944. *Engineering Education After the War.* Society for the Promotion of Engineering Education. Report of the Committee on Aims and Scope of Engineering Curricula. http://web.mit.edu/jwk/www/docs/Hammond%20Report%201944.pdf.

Hannon, A. 2022. "Bulkheads Caused the Gold King Mine Spill: Could They Also Be Part of the Solution?" *Durango Herald*, March 30. https://www.durangoherald.com/articles/ bulkheads-caused-the-gold-king-mine-spill-could-they-also-be-part-of-the-solution/.

Harrell, J. A., and V. M. Brown. 1992. "The World's Oldest Surviving Geological Map: The 1150 B.C. Turin Papyrus from Egypt." *Journal of Geology* 100 (1): 3–18. http://www.jstor.org/stable/30082315.

Hartshorn, J. K. 1977. "Imperial Valley and Imperial Irrigation District: A Brief History." In *Desert Wasteland to Agricultural Wonder: The Story of Water and Power*, edited by Imperial Irrigation District Community and Special Services, 1–11. October. https://cawaterlibrary.net/wp-content/uploads/2019/10/Imperial-Valley-Desert-Wasteland-to-Ag-Wonderland.pdf.

Harvey, D. 1999. "The Environment of Justice." In *Living with Nature: Environmental Politics as Cultural Discourse*, edited by F. Fischer and M. A. Hajer, 153–85. Oxford University Press.

Hawhee, D., and C. J. Olson. 2013. "Pan-Historiography: The Challenges of Writing History Across Time and Space." In *Theorizing Histories of Rhetoric*, edited by M. Bailiff, 90–105. Southern Illinois University Press.

Hayhoe, G. F., and P. E. Brewer. 2021. *A Research Primer for Technical Communication: Methods, Exemplars, and Analyses*. Routledge.

Healy, J. F. 1978. *Mining and Metallurgy in the Greek and Roman World*. Thames and Hudson.

Heath, R. L., and H. D. O'Hair. 2009. "The Significance of Crisis in Risk Communication." In *Handbook of Risk and Crisis Communication*, edited by R. L. Heath and H. D. O'Hair, 5–30. Routledge.

Herndl, C. G. 1993. "Teaching Discourse and Reproducing Culture: A Critique of Research and Pedagogy in Professional and Non-Academic Writing." *College Composition and Communication* 44 (3): 349–63. https://doi.org/10.2307/358988.

Herndl, C. G. 1996. "Tactics and the Quotidian: Resistance and Professional Discourse." *JAC* 163 (3): 455–70. https://www.jstor.org/stable/20866093.

Herndl, C. G., B. A. Fennell, and C. R. Miller. 1991. "Understanding Failures in Organizational Discourse: The Accident at Three Mile Island and the Shuttle *Challenger* Disaster." In *Textual Dynamics of the Professions*, edited by C. Bazerman and J. Paradis, 279–305. University of Wisconsin Press.

Hill Collins, P. 1990. *Black Feminist Thought: Knowledge, Consciousness, and the Politics of Empowerment*. Unwin Hyman.

Hinojosa-Huerta, O., E. Soto-Montoya, M. Gómez-Sapiens, A. Calvo-Fonseca, R. Guzmán-Olachea, J. Butrón-Méndez, J. J. Butrón-Rodríguez, and M. Román-Rodríguez. 2013. "The Birds of the Ciénega de Santa Clara, a Wetland of International Importance Within the Colorado River Delta." *Ecological Engineering* 59: 61–73.

Hoffman, K. S. 2002. "'Going Public' in the Nineteenth Century: Grover Cleveland's Repeal of the Sherman Silver Purchase Act." *Rhetoric and Public Affairs* 5 (1): 57–77. http://www.jstor.org/stable/41939717.

Holcombe, S., and B. Fredericks. 2021. "Beyond Juukan Gorge, the Relentless Threat Mining Poses to the Pilbara Cultural Landscape." *The Conversation*, February 24. https://theconversation.com/beyond-juukan-gorge-the-relentless-threat-mining-poses-to-the-pilbara-cultural-landscape-155941.

Homestead Act Public Law 37–64 (12 STAT 392). 1862. "Enrolled Acts and Resolutions of Congress, 1789–2011." General Records of the United States Government, Record Group 11. National Archives.

Hopper, R. J. 1961. "The Mines and Miners of Ancient Athens." *Greece and Rome* 8 (2): 138–51. http://www.jstor.org/stable/641645.

Hopton, S. B., and P. Rajan. 2023. "Critical Approaches to Climate Justice, Technology, and Technical Communication: Special Issue Introduction." *Technical Communication Quarterly* 32 (3): 217–23.

Horton, Z. 2021. *The Cosmic Zoom: Scale, Knowledge, and Mediation*. University of Chicago Press.

Howden, C. M., E. T. Stone, V. Nallur, M. R. McClung, and M. D. Moran,. 2019. "Impact of the Bakken/Three Forks Unconventional Oil and Gas Development on Natural Habitats in North Dakota." *Land Degradation and Development* 30: 524–32. https://doi.org/10.1002/ldr.3245.

Howe, E. F., and W. J. Hall,. 1910. *The Story of the First Decade in Imperial Valley, California*. Howe and Sons.

Hundley, N. 1973. "The Politics of Reclamation: California, the Federal Government, and the Origins of the Boulder Canyon Act." *California Historical Quarterly* 52 (4): 292–325.

Imperial Irrigation District (Calif.), United States. Bureau of Reclamation. Lower Colorado Region. 1994. *All-American Canal Lining Project, Imperial County, California: Final Environmental Impact Statement/Final Environmental Impact Report*. U.S. Department of the Interior, Bureau of Reclamation, Lower Colorado Region.

International Boundary and Water Commission (IBWC). 1973. Minute 242. Permanent and Definitive Solution to the International Problem of the Salinity of the Colorado River. https://www.ibwc.gov/wp-content/uploads/2023/05/Min242.pdf.

International Boundary and Water Commissions (IBWC). 2012. Minute 319. Interim International Cooperative Measures in the Colorado River Basin Through 2017 and Extension of Minute 318 Cooperative Measures to Address the Continued Effects of the April 2010 Earthquake in the Mexicali Valley, Baja California. https://www.ibwc.gov/wp-content/uploads/2012/11/Minute_319.pdf.

International Boundary and Water Commission (IBWC). 2024a. Minute 323. Construction of a Composite Cutoff Wall to Reduce the Risk of Failure at Amistad

International Dam. https://www.ibwc.gov/wp-content/uploads/2025/01/Minute-332-and-Joint-Report-PE-12-10-2024.pdf.

International Boundary and Water Commission (IBWC). 2024b. Minute 330. Expansion of Colorado River Temporary Measures. https://ibwc.azurewebsites.net/wp-content/uploads/2024/04/Minute-330-English-Spanish-Version-Signed-Clean.pdf.

International Boundary and Water Commission (IBWC). 2024c. "United States and Mexico. U.S. Section. History." https://www.ibwc.gov/about-us/history/.

Irving, S. 2008. *Natural Science and the Origins of the British Empire.* Routledge.

Itchuaqiyaq, C. U. 2023. "When Sound Is Frozen: Extracting Climate Data from Inuit Narratives." In *Technical Communication for Environmental Action,* edited by S. D. Williams, 19–38. State University of New York Press.

Itchuaqiyaq, C. U., A. C. Edenfield, and K. Grant-Davie. 2022. "Sex Work and Professional Risk Communication: Keeping Safe on the Streets." *Journal of Business and Technical Communication* 36 (1): 1–37. https://doi.org/10.1177/10506519211044190.

Jacobsen, T., and R. M. Adams. 1958. "Salt and Silt in Ancient Mesopotamian Agriculture." *Science* 128: 1251–58. https://doi.org/10.1126/science.128.3334.1251.

James, T., A. Evans, E. Madly, and C. Kell. 2014. *The Economic Importance of the Colorado River to the Basin Region.* December 18. L. William Seidman Research Institute, Arizona State University. https://businessforwater.org/wp-content/uploads/2016/12/PTF-Final-121814.pdf.

Jha, G., S. Mukhopadhyay, A. L. Ulery, K. Lombard, S. Chakraborty, D. C. Weindorf, D. VanLeeuwen, and C. Brungard. 2016. "Agricultural Soils of the Animas River Watershed After the Gold King Mine Spill: An Elemental Spatiotemporal Analysis via Portable X-ray Fluorescence Spectroscopy." *Journal of Environmental Quality* 50 (3): 730–43. https://doi.org/10.1002/jeq2.2020.

Johnson, N. R., and M. A. Johnson. 2020. "Precarious Data: Affect, Infrastructure, and Public Education." *Rhetoric Society Quarterly* 50 (5): 368–82. https://doi.org/10.1080/02773945.2020.1814397.

Jones, M. 2021. "A Counter-History of Rhetorical Ecologies." *Rhetoric Society Quarterly* 51 (4): 336–52. https://doi.org/10.1080/02773945.2021.1947517.

Jones, N. N., K. R. Moore, and R. Walton. 2016. "Disrupting the Past to Disrupt the Future: An Antenarrative of Technical Communication." *Technical Communication Quarterly* 25 (4): 211–29. https://doi.org/10.1080/10572252.2016.1224655.

Jones, N. N., and M. F. Williams. 2018. "Technologies of Disenfranchisement: Literacy Tests and Black Voters in the U.S. from 1890 to 1965." *Technical Communication* 65 (4): 371–85.

Jones, N. N. and M. F. Williams. 2022. "Archives, Rhetorical Absence, and Critical Imagination: Examining Black Women's Mental Health Narratives at Virginia's

Central State Hospital." *IEEE Transactions on Professional Communication* 65 (1): 179–96. https://doi.org/10.1109/TPC.2022.3140883.

Jones, W. N.d. "Petroleum." *Utah History Encyclopedia*. https://www.uen.org/utah_history_encyclopedia/p/PETROLEUM.shtml.

Juskus, R. 2023. "Sacrifice Zones: A Genealogy and Analysis of an Environmental Justice Concept." *Environmental Humanities* 15 (1): 3–24. https://doi.org/10.1215/22011919-10216129.

Karl, Terry L. 2017. *The Paradox of Plenty: Oil Booms and Petro-States*. University of California Press.

Kasperson, R. E., O. Renn, P. Slovic, H. S. Brown, J. Emel, R. Goble, J. X. Kasperson, and S. Ratick. 1988. "The Social Amplification of Risk: A Conceptual Framework." *Risk Analysis* 8 (2): 177–87. https://doi.org/10.1111/j.1539-6924.1988.tb01168.x.

Kasperson, R. E., and P. J. M. Stallen. 1991. Introduction to *Communicating Risks to the Public: International Perspectives*, edited by R. E. Kasperson and P. J. M. Stallen. Springer. https://doi.org/10.1007/978-94-009-1952-5_1.

Katz, S. B. 1992. "The Ethic of Expediency: Classical Rhetoric, Technology, and the Holocaust." *College English* 54 (3): 255–75. https://doi.org/10.2307/378062.

Katz, S. B., and C. R. Miller. 1996. "The Low-Level Radioactive Waste Siting Controversy in North Carolina: Toward a Rhetorical Model of Risk Communication." In *Green Culture: Environmental Rhetoric in Contemporary America*, edited by C. G. Herndl and S. Brown, 111–40. University of Wisconsin Press.

Katz-Rosene, R. M. 201. "From Narrative of Promise to Rhetoric of Sustainability: A Genealogy of Oil Sands." *Environmental Communication* 11 (3): 401–14. https://doi.org/10.1080/17524032.2016.1253597.

Keighin, C. W., and M. H. Hibpshman. 1975. "Preliminary Mineral Resource Study of the Uintah and Ouray Reservation, Utah." *Administrative Report: BIA-4*. United States Geological Survey, United States Bureau of Mines. https://www1.eere.energy.gov/tribalenergy/guide/pdfs/unitah_ouray_4.pdf.

Kelly, J. F., and R. L. Hutto. 2005. "An East-West Comparison of Migration in North American Wood Warblers." *The Condor* 107: 197–211.

Kempter, H., and B. Frenzel. 2000. "The Impact of Early Mining and Smelting on the Local Tropospheric Aerosol Detected in Ombrotrophic Peat Bogs in the Harz, Germany." *Water, Air, and Soil Pollution* 121: 93–108. https://doi.org/10.1023/A:1005253716497.

Kendall, L. 2009. "A Response to Christine Hine's 'Defining Project Boundaries.'" In *Internet Inquiry: Conversations about Method*, edited by A.N. Markham and N. Baym, 21–25. Sage.

Kendy, E., K. W. Flessa, K. J. Schlatter, C. A. de la Parra, O. M. Hinojosa Huerta, Y. K. Carillo-Guerrero, and E. Guillen. 2017. "Leveraging Environmental

Flows to Reform Water Management Policy: Lessons Learned from the 2014 Colorado River Delta Pulse Flow." *Ecological Engineering* 106 (B): 683–94. https://doi.org/10.1016/j.ecoleng.2017.02.012.

Killingsworth, M. J. 2007. "A Phenomenological Perspective on Ethical Duty in Environmental Communication." *Environmental Communication* 1: 58–63. https://doi.org/10.1080/17524030701334243.

Killingsworth, M. J., and D. Steffens. 1989. "Effectiveness in the Environmental Impact Statement: A Study in Public Rhetoric." *Written Communication* 6 (2): 155–80. https://doi.org/10.1177/0741088389006002002.

Kimball, M. A. 2017. "The Golden Age of Technical Communication." *Journal of Technical Writing and Communication* 47 (3): 330–58. https://doi.org/10.1177/0047281616641927.

King, L. M. 1923. *A History of Sumer and Akkad: An Account of the Early Races of Babylonia from Prehistoric Times to the Foundation of the Babylonian Monarchy (volume 1*). Chatto and Windus.

King, M. L., Jr. 1967. "The Three Evils of Society." Address delivered at the National Conference on New Politics, August 31, Chicago. https://okra.stanford.edu.

Kishel, J. 1993. "Lining the All-American Canal: Legal Problems and Physical Solutions." *Natural Resources Journal* 33 (3): 697–726. http://www.jstor.org/stable/24884624.

Kriebel, D., J. Tickner, P. Epstein, J. Lemons, R. Levins, E. L. Loechler, M. Quinn, R. Rudel, T. Schettler, and M. Stoto. 2001. "The Precautionary Principle in Environmental Science." *Environmental Health Perspectives* 109 (9): 871–76. https://doi.org/10.1289/ehp.01109871.

Kruse, K. M., and J. E. Zelizer. 2019. *Fault Lines: A History of the United States Since 1974*. W. W. Norton.

Kuhl, E. 2022. "The Hard(Rock) Truth About Abandoned Mines in the Western United States: Why the Pressure Is on to Enact Good Samaritan Legislation as a Way to Recover." *Colorado Environmental Law Journal* 28 (1): 256–81.

Kuhn, E., and J. Fleck. 2019. *Science Be Dammed: How Ignoring Inconvenient Science Drained the Colorado River*. University of Arizona Press.

Kurwadkar, S., J. Dane, S. R. Kanel, M. N. Nadagouda, R.W. Cawdrey, B. Ambade, G. C. Struckhoff, and R. Wilkin. 2022. "Per- and Polyfluoroalkyl Substances in Water and Wastewater: A Critical Review of Their Global Occurrence and Distribution." *Science of the Total Environment* 809: 1–19.

Kwiatkowska, T. 2007. "The Sadness of the Woods Is Bright: Deforestation and Conservation in the Middle Ages." *Medievalia* 39: 40–47.

Kynell-Hunt, T. 2000. *Writing in a Milieu of Utility: The Move to Technical Communication in American Engineering Programs, 1850–1950*. 2nd ed. Ablex.

Kynell-Hunt, T. 2004. *Power and Legitimacy in Technical Communication: Volume II, Strategies for Professional Status*. Baywood.

Kynell-Hunt, T., and G. J. Savage, eds. 2003. *Power and Legitimacy in Technical Communication: Volume I, The Historical and Contemporary Struggle for Professional Status.* Baywood.

Lake, R. A. 1991. "Between Myth and History: Enacting Time in Native American Protest Rhetoric." *Quarterly Journal of Speech* 77 (2): 123–51. https://doi.org/10.1080/ 00335639109383949.

Lartey, J. 2023. "Ohio Train Derailment Is a Wake-up Call." *Guardian*, February 11. https://www.theguardian.com/us-news/2023/feb/11/ohio-train-derailment-wake-up-call.

Lee, S. 2021. "Language Minorities' Localization in COVID-19 Recovery: An Ecological Approach to Navigating Community-Based User Experience." In *Proceedings of the 39th ACM International Conference on Design of Communication (SIGDOC '21)*, 183–89. Association for Computing Machinery. https://doi.org/10.1145/3472714.3473640.

Lee, S. 2022. "Translingual and Translational Practices as Rhetorical Care Technologies in COVID-19 Recovery." *Journal of Rhetoric, Professional Communication, and Globalization* 11 (1): 35–56.

Leff, M. 1988. "Serious Comedy: The Strange Case History of Dr. Vitanza." *Rhetoric Review* 6 (2): 237–45. http://www.jstor.org/stable/465941.

Leiss, W. 1996. "Three Phases in the Evolution of Risk Communication Practice." *Annals of the American Academy of Political and Social Science* 545 (1): 85–94. https://doi.org/10.1177/0002716296545001009.

Leiss, W., and D. Powell. 2004. *Mad Cows and Mother's Milk: The Perils of Poor Risk Communication.* 2nd ed. McGill-Queen's University Press.

Lennon, M. 2017. "Decolonizing Energy: Black Lives Matter and Technoscientific Expertise amid Solar Transitions." *Energy Research and Social Science* 30: 18–27. https://doi.org/10.1016/j.erss.2017.06.002.

Leopold, A. 1949. *A Sand County Almanac: And Sketches Here and There.* Oxford University Press.

Levin, S. A. 1992, "The Problem of Pattern and Scale in Ecology: The Robert H. MacArthur Award Lecture." *Ecology* 73 (6): 1943–67. https://doi.org/10.2307/1941447.

Lewis, D. R. N.d. "Uintah-Ouray Indian Reservation." *Utah History Encyclopedia.* https://www.uen.org/utah_history_encyclopedia/u/uintah-ouray_indian_reservation.shtml.

Liang, Q., and L. Yu. 2023. "Assessment of Carbon Emission Potential of Polyvinyl Chloride Plastics." *E3S Web of Conferences* 393: 1–4. https://doi.org/10.1051/e3sconf/202339301031.

Lillis, P. G., A. Warden, and D. J. King. 2003. "Petroleum Systems of the Uinta and Piceance Basins—Geochemical Characteristics of Oil Types." In *Petroleum Systems and Geologic Assessment of Oil and Gas in the Uinta-Piceance Province, Utah and Colorado, U.S. Geological Survey Digital Data Series DDS–69–B,* edited by USGS Uinta-Piceance Assessment Team, 1–13. https://pubs.usgs.gov/dds/dds-069/dds-069-b/REPORTS/Chapter_3.pdf.

Lim, X. 2021. "Microplastics Are Everywhere—but Are They Harmful? Scientists Are Rushing to Study the Tiny Plastic Specs That Are in Marine Animals—and in Us." *Nature*, May 4. https://www.nature.com/articles/d41586-021-01143-3.

Lisabeth, L. 2021. "Strunk and White and Whiteness." *College Composition and Communication* 73 (1): 80–102. doi.org/10.58680/ccc202131588.

Liu, W. G. 2015. *The Chinese Market Economy, 1000–1500*. State University of New York Press.

Lohmann, L. 2013. *Energy Alternatives: Surveying the Territory*. Corner House. https://www.thecornerhouse.org.uk/sites/thecornerhouse.org.uk/files/ENERGY%20ALTERNATIVES%20--%20SURVEYING%20THE%20TERRITORY.pdf.

Longo, B. 2000. *Spurious Coin: A History of Science, Management, and Technical Writing*. State University of New York Press.

Lopez, M. 2020. "Tribal Rights: The 1872 Mining Law's Past and Future." *Natural Resources and Environment* 34 (3): 53–55. https://www.jstor.org/stable/27010602.

Lorde, A. 1984. *Sister Outsider: Essays and Speeches*. Crossing Press.

Luft, R. E. 2009. "Beyond Disaster Exceptionalism: Social Movement Developments in New Orleans After Hurricane Katrina." *American Quarterly* 61 (3): 499–528.

Luft, R. E. 2016. "Governing Disaster: The Politics of Tribal Sovereignty in the Context of (un)Natural Disaster." *Ethnic and Racial Studies* 39 (5): 802–20. https://doi.org/10.1080/01419870.2015.1080376.

Lundberg, E., C. G. Druschke, B. McGreavy, S. Randall, T. Quiring, A. Fisher, F. Soluri, et al. 2017. "Communicating About Hydropower, Dams, and Climate Change." *Oxford Research Encyclopedia of Climate Science*, September 26. https://oxfordre.com/climatescience/view/10.1093/acrefore/9780190228620.001.0001/acrefore-9780190228620-e-442.

Lundgren, R. E., and A. H. McMakin. 2018. *Risk Communication: A Handbook for Communicating Environmental, Safety, and Health Risks*. 6th ed. John Wiley and Sons.

Maffly, B. 2022. "Uinta Basin Railway on Track After Court Ruling." *Salt Lake Tribune*, July 16. https://www.sltrib.com/news/environment/2022/07/16/uinta-basin-railway-track-after/.

Mailloux, S. 1998. *Reception Histories: Rhetoric, Pragmatism, and American Cultural Politics*. Cornell University Press.

Malm, A. 2016. "Who Lit This Fire? Approaching the History of the Fossil Economy." *Critical Historical Studies* 3 (2): 215–48. https://doi.org/10.1086/688347.

Malone, M. 1986. "The Collapse of Western Metal Mining: An Historical Epitaph." *Pacific Historical Review* 55 (3): 455–64. https://doi.org/10.2307/3639707.

Maraniss, D., and M. Weisskopf. 1988. "The Faces of Pollution: As Cancer, Miscarriages Mount, Louisiana Wonders if It Is a 'National Sacrifice Zone.' "

Los Angeles Times, January 24. www.latimes.com/archives/la-xpm-1988-01-24-mn-37913-story.html.

Marten, G. G. 1972. "Censusing Mouse Populations by Means of Tracking." *Ecology* 53: 859–67.

Mashallah ibn Athari. N.d. *Construction and Operation of Astrolabes*. [Translated from Arabic].

McGreavy, B., D. Ranco, J. Daigle, S. Greenlaw, N. Altvater, T. Quiring, N. Michelle, et al. 2021. "Science in Indigenous Homelands: Addressing Power and Justice in Sustainability Science from/with/in the Penobscot River." *Sustainability Science* 16 (3): 937–47.

McMichael, A. J. 2017. "Spread of Farming, New Diseases, and Rising Civilizations mid-Holocene Optimum." In *Climate Change and the Health of Nations: Famines, Fevers, and the Fate of Populations*, ed. A. J. McMichael, 108–25. Oxford. https://doi.org/10.1093/oso/9780190262952.003.0010.

McWilliams, C. 1949. *California: The Great Exception*. University of California.

Merchant, C. 1989. *The Death of Nature: Women, Ecology, and the Scientific Revolution*. Harper and Row.

Merriam, S. B. 1998. *Qualitative Research and Case Study Applications in Education*. Jossey-Bass.

Mignolo, W. D. 2011. *The Darker Side of Western Modernity: Global Futures, Decolonial Options*. Duke University Press. https://doi.org/10.1215/9780822394501.

Miller, C. R. 1979. "A Humanistic Rationale for Technical Writing." *College English* 40 (6): 610–17. https://doi.org/10.2307/375964.

Miller, C. R. 1980. "Environmental Impact Statements and Rhetorical Genres: An Application of Rhetorical Theory to Technical Communication." PhD diss., Rensselaer Polytechnic Institute.

Miller, C. R. 2003. "The Presumptions of Expertise: The Role of Ethos in Risk Analysis." *Configurations* 11 (2): 163–202. https://doi.org/10.1353/con.2004.0022.

Mills, G. H., and J. A. Walter. 1954. *Technical Writing*. Holt, Rinehart and Winston.

Mirel, B. 1994. "Debating Nuclear Energy: Theories of Risk and Purposes of Communication." *Technical Communication Quarterly* 3 (1): 41–65. https://doi.org/10.1080/10572259409364557.

Mitchell, J. H. 1976. "It's a Craft Course: Indoctrinate, Don't Educate." *Technical Writing Teacher* 4 (1): 2–6.

Mohun, A. P. 2016. "Constructing the History of Risk: Foundations, Tools, and Reasons Why." *Historical Social Research* 41 (1): 30–47. https://doi.org/10.12759/hsr.41.2016.1.30-47.

Moore, K. R. 2016. "Public Engagement in Environmental Impact Studies: A Case Study of Professional Communication in Transportation Planning." *IEEE Transactions on Professional Communication* 59 (3): 245–60. https://doi.org/10.1109/TPC.2016.2583278.

Moore, P. 1997. "Rhetorical vs. Instrumental Approaches to Teaching Technical Communication." *Technical Communication* 44 (2): 163–73.

Moran, M. G. 1985. "The History of Technical and Scientific Writing." In *Research in Technical Communication: A Bibliographic Sourcebook*, edited by M. G. Moran and D. Journey, 25–38. Greenwood.

Moran, M. G. 2005. "Figures of Speech as Persuasive Strategies in Early Commercial Communication: The Use of Dominant Figures in the Raleigh Reports About Virginia in the 1580s." *Technical Communication Quarterly* 14 (2): 183–96.

Morgan, M. G., B. Fischhoff, A. Bostrom, and C. J. Atman. 2001. *Risk Communication: A Mental Models Approach*. Cambridge University Press.

Moscato, D. 2019. "The Metanarrative of Rural Environmentalism: Rhetorical Activism in Bold Nebraska's Harvest the Hope." *Public Relations Inquiry* 8 (1): 23–47. https://doi.org/10.1177/2046147X18810733.

Moscato, D. 2022. *Dirt Persuasion: Civic Environmental Populism and the Heartland's Pipeline Fight*. University of Nebraska Press.

Moxon, J. 1687. *Mechanick Exercises*. J. Moxon.

Mrozowski, S. A. 1999. "Colonization and the Commodification of Nature." *International Journal of Historical Archaeology* 3 (3): 153–66. https://doi.org/10.1023/A:1021957902956.

Müller-Mahn, D., and J. Everts. 2012. "Riskscapes: The Spatial Dimensions of Risk." In *The Spatial Dimensions of Risk*, edited by D. Müller-Mahn, 22–36. Routledge. https://doi.org/10.4324/9780203109595.

National Archives. N.d. "British Transatlantic Slave Trade Records." https://nationalarchives.gov.uk/help-with-your-research/research-guides/british-transatlantic-slave-trade-records/.

National Association for the Advancement of Colored People of Warren County, et al. v. Anne Gorsuch, et al. 1982. Civil Action No. 82-768-CIV-5, U.S. District Court, Eastern District of North Carolina, Raleigh Division, RC-AG, File 2363, Division of Records, State of North Carolina Archives, Raleigh, N.C., 9–10.

National Cancer Institute. 2024. "Vinyl Chloride." June 13. https://www.cancer.gov/about-cancer/causes-prevention/risk/substances/vinyl-chloride.

National Drought Mitigation Center. 2022. *U.S. Drought Monitor*. https://droughtmonitor.unl.edu

National Oceanic and Atmospheric Administration. N.d. "Chemical Datasheet: Benzene." CAMEO Chemicals. https://cameochemicals.noaa.gov/chemical/1692.

National Research Council. 1989. *Improving Risk Communication*. National Academy Press.

Natural Resources Defense Council. 2023. *The Environmental Justice Movement*. August 22. https://www.nrdc.org/stories/environmental-justice-movement.

National Toxicology Program. 1981. *Phthalic Acid Esters: Toxicological Evaluation and Suggestions for Additional Safety Testing (Draft)*. National Institutes of Health, U.S. Department of Health and Human Services.

National Transportation Safety Board. N.d. *Norfolk Southern Railway Train Derailment*. https://www.ntsb.gov/investigations/Pages/RRD23MR005.aspx.

Navajo Nation EPA. 2017. "Navajo Nation Surface Water Quality Standards." May 23. https://www.epa.gov/sites/default/files/2014-12/documents/navajo-tribe.pdf.

Nielsen, J., B. Åkesson, and S. Skerfving. 1985. "Phthalate Ester Exposure—Air Levels and Health of Workers Processing Polyvinylchloride." *American Industrial Hygiene Association Journal* 46 (11): 643–47. https://doi.org/10.1080/15298668591395463.

Nikiforuk, A. 2012. *The Energy of Slaves: Oil and the New Servitude.* Greystone Books.

Nixon, R. 2013. *Slow Violence and the Environmentalism of the Poor.* Harvard University Press.

November, V. 2004. "Being Close to Risk: From Proximity to Connexity." *International Journal of Sustainable Development* 7 (3): 273–86.

November, V. 2008. "Spatiality of Risk." *Environment and Planning A* 40: 1523–27.

Occupational Safety and Health Administration (OSHA) Hazard Communication Standard (HCS). 29 CFR 1910.1200. https://www.osha.gov/laws-regs/federalregister/1983-11-25.

O'Connor, D. 2012. "From Topography to Cosmos." In *Ancient Perspectives: Maps and Their Place in Mesopotamia, Egypt, Greece, and Rome*, edited by R. J. A. Talbert, 193–234. University of Chicago Press.

Ohio Department of Natural Resources. 2023. "ODNR Update on East Palestine Train Derailment Impact to Wildlife." February 23. https://ohiodnr.gov/discover-and-learn/safety-conservation/about-ODNR/news/Train-Derailment.

Ohmann, R. 1976. *English in America: A Radical View of the Profession.* Oxford University Press.

Olivarius-McAllister, C. 2013. "Superfund: A Dirty Word to Some in Silverton." *Durango Herald*, August 3. https://www.durangoherald.com/articles/superfund-a-dirty-word-to-some-in-silverton/.

Olman, L., and D. DeVasto. 2020. "Hybrid Collectivity: Hacking Environmental Risk Visualization for the Anthropocene." *Communication Design Quarterly* 8 (4): 15–28. https://doi.org/10.1145/3431932.3431934.

Olson, K. R., and J. M. Lang. 2021. "The Disappearing Colorado River: Historic and Modern Attempts to Manage the Lifeline of the United States Southwest." *Open Journal of Soil Science* 11 (11): 538–66. https://doi.org/10.4236/ojss.2021.1111027.

O'Rourke, P. M. 1980. *Frontier in Transition.* Bureau of Land Management, Colorado State Office. https://ia801308.us.archive.org/22/items/ frontierintransi00orou/frontierintransi00orou.pdf.

Overpeck, J. T., and B. Udall. 2020. "Climate Change and the Aridification of North America." *PNAS* 117 (22): 11856–58. https://doi.org/10.1073/pnas.2006323117.

Ovintiv Inc. N.d. "Sustainability." Ovintiv Inc. https://sustainability.ovintiv.com

Özden-Schilling, C. 2015. "Economy Electric." *Cultural Anthropology* 30 (4): 578–88. https://doi.org/10.14506/ca30.4.06.

Pain, R., and C. Cahill. 2021. "Critical Political Geographies of Slow Violence and Resistance." *Environment and Planning C: Politics and Space* (November 22). https://doi.org/10.1177/23996544211052051.

Paliewicz, N. S. 2018. "The Country, the City, and the Corporation: Rio Tinto Kennecott and the Materiality of Corporate Rhetoric." *Environmental Communication* 12 (6): 744–762. https://doi.org/10.1080/17524032.2017.1416421.

Paliewicz, N. S. 2023. "Thinking Like a Copper Mine: An Ecological Approach to Corporate Ethos and Prosōpon." *Rhetoric Society Quarterly* 53 (2): 231–46. https://doi.org/10.1080/02773945.2022.2129757.

Paradis, J., D. Dobrin, and R. Miller. 1985. "Writing at Exxon ITD: Notes on the Writing Environment of an R and D Organization." In *Writing in Nonacademic Settings*, edited by L. Odell and D. Goswami, 281–307. Guilford Press.

Parliament of the Commonwealth of Australia, Joint Standing Committee on Northern Australia. 2020. "Never Again: Inquiry into the Destruction of 46,000 Year Old Caves at the Juukan Gorge in the Pilbara Region of Western Australia—Interim Report." https://parlinfo.aph.gov.au/parlInfo/download/committees/reportjnt/024579/toc_pdf/NeverAgain.pdf.

Peña, D. G. 1999. "Cultural Landscapes and Biodiversity: The Ethnoecology of an Upper Río Grande Watershed Commons." In *Ethnoecology: Situated Knowledge/Located Lives*, edited by V. D. Nazarea, 107–32. University of Arizona Press.

Pender, K. 2018. *Being at Genetic Risk: Toward a Rhetoric of Care*. Pennsylvania State University Press.

Perkins, T. 2024. "Chemicals from East Palestine Derailment Spread to 16 US States, Data Shows." *Guardian*, June 19. https://www.theguardian.com/us-news/article/2024/jun/19/east-palestine-toxic-derailment-chemicals-spread.

Petrocultures Research Group. 2016. *After Oil*. University of Alberta. https://afteroil.ca/wp-content/uploads/2022/04/After-Oil.pdf.

Pezzullo, P. C. 2017. "Environment." *Oxford Research Encyclopedia of Communication*.

Pfaff, C., R. L. Queen, and D. Clark. 1992. *The Historic Yuma Project: History, Resources Overview, and Assessment*. Bureau of Reclamation: Cultural Resources Program. https://www.usbr.gov/lc/phoenix/AZ100/1900/yuma_project.html.

Pflugfelder, E. H. 2018. "Failure Matters: Conflicting Practices in a High-Tech Case." *Journal of Technical Writing and Communication* 48 (1): 31–52. https://doi.org/10.1177/0047281616662984.

Pflugleder, E. H. 2019. "Risk Selfies and Nonrational Environmental Communication." *Communication Design Quarterly* 7 (1): 73–84. https://doi.org/10.1145/3331558.3331565.

Pflugfelder, E. H. 2022. *Geoengineering, Persuasion, and the Climate Crisis: A Geologic Rhetoric*. University of Alabama Press.

Pflugfelder, E. H., T, R. Amidon, D. J. Sackey, and D. P. Richards. 2023. "Expanding the Scope and Scale of Risk in TPC: Water Access and the Colorado River

Basin." *Technical Communication Quarterly* 32 (3): 224–41. https://doi.org/10.1080/10572252.2023.2210194.

Pinelli, T. E. 1985. "Introduction." *Technical Communication* 32 (4): 6–7.

Piotrowski, M. 2013. "Rhetoric of Oil in Canadian News: Framed for Indigenous Care." *Canadian Journal of Communication* 38 (4): 629–38. https://doi.org/10.22230/cjc.2013v38n4a2649.

Pitt, J., D. F. Luecke, M. J. Cohen, and E. P. Glenn. 2000. "Two Nations, One River: Managing Ecosystem Conservation in the Colorado River Delta." *Natural Resources Journal* 40 (4): 819–64.

Plec, E., and M. Pettenger. 2012. "Greenwashing Consumption: The Didactic Framing of ExxonMobil's Energy Solutions." *Environmental Communication,* 6 (4): 459–76. https://doi.org/10.1080/17524032.2012.720270.

Plough, A., and S. Krimsky. 1987. "The Emergence of Risk Communication Studies: Social and Political Context." *Science, Technology, and Human Values* 12 (3–4): 4–10. http://www.jstor.org/stable/689375.

Porter, J. E., P. Sullivan, S. Blythe, J. T. Grabill, and L. Miles. 2000. "Institutional Critique: A Rhetorical Methodology for Change." *College Composition and Communication* 51 (4): 610–42. https://doi.org/10.2307/358914.

Posch, B. C., S. E. Bush, D. F. Koepke, A. Schuessler, L. L. A. Anderegg, L. M. T. Aparecido, B. W. Blonder, et al. 2024. "Intensive Leaf Cooling Promotes Tree Survival During a Record Heatwave." *PNAS* 121 (43): 1–9.

Potts, L. 2013. *Social Media in Disaster Response: How Experience Architects Can Build for Participation*. Routledge.

Potts, M. 1986. "Exxon to Shed South Africa Holdings." *Washington Post,* December 31. https://www.washingtonpost.com/archive/politics/1986/12/31/exxon-to-shed-south-africa-holdings/473cd1f7-6803-4e59-ba59-6df8895e217a/.

Power, T., D. Wilson, O. Best, T. Brockie, L. Bourque Bearskin, E. Millender, and J. Lowe. 2020. "COVID-19 and Indigenous Peoples: An Imperative for Action." *Journal of Clinical Nursing* 29 (15–16): 2737–41. https://doi.org/10.1111/jocn.15320.

Raign, K. R. 2024. *The Origins of the Art and Practice of Professional Writing: The Written Word as a Tool for Social Justice Then and Now*. State University of New York Press.

Rainey, A. F. 2009. "The Origins of the West Semitic Alphabet in Egyptian Scripts." *Bulletin of the American Schools of Oriental Research* 354: 83–86.

Ravitch, S. M., and M. Riggan. 2016. *Reason and Rigor: How Conceptual Frameworks Guide Research*. 2nd ed. SAGE.

Read, S. 2019. "The Infrastructural Function: A Relational Theory of Infrastructure for Writing Studies." *Journal of Business and Technical Communication* 33 (3): 233–67. https://doi.org/10.1177/1050651919834980.

Reamer, D. 2015. "Risk = Probability × Consequences: Probability, Uncertainty, and the Nuclear Regulatory Commission's Evolving Risk Communication

Rhetoric." *Technical Communication Quarterly* 24 (4): 349–73. https://doi.org/10.1080/10572252.2015.1079334.

Richards, D. P. 2015. "Testing the Waters: Local Users, Sea Level Rise, and the Productive Usability of Interactive Geovisualizations." *Communication Design Quarterly* 3 (3): 25–29.

Richards, D. P. 2017. "Reconstituting Causality: Accident Reports as Posthuman Documentation." In *Topic-Driven Environmental Rhetoric*, edited by D. G. Ross, 149–67. Routledge.

Richards, D. P. 2018. "Not a Cape, but a Life Preserver: The Importance of Designer Localization in Interactive Sea Level Rise Viewers." *Communication Design Quarterly* 6 (2): 57–69.

Richards, D. P. 2019. "An Ethic of Constraint: Citizens, Sea-Level Rise Viewers, and the Limits of Agency." *Journal of Business and Technical Communication* 33 (3): 292–337. https://doi.org/10.1177/1050651919834983.

Richards, D. P. 2023. "Flood Insurance Rate Maps as Communicative Sites of Pragmatic Environmental Action." In *Technical Communication for Environmental Action*, edited by S. Williams, 95–120. State University of New York Press.

Richards, D. P. 2025. "Dead Man's Switch: Blame and Causality in the Epideictic Scenes of Disaster." *Rhetoric Society Quarterly* 55 (1): 26–41.

Richards, D. P., and E. E. Jacobson. 2022. "How Real Is Too Real? User-Testing the Effects of Realism as a Risk Communication Strategy in Sea Level Rise Visualizations." *Technical Communication Quarterly* 31 (2): 190–206. https://doi.org/10.1080/10572252.2021.1986135.

Richards, D. P., and S. H. Stephens. 2022. "Do Voices Really Make a Difference? Investigating the Value of Local Video Narratives in Risk Perceptions and Attitudes Towards Sea-Level Rise." *Technical Communication* 69 (4): 79–96. https://doi.org/10.55177/tc105639.

Richerson, P. J., R. Boyd, and R. L. Bettinger. 2001. "Was Agriculture Impossible During the Pleistocene but Mandatory During the Holocene? A Climate Change Hypothesis." *American Antiquity* 66 (3): 387–411. https://doi.org/10.2307/2694241.

Rickard, T. A. 1908. *A Guide to Technical Writing*. Mining and Scientific Press.

Rickard, T. A. 1910. *A Guide to Technical Writing*. 2nd ed. Mining and Scientific Press.

Rickard, T. A. 1932. *Man and Metals: A History of Mining in Relation to the Development of Civilization*. McGraw-Hill.

Ridolfo, J. 2005. "Rhetoric, Economy and the Technologies of Activist Delivery." Master's thesis, Michigan State University.

Ridolfo, J., and D. N. DeVoss. 2009. "Composing for Recomposition: Rhetorical Velocity and Delivery." *Kairos: A Journal of Rhetoric, Technology, and Pedagogy* 13 (2). https://kairos.technorhetoric.net/13.2/topoi/ridolfo_devoss/intro.html.

Rio Tinto. 2023. "Community Agreements." https://www.riotinto.com/en/sustainability/communities/community-agreements.

Robins, N. A. 2011. *Mercury, Mining, and Empire: The Human and Ecological Cost of Colonial Silver Mining in the Andes*. Indiana University Press. https://doi.org/10.2307/j.ctt1npf8h.

Rogers, E. M., and D. L. Kincaid. 1981. *Communications Networks: Toward a New Paradigm for Research*. Free Press.

Rosenberg, K. V., A. M. Dokter, P. J. Blancher, J. R. Sauer, A. C. Smith, P. A. Smith, J. C. Stanton, et al. 2019. "Decline of the North American Avifauna." *Science* 366: 120–24. https://doi.org/10.1126/science.aaw1313.

Rosner, D., and G. E. Markowitz. 1987. *Dying for Work: Workers' Safety and Health in Twentieth-Century America*. Indiana University Press.

Rosner, D., and G. E. Markowitz. 2013. *Deceit and Denial: The Deadly Politics of Industrial Pollution*. University of California Press.

Ross, D. G., ed. 2017. *Topic-Driven Environmental Rhetoric*. Routledge.

Rowan, K. E. 1991. "Goals, Obstacles, and Strategies in Risk Communication: A Problem-Solving Approach to Improving Communication about Risks." *Journal of Applied Communication Research* 19 (4): 300–329. https://doi.org/10.1080/00909889109365311.

Rubiano, M. P. 2022. "Oil Terminal Canceled in Louisiana's Plaquemines Parish." *Grist*, July 16. https://grist.org/climate-energy/oil-terminal-cancelled-in-louisianas-plaquemines-parish/.

Ruckelshaus, W. D. 1987. "Overviews of the Problem: Communicating About Risk." In *Risk Communication: Proceedings of the National Conference on Risk Communication Held in Washington, D.C., January 29–31, 1986*, edited by J. C. Davies, V. T. Covello, and F. W. Allen, 3–10. Conservation Foundation.

Runwal, P. 2024. "Decision to Vent and Burn Was Unnecessary, National Transportation Safety Board Says." *Chemical and Engineering News*, May 26. https://cen.acs.org/environment/Decision-vent-burn-unnecessary-National/102/i20.

Rupp, S. 2013. "Considering Energy: $E = mc^2 = (\text{Magic}\cdot\text{Culture})^2$." In *Cultures of Energy: Power, Practices, Technologies*, edited by S. Strauss, S. Rupp, and T. Love, 79–95. Routledge.

Russell, D. R. 2002. *Writing in the Academic Disciplines: A Curricular History*. Southern Illinois University Press.

Russell, L. D., and A. S. Babrow. 2011. "Risk in the Making: Narrative, Problematic Integration, and the Social Construction of Risk." *Communication Theory* 21 (3): 239–60. https://doi.org/10.1111/j.1468-2885.2011.01386.x.

Ryan, C. 1993. "Using Environmental Impact Statements as an Introduction to Technical Writing." *Technical Communication Quarterly* 2 (2): 205–13. https://doi.org/10.1080/10572259309364534.

Rylko-Bauer, B., and P. Farmer. 2016. "Structural Violence, Poverty, and Social Suffering." In *The Oxford Handbook of the Social Science of Poverty*, edited by D. Brady and L. M. Burton, 47–74. Oxford University Press.

Sackey, D. J. 2020. "One-Size-Fits-None: A Heuristic for Proactive Value-Sensitive Design." *Technical Communication Quarterly* 29 (1): 33–48. https://doi.org/10.1080/10572252.2019.1634767.

Sackey, D. J., J. Ridolfo, and D. N. DeVoss. 2018. "Making Space in Lansing, Michigan: Communities and/in Circulation." In *Circulation, Writing, and Rhetoric*, edited by L. E. Gries. Utah State University Press.

Sadar, A. J., and M. Shull. 2000. *Environmental Risk Communication: Principles and Practices for Industry*. Routledge.

Saldanha, R. 2020. "What Can We Learn from the Rio Tinto Disaster?" *Morning Star*, September 22. https://www.morningstar.ca/ca/news/205544/what-can-we-learn-from-the-rio-tinto-disaster.aspx.

Sanchez, R., J. A. Breña-Naranjo, A. Rivera, R. T. Hanson, A. Hernández-Espriú, R. J. Hogeboom, A. Milman, et al. 2021. "Binational Reflections on Pathways to Groundwater Security in the Mexico–United States Borderlands." *Water International* 46 (7–8): 1017–36. https://doi.org/10.1080/02508060.2021.1999594.

Sandman, P. M. 1987. "Risk Communication: Facing Public Outrage." *EPA Journal* (U.S. Environmental Protection Agency) (November): 21–22.

Sandman, P. M. 1993. *Responding to Community Outrage: Strategies for Effective Risk Communication*. AIHA Press.

Sass, B. 2005. *The Alphabet at the Turn of the Millennium: The West Semitic Alphabet ca. 1150–850 BCE; The Antiquity of the Arabian, Greek and Phrygian Alphabets*. Tel Aviv University Institute of Archaeology Occasional Publications No. 4. Tel Aviv University.

Sauer, B. 1993. "Sense and Sensibility in Technical Documentation: How Feminist Interpretation Strategies Can Save Lives in the Nation's Mines." *Journal of Business and Technical Communication* 7 (1): 63–83.

Sauer, B. 1994. "Fatal Grammar: The Rhetoric of Disasters." *Technical Communication* 41 (1): 154–60.

Sauer, B. 1996. "Communicating Risk in a Cross-Cultural Context: A Cross-Cultural Comparison of Rhetorical and Social Understandings in U.S. and British Mine Safety Training Programs." *Journal of Business and Technical Communication* 10 (3): 306–29. https://doi.org/10.1177/1050651996010003002.

Sauer, B. 2002. *The Rhetoric of Risk: Technical Documentation in Hazardous Environments*. Routledge.

Scalercio, M. 2018. "Dominating Nature and Colonialism: Francis Bacon's View of Europe and the New World." *History of European Ideas* 44 (8): 1076–91.

Schandorf, M., and A. Karatzogianni. 2018. "#NODAPL: Distributed Rhetorical Praxis at Standing Rock." In *The Routledge Handbook of Digital Writing and Rhetoric*, edited by S. A. Selber, 235–56. Routledge. https://doi.org/10.4324/9781315518497-15.

Schatzki, T. 1996. *Social Practices: A Wittgensteinian Approach to Human Activity and the Social*. Pennsylvania State University Press.

Schatzki, T. 2002. *The Site of the Social: A Philosophical Account of the Constitution of Social Life and Change*. Pennsylvania State University Press.

Schatzki, T. 2010. *The Timespace of Human Activity: On Performance, Society, and History as Indeterminate Teleological Events*. Lexington Books.

Scherer, C. W., and H. Cho. 2003. "A Social Network Contagion Theory of Risk Perception." *Risk Analysis* 23 (2): 261–67. https://doi.org/10.1111/1539-6924.00306.

Schillmeier, M. 2008. "Risk as Mediation—Societal Change, Self-Endangerment and Self-Education." *Beyond Current Horizons Review–Future Lab*, 1–18.

Schmandt-Besserat, D. 1996. *How Writing Came About*. University of Texas Press.

Scott, H. 2008. "Colonialism, Landscape and the Subterranean." *Geography Compass* 2 (6): 1853–69.

Scott, J. B. 2003. *Risky Rhetoric: AIDS and the Cultural Practices of HIV Testing*. Southern Illinois University Press.

Scott, J. B. 2006. "Kairos as Indeterminate Risk Management: The Pharmaceutical Industry's Response to Bioterrorism." *Quarterly Journal of Speech* 92 (2): 115–43.

Scott, J. B., B. Longo, and Katherine V. Wills, eds. 2006. *Critical Power Tools: Technical Communication and Cultural Studies*. State University of New York Press.

Segal, R., and E. Weizman, eds. 2003. *A Civilian Occupation: The Politics of Israeli Architecture*. Babel; Verso.

Senda-Cook, S., D. Endres, S. K. Sowards, and B. McGreavy. 2023. "Engaging Complex Temporalities in Environmental Rhetoric." *Frontiers in Communication* 8: 1–12. https://doi.org/10.3389/fcomm.2023.1176887.

Seven County Infrastructure Coalition. N.d. "Projects." https://scic-utah.org/projects/.

Seven County Infrastructure Coalition et al. v. Eagle County, Colorado, et al., 605 U.S. ____ 2025. https://www.supremecourt.gov/opinions/24pdf/23-975_m648.pdf.

Shannon, C. E., and W. Weaver. 1949. *The Mathematical Theory of Communication*. University of Illinois Press.

Shapin, S., and S. Schaffer. 1985. *Leviathan and the Air-Pump: Hobbes, Boyle, and the Experimental Life*. Princeton University Press.

Shelton, C., and S. Warren-Riley. 2023. "Historicizing Power and Legitimacy After the Social Justice Turn: Resisting Narcissistic Tendencies." *Technical Communication Quarterly* 32 (4): 313–26. https://doi.org/10.1080/10572252.2022.2141898.

Shen, K. 2011. *Brush Talks from Dream Brook*. Translated by W. Hong and Z. Zheng. Paths International; Sichuan People's Publishing House.

Shrestha, N., G. Chilkoor, J. Wilder, V. Gadhamshetty, and J. J. Stone. 2017. "Potential Water Resource Impacts of Hydraulic Fracturing from Unconventional Oil Production in the Bakken Shale." *Water Research* 108: 1–24. https://doi.org/10.1016/j.watres.2016.11.006.

Simmons, W. M. 2007. *Power and Participation: Civic Discourse in Environmental Policy Decisions*. State University of New York Press.

Simonds, W. J. 2015. "The Boulder Canyon Project: Hoover Dam. Reclamation History." August 4. US Bureau of Reclamation. https://www.usbr.gov/history/hoover.html.

Slack, M., M. Fillios, and R. Fullagar. 2009, "Aboriginal Settlement During the LGM at Brockman, Pilbara Region, Western Australia." *Archaeology in Oceania* 44: 32–39. https://doi.org/10.1002/j.1834-4453.2009.tb00066.x.

Slovic, P. 2010. *Risk as Feeling: New Perspectives on Risk Perception*. Earthscan. SM Energy. https://www.sm-energy.com

Smith, C. S., T. P. Reust, and R. D. Richard. 2003. "Site 48UT375: Late Paleoindian Period Subsistence and Land Use Patterns in the Green River Basin, Wyoming." *Plains Anthropologist* 48 (186): 133–49. https://doi.org/10.1080/2052546.2003.11949302.

Smith, D. 1996. "The Miners: 'They Builded Better Than They Knew.'" In *The Western San Juan Mountains: Their Geology, Ecology, and Human History*, edited by R. Blair. University Press of Colorado.

Smith, D. 2009. *The Trail of Gold and Silver: Mining in Colorado, 1859–2009*. University Press of Colorado.

Smith, F. R. 1985. "Editorial: The Importance of Research in Technical Communication." *Technical Communication* 32 (4): 4–5.

Smith, J. E. 1969. "Time, Times, and the 'Right Time': 'Chronos' and 'Kairos.'" *The Monist* 53 (1): 1–13.

Smith, J. E. 1986. "Time and Qualitative Time." *Review of Metaphysics* 40 (1): 3–16.

Smith, J. M., and T. van Ierland. 2018. "Framing Controversy on Social Media: #NoDAPL and the Debate About the Dakota Access Pipeline on Twitter." *IEEE Transactions on Professional Communication* 61 (3): 226–41. https://doi.org/10.1109/TPC.2018.2833753.

Souther, J. W. 1957. *Technical Report Writing*. Wiley.

Southern Ute Indian Tribe. N.d. "History." https://www.southernute-nsn.gov/history/.

Spangler, J. D. 2000. "Radiocarbon Dates, Acquired Wisdom, and the Search for Temporal Order in the Uinta Basin." In *Intermountain Archeology*, edited by D. B. Madsen and M. D. Metcalf, 48–68. University of Utah Press.

Sperry, R. L. 1975. "When the Imperial Valley Fought for Its Life." *Journal of San Diego History* 21 (1). https://sandiegohistory.org/journal/1975/january/index-htm-42/.

Spoel, P., and C. Barriault. 2011. "Risk Knowledge and Risk Communication: The Rhetorical Challenge of Public Dialogue." In *Writing (in) the Knowledge Society*, edited by D. Starke-Meyerring, A. Paré, N. Artemeva, M. Horne, and L. Yousoubova, 87–112. Parlor Press.

Spoel, P., and R. C. Den Hoed. 2014. "Places and People: Rhetorical Constructions of 'Community' in a Canadian Environmental Risk Assessment." *Environmental Communication* 8 (3): 267–85. https://doi.org/10.1080/17524032.2013.850108.

Sprat, T. 1667. *The History of the Royal-Society of London for the Improving of Natural Knowledge by Tho. Sprat.* In the digital collection Early English Books Online, University of Michigan Library Digital Collections. https://name.umdl.umich.edu/A61158.0001.001.

Stake, R. E. 2005. *Multiple Case Study Analysis.* Guilford Press.

Steinberg, T. 2000. *Acts of God: The Unnatural History of Natural Disaster in America.* Oxford University Press.

Stene, E. A. 1995. "All-American Canal: Boulder Canyon Project." Bureau of Reclamation. https://www.usbr.gov/projects/pdf.php?id=80.

Stene, E. A. 1996. "The Historical Statistics of the Colorado Mining Industry." *Mining History Journal* 3: 121–28.

Stinson, S., and M. Le Rouge, eds. 2022. *Embodied Environmental Risk in Technical Communication: Problems and Solutions Toward Social Sustainability.* Routledge.

Stop Uinta Basin Railway. N.d. "Stop Uinta Basin Railway." https://www.stopuintabasinrailway.com.

Stratman, J. F., C. Boykin, M. C. Holmes, M. J. Laufer, and M. Breen. 1995. "Risk Communication, Metacommunication, and Rhetorical Stases in the Aspen-EPA Superfund Controversy." *Journal of Business and Technical Communication* 9 (1): 5–41. https://doi.org/10.1177/1050651995009001010.

Stormer, N., and B. McGreavy. 2017. "Thinking Ecologically About Rhetoric's Ontology: Capacity, Vulnerability, and Resilience." *Philosophy and Rhetoric* 50 (1): 1–25. https://doi.org/10.5325/philrhet.50.1.0001.

Strunk, W., Jr. 1918. *The Elements of Style.* Harcourt, Brace and Company.

Sullivan, D. L. 1990. "Political-Ethical Implications of Defining Technical Communication as a Practice." *Journal of Advanced Composition* 10 (2): 375–86. jstor.org/stable/20865737.

Summers, S. 2020. "Northern Ute Bands Displaced to Utah." *Leadville Herald*, November 11. https://www.leadvilleherald.com/free_content/article_9b6ac79c-2434-11eb-9713-6fa27da196db.html.

Summitt, A. R. 2013. *Contested Waters: An Environmental History of the Colorado River.* Utah State University Press.

Swyngedouw, E. 1997a. "Neither Global nor Local: "Glocalisation" and the Politics of Scale." In *Spaces of Globalization: Reasserting the Power of the Local*, edited by K. Cox. Guilford/Longman.

Swyngedouw, E. 1997b. "Excluding the Other: The Contested Production of a New 'Gestalt of Scale' and the Politics of Marginalisation." In *Society, Place, Economy: States of the Art in Economic Geography*, edited by R. Lee and J. Wills. Edward Arnold.

Swyngedouw, E. 2000. "Authoritarian Governance, Power and the Politics of Rescaling." *Environment and Planning D: Society and Space* 18 (1): 63–76.

Swyngedouw, E. 2004. "Globalisation or 'Glocalisation'? Networks, Territories and Rescaling." *Cambridge Review of International Affairs* 17 (1): 25–48. https://doi.org/10.1080/0955757042000203632.

Szeman, I., and D. Boyer, eds. 2017. *Energy Humanities: An Anthology*. Johns Hopkins University Press.

Szymanski, E. A. 2023. "Conversations with Other-Than-Human Creatures: Unpacking the Ambiguity of 'with' for Multispecies Rhetorics." *Rhetoric Society Quarterly* 53 (2): 138–52. https://doi.org/10.1080/02773945.2022.2095423.

Taussig, F. W. 1893. "The Crisis in the United States and the Repeal of Silver Purchase." *Economic Journal* 3 (12): 733–45. https://doi.org/10.2307/2956215.

Taylor, F. W. 1911. *The Principles of Scientific Management.* Harper and Brothers.

Tebeaux, E. 1980. "Let's Not Ruin Technical Writing, Too: A Comment on the Essays of Carolyn Miller and Elizabeth Harris." *College English* 41 (7): 822–25. https://doi.org/10.2307/376223.

Tebeaux, E. 2008. "Technical Writing in English Renaissance Shipwrightery: Breaching the Shoals of Orality." *Journal of Technical Writing and Communication* 38 (1): 3–25. https://doi.org/10.2190/TW.38.1.b.

Thomlison, A. 2019. "From Pipeline to Plate: The Domestication of Oil Sands Through Visual Food Analogies." In *The Rhetoric of Oil in the Twenty-First Century*, edited by H. Graves and D. E. Beard, 189–210. Routledge. https://journals.sagepub.com/doi/full/10.1177/13678779231159697.

Thompson. J. 2015. "When Our River Turned Orange: Nine Things You Need to Know About the Animas River Mine Waste Spill." *High Country News*, August 10. https://www.hcn.org/articles/when-our-river-turned-orange-animas-river-spill/.

Thompson, J. 2016a. "Silverton's Gold King Reckoning: How the Animas River Disaster Forced Silverton to Face Its Pollution Problem—and Its Destiny." *High Country News*, May 2. https://www.hcn.org/issues/48-7/silvertons-gold-king-reckoning/.

Thompson, J. 2016b. "A Gold King Mine Timeline: A Tangled History of Profit, Tragedy, and Unfulfilled Dreams." *High Country News*, May 2. https://www.hcn.org/issues/48-7/a-gold-king-mine-timeline/.

Thompson, J. 2018. *River of Lost Souls: The Science, Politics, and Green Behind the Gold King Mine Disaster.* Torrey House Press.

Tianduowa, Z., K. C. Woodson, and M. W. Ertsen. 2018. "Reconstructing Ancient Hohokam Irrigation Systems in the Middle Gila River Valley, Arizona, United States of America." *Human Ecology* 46 (5): 735–46. https://doi.org/10.1007/s10745-018-0023-x.

Tiki, W., G. Oba, and T. Tvedt. 2013." An Indigenous Time-Related Framework for Reconstructing the Impact of Disasters on Ancient Water Systems in Southern Ethiopia, 1560–1950." *Journal of Historical Geography* 41: 33–43.

Tillery, Denise 2005. "The Plain Style in the Seventeenth Century: Gender and the History of Scientific Discourse." *Journal of Technical Writing and Communication* 35 (3): 273–89. https://doi.org/10.2190/MRQQ-K2U6-LTQU-0X56.

Toxic-Free Future. 2024. "Toxic Cargo: How Rail Transport of Vinyl Chloride Puts Millions at Risk, an Analysis One Year After the Ohio Train Derailment." January 22. https://toxicfreefuture.org/research/toxic-cargo/key-findings/.

Transportation Safety Board of Canada. 2014. *Railway Investigation Report R13D0054*. https://www.tsb.gc.ca/sites/default/files/ rapports-reports/rail/R13D0054/eng/r13d0054.pdf.

Trasande, L., R. T. Zoeller, U. Hass, A. Kortenkamp, P. Grandjean, J. P. Myers, J. DiGangi, et al. 2016. "Burden of Disease and Costs of Exposure to Endocrine Disrupting Chemicals in the European Union: An Updated Analysis." *Andrology* 4 (4): 565–72. https://doi.org/10.1111/andr.12178.

Tucker, W. T., and S. Ferson. 2008. "Strategies for Risk Communication: Evolution, Evidence, Experience." *Annals of the New York Academy of Sciences* 1128: ix–xii. https://doi.org/10.1196/annals.1399.000.

Udall, B., and J. Overpeck. 2017. "The Twenty-First Century Colorado River Hot Drought and Implications for the Future." *Water Resources Research* 53 (3): 2404–18. https://doi.org/10.1002/2016WR019638.

United Nations General Assembly. 2015. *Transforming Our World: The 2030 Agenda for Sustainable Development, A/RES/70/1*. October 21. https://sdgs.un.org/2030agenda

United States Bureau of Reclamation. 2007. "Colorado River Interim Guidelines for Lower Basin Shortages and Coordinated Operations for Lake Powell and Lake Mead." https://www.federalregister.gov/documents/2007/11/02/E7-21417/colorado-river-interim-guidelines-for-lower-basin-shortages-and-coordinated-operations-for-lake.

United States Bureau of Reclamation. 2008. "The Law of the River." US Department of the Interior, Bureau of Reclamation, Lower Colorado Region. March. https://www.usbr.gov/lc/region/g1000/lawofrvr.html.

United States Bureau of Reclamation. 2022. "Lake Mead Annual High and Low Elevations (1935–2022)." https://www.usbr.gov/lc/region/g4000/lakemead_line.pdf.

United States Bureau of Reclamation. 2024. "Colorado River Basin." December 6. https://www.usbr.gov/ColoradoRiverBasin/.

United States Bureau of Reclamation. 2025. "Colorado River Post 2026 Operations." https://www.usbr.gov/ColoradoRiverBasin/post2026/index.html.

United States Congress. 1830. The Indian Removal Act of 1830, ch. 148, §§ 7, 8, 4 Stat. 412.

United States Congress. 1862. Morrill Land-Grant Act of 1862, 7 U.S.C. § 301 et. seq. (1862).

United States Congress. 1864. Treaty with the Utah-Tabeguache Band, 1863 [Conejos Treaty]. 13 Stat. 673. https://treaties.okstate.edu/treaties/treaty-with-the-utah-tabeguache-band-1863-0856#.

United States Congress. 1871. Indian Appropriations Act of 1871, Pub. L. No. 41–120, 16 Stat. 544 (1871).

United States Congress. 1872. General Mining Act of 1872. (Amended by P.L.1033–66, 1992.)

United States Congress. 1890. Sherman Silver Purchase Act of 1890. 31 U.S.C. § 408, 410, 412, 453.

United States Congress. 1902. Reclamation Act of 1902. Ch. 1093, 32 Stat. 388. 43 U.S.C. Chapter One2. (1902).

United States Congress. 1928. Boulder Canyon Project Act, 43 U.S.C. § 617. (1928).

United States Congress. 1958. National Defense Education Act of 1958, Pub. L. No. 85–864, 72 Stat. 1580.

United States Congress. 1970a. National Environmental Policy Act of 1969 (P.L. 91–190). U.S. Government Publishing Office. https://www.govinfo.gov/app/details/COMPS-10352.

United States Congress. 1970b. Occupational Safety and Health Act of 1970. U.S. Government Publishing Office. https://www.govinfo.gov/app/details/COMPS-1523.

United States Congress. 1972. Clean Water Act (P.L. 92–500). U.S. Government Publishing Office.

United States Congress. 1977. Federal Mine Safety and Health Act of 1977 (P.L. 95–164). U.S. Government Publishing Office.

United States Congress. 1980. Comprehensive Environmental Response, Compensation, and Liability Act of 1980 (P.L. 96–510). U.S. Government Publishing Office.

United States Congress. 2019. H.R. 2030 Colorado River Drought Contingency Plan Authorization Act (Public Law 116–14).

United States Congress. 2023. Fiscal Responsibility Act of 2023 (P.L. 118–5). U.S. Government Publishing Office.

United States Department of Agriculture. N.d. "Focus on Croplands in the Southwest. Climate Hubs." https://www.climatehubs.usda.gov/ hubs/southwest/topic/focus-croplands-southwest.

United States Department of the Interior. 2019. "Colorado River Delta Ecosystem Changes in Response to the Minute 319 Pulse Flow." https://eros.usgs.gov/doi-remote-sensing-activities/2019/usgs/colorado-river-delta-ecosystem-changes-response-minute-319-pulse-flow.

United States Department of the Interior, Bureau of Land Management. 2021. *Uinta Basin Natural Gas Development Project: Final Environmental Impact Statement* (Volume I: Summary and Chapters 1–9). August 6. https://icfbiometrics.blob.core.windows.net/ uinta-basin/Volume_I_Summary_and_Chapters_1_9_FEIS.pdf.

United States Department of the Interior, Bureau of Reclamation, Ten Tribes Partnership. 2018. "Colorado River Basin Ten Tribes Partnership Tribal Water Study Report." https://www.usbr.gov/lc/region/programs/crbstudy/tws/finalreport.html.

United States Environmental Protection Agency. N.d. "Red and Bonita Mine Site." https://response.epa.gov/site/site_profile.aspx.

United States Environmental Protection Agency. 2016. "One Year After the Gold King Mine Incident: A Retrospective of EPA's Efforts to Restore and Protect Impacted Communities." August 1. https://www.epa.gov/sites/default/files/2016-08/documents/mstanislausgkm1yrreportwhole8-1-16.pdf.

United States Environmental Protection Agency. 2017. "Frequent Questions Related to the Gold King Mine Response." March 16. https://www.epa.gov/goldkingmine/frequent-questions-related-gold-king-mine-response.

United States Environmental Protection Agency. 2023a. "Superfund Site: Bonita Peak Mining District Unincorporated, CO." September 30. https://cumulis.epa.gov/supercpad/SiteProfiles/index.cfm.

United States Environmental Protection Agency. 2023b. "Norfolk Southern East Palestine Train Derailment General Notice Letter." Uhttps://www.epa.gov/system/files/documents/2023-02/Norfolk%20Southern%20East%20Palestine%20Train%20Derailment%20General%20Notice%20Letter%202.10.2023%20%281%29.pdf.

United States Environmental Protection Agency. 2024. "Deepwater Horizon—BP Gulf of Mexico Oil Spill." July 24. https://www.epa.gov/enforcement/deepwater-horizon-bp-gulf-mexico-oil-spill.

United States Forest Service. N.d. "Ashley National Forest: History and Culture." U.S. Department of Agriculture. https://www.fs.usda.gov/detail/ashley/learning/history-culture/?cid=fsm9_002407.

United States Forest Service. N.d. "Uinta-Wasatch-Cache National Forest: History and Culture." U.S. Department of Agriculture. https://www.fs.usda.gov/detail/uwcnf/learning/history-culture?cid=FSEM_035530.

United States Geological Survey. N.d. *Geological Survey Bulletin 1291: The Geologic Story of the Uinta Mountains*. National Park Service.

United States Geological Survey. 2007. "Environmental Effects of Historical Mining in the Animas River Watershed, Southwestern Colorado (Fact Sheet No. 2007–3051)." United States Department of the Interior. https://www.arlis.org/docs/vol1/176637104.pdf.

United States Geological Survey. 2016. "A River Ran Through It: Scientists Study Effects of Water Released Across U.S.-Mexico Border." October 24. https://www.usgs.gov/news/featured-story/river-ran-through-it-and-brought-life-least-while.

United States Geological Survey. 2019. "The Four Great Surveys of the West." September 30. United States Department of the Interior. https://pubs.usgs.gov/circ/c1050/surveys.htm.

United States Geological Survey. 2022. "Water-Year Summary for Site USGS 09380000." https://waterdata.usgs.gov/nwis/wys_rpt/.

United State Government Publishing Office. N.d. "Title 40: Protection of Environment. Code of Federal Regulations." https://www.ecfr.gov/current/title-40/chapter-V/subchapter-A/part-1502.

United States Government Print Office. 1946. "Utilization of Waters of the Colorado and Tijuana Rivers and of the Rio Grande: Treaty Between the United States of America and Mexico" [US-Mexico Water Treaty of 1944]. https://www.usbr.gov/lc/region/pao/pdfiles/mextrety.pdf.

United States National Park Service. 2008. "The Utes in Southwestern Colorado: A Confrontation of Cultures" [image of Ute expatriation between 1800 and

2000]. *Frontier in Transition: A History of Southwestern Colorado.* BLM Cultural Resources Series (Colorado: No. 10). https://www.nps.gov/parkhistory/online_books/blm/co/10/chap5.htm.

United States National Park Service. 2023a. "Endangered Fish. Glen Canyon National Recreation Area AZ, UT." March 14. https://www.nps.gov/glca/learn/nature/endangeredfish.htm.

United States National Park Service. 2023b. "Sentry Milk-Vetch: Endangered Plant. Grand Canyon National Park, Arizona." September 16. https://www.nps.gov/grca/learn/nature/astragalus.htm.

United States Senate. 2015. *Oversight of the Cause, Response, and Impacts of EPA's Gold King Mine Spill.* September 16. Committee on the Environment and Public Works. Washington, D.C.

United States v. Ward. 1980. 448 U.S. 242. https://supreme.justia.com/cases/federal/us/448/242/.

Utah Department of Transportation. 2021. "Uinta Basin Railway: Summary Report." Utah Department of Transportation. https://uintabasinrailwayeis.com/documents/

UDOT_TM_Uinta_Basin_Summary_Report.pdf.

Utah Division of Indian Affairs. N.d. "Ute Indian Tribe of the Uintah and Ouray Reservation." https://indian.utah.gov/ute-indian-tribe-of-the-uintah-ouray-reservation/.

Utah Energy Research Triangle Project. 2015, March 31. "Characterization of Waxy Crude Deposition in Pipelines." https://www.usu.edu/binghamresearch/files/reports/Utah-Energy-Research-Triangle-Project-Final-Report-March-2015.pdf.

Utah Indians. N.d. "Early Peoples: The Utes." Utah American Indian Digital Archive. https://utahindians.org/archives/ute/earlyPeoples.html

Valencia, J. 2024. "Meet the Cucuapa, First People of Calexico, Mexicali." *Calexico Chronicle*, December 5. https://calexicochronicle.com/2024/12/05/guest-column-meet-the-cucapa-1st-peoples-of-calexico-mexicali/.

Van Horne, Y. O., K. Chief, P. H. Charley, M. G. Begay, N. Lothrop, M. L. Bell, R. A. Canales, N. I. Teufel-Shone, and P. I. Beamer. 2021. "Impacts to Diné Activities with the San Juan River After the Gold King Mine Spill." *Journal of Exposure Science and Environmental Epidemiology* 31 (5): 852–66. https://doi.org/10.1038/s41370-021-00290-z.

Van Winkle, K. 2021. "Above All Made by Themselves: The Visual Rhetoric of W. E. B. Du Bois's Data Visualizations." *Technical Communication Quarterly* 31 (1): 17–32. https://doi.org/10.1080/10572252.2021.1906450.

Van Wynsberghe, R., and S. Khan. 2007. "Redefining Case Study." *International Journal of Qualitative Methods* 6 (2): 80–94.

Vendel, K. A., and M. A. Vendel, with the San Juan County Historical Society. 2015. *Mines Around Silverton.* Images of America Series. Arcadia Publishing.

Vitanza, V. 1987. "Notes Toward Historiographies of Rhetoric, or the Rhetorics of the Historics of Rhetorics: Tradition, Revisionary, and Sub/versive." *Pre/text* 8 (1–2): 63–125.

Vitanza, V. 1996a. "Historiographies of Rhetoric." In *Encyclopedia of Rhetoric and Composition: Communication from Ancient Times to the Information Age*, edited by T. Enos, 324–25. Routledge.

Vitanza, V. 1996b. *Negation, Subjectivity, and the History of Rhetoric.* State University of New York Press.

von Guerard, P., S. E. Church, D. B. Yager, and J. M. Besser. N.d. "The Animas River Watershed, San Juan County, Colorado." In *Integrated Investigations of Environmental Effects of Historical Mining in the Animas River Watershed, San Juan County, Colorado*, chapter B, edited by S. E. Church, P. von Guerard, and S. E. Finger, #1651, 17–38. US Department of the Interior / US Geological Survey. https://pubs.usgs.gov/pp/1651/downloads/Vol1_combinedChapters/vol1_chapB.pdf.

Waddell, C. 1995. "Defining Sustainable Development: A Case Study in Environmental Communication." *Technical Communication Quarterly* 4 (2): 201–16. https://doi.org/10.1080/10572259509364597.

Wagnon, M., and S. Baniya. 2024. "Protesting Locally, Impacting Globally: Rhetorical Narratives of Mountain Valley Pipeline Activists." *Technical Communication Quarterly* (December 23): 1–17. https://doi.org/10.1080/10572252.2024.2441122.

Walaski, P. F. 2011. *Risk and Crisis Communications: Methods and Messages.* Wiley.

Walton, R., K. R. Moore, and N. N. Jones. 2019. *Technical Communication After the Social Justice Turn.* Routledge.

Walwema, J. 2023. "Participatory Policy: Enacting Technical Communication for a Shared Water Future." In *Technical Communication for Environmental Action*, edited by S. D. Williams, 245–66. State University of New York Press.

Walwema, J., J. S. Colton, and S. Holmes. 2022. "Introduction to Special Issue on 21st-Century Ethics in Technical Communication: Ethics and the Social Justice Movement in Technical and Professional Communication." *Journal of Business and Technical Communication* 36 (3): 257–69. https://doi.org/10.1177/10506519221087694.

Ward, E. 2001. "Salt of the River, Salt of the Earth: Politics, Science and Ecological Diplomacy in the Mexicali Valley (1961–1965)." *Frontera norte* 13 (26): 105–39.

Webb, C. 1981. "A Federal Judge Monday Sentenced Robert E. 'Buck' Ward." United Press International, June 22. https://www.upi.com/Archives/1981/06/22/A-federal-judge-Monday-sentenced-Robert-E-Buck-Ward/9763362030400/

Webb, D. 2023. "Colorado's Tennessee Pass Rail Line." *Colorado Newsline*, May 4. https://coloradonewsline.com/2023/05/04/colorado-tennessee-pass-rail-line/.

Weber, B. A., J. Geigle, and C. Barkdull. 2014. "Rural North Dakota's Oil Boom and Its Impact on Social Services." *Social Work* 59 (1): 62–72. https://doi.org/10.1093/sw/swt068.

Weizman, E. 2007. *Hollow Land: Israel's Architecture of Occupation.* Verso.

Welch, R., and M. Scott. 2019. "North Dakota Access Pipeline and the Value of Rhetorical Ethics." *Works and Days* 37 (1–2): 235–56.

Welhausen, C. A. 2017. "At Your Own Risk: User-Contributed Flu Maps, Participatory Surveillance, and an Emergent DIY Risk Assessment Ethic." *Communication Design Quarterly* 5 (2): 51–61. https://doi.org/10.1145/3131201.3131206.

Werry, C. 2001. "The Rhetorical Self-Fashioning of Technical Communication, 1984–1994." *Lore: A Journal of Writing and Communication* 1 (1). rhetoric.sdsm.edu/lore/1_2_contents.html.

White, L. A. 1943. "Energy and the Evolution of Culture." *American Anthropologist* 45 (3): 335–56. https://doi.org/10.1525/aa.1943.45.3.02a00010.

White, L.A. 1949. *The Science of Culture: A Study of Man and Civilization*. Farrar, Straus.

White, L. A. 1959. *The Evolution of Culture: The Development of Civilization to the Fall of Rome*. McGraw-Hill.

Whyte, K. 2021. "Time as Kinship." In *The Cambridge Companion to Environmental Humanities*, edited by J. Cohen and S. Foote, 39–55. Cambridge University Press.

Wickliff, G. A. 1997. "Geology, Photography, and Environmental Rhetoric in the American West of 1860–1890." *Technical Communication Quarterly* 6 (1): 41–75. https://doi.org/10.1109/TPC.2007.908732.

Wiens, J. A. 1973. "Pattern and Process in Grassland Bird Communities." *Ecological Monographs* 43: 237–70.

Wijkman, A., and L. Timberlake. 1984. *Natural Disasters: Acts of God, or Acts of Man?* International Institute for Environment and Development.

Wilcox, D. J. 1987. *The Measure of Times Past: Pre-Newtonian Chronologies and the Rhetoric of Relative Time*. University of Chicago Press.

Williams, A. P., B. I. Cook, and J. E. Smerdon. 2022. "Rapid Intensification of the Emerging Southwestern North American Megadrought in 2020–2021." *Nature Climate Change* 12: 232–34. https://doi.org/10.1038/s41558-022-01290-z.

Williams, M. F. 2006. "Tracing W.E.B. Dubois' 'Color Line' in Government Regulations." *Journal of Technical Writing and Communication* 36 (2): 141–65.

Williams, M. F. 2010. *From Black Codes to Recodification: Removing the Veil from Regulatory Writing*. Routledge.

Williams, M. F., and O. Pimental. 2014. *Communicating Race, Ethnicity, and Identity in Technical Communication*. Baywood Publishing.

Williams, S., ed. 2023. *Technical Communication for Environmental Action*. Routledge.

Wilshusen, R. H., M. J. Churchill, and J. M. Potter. 1997. "Prehistoric Reservoirs and Water Basins in the Mesa Verde Region: Intensification of Water Collection Strategies During the Great Pueblo Period." *American Antiquity* 62 (4): 664–81.

Wilson, J., and N. Lash. 2023. "The Historic Claims That Put a Few California Farming Families First in Line for Colorado River Water." *ProPublica*, November 9. https://www.propublica.org/article/california-farm-families-gained-control-colorado-river.

Wilson, S., I. Szeman, and A. Carlson. 2017. "On Petrocultures: Or, Why We Need to Understand Oil to Understand Everything Else." In *Petrocultures: Oil, Politics, Culture*, edited by S. Wilson, A. Carlson, and I. Szeman, 3–20. McGill-Queen's University Press.

Winsor, D. A. 1998. "Communication Failures Contributing to the *Challenger* Accident: An Example for Technical Communicators." *IEEE Transactions on Professional Communication* 31 (3): 101–7.

Winsor, D. A. 2001. "Learning to Do Knowledge Work in Systems of Distributed Cognition." *Journal of Business and Technical Communication* 15 (1): 5–28.

Winters v. United States, 207 U.S. 564 1908.

Witte, K., G. Meyer, and D. Martell. 2001. *Effective Health Risk Messages*. Sage.

Wolfe, N. L., L. A. Burns, and W. C. Steen. 1980. "Use of Linear Free Energy Relationships and an Evaluative Model to Assess the Fate and Transport of Phthalate Esters in the Aquatic Environment." *Chemosphere* 9 (7–8): 393–402. https://doi.org/10.1016/0045-6535(80)90022-3.

Wyoming v. Colorado, 259 U.S. 419 1922.

Yin, R. K. 2018. *Case Study Research and Applications: Design and Methods*. 6th ed. Sage.

Young, E., and T. Ingram. 2021. "A Year on from the Destruction at Juukan, Could It Happen Again?" *Sydney Morning Herald*, May 21. https://www.smh.com.au/national/a-year-on-from-the-destruction-at-juukan-could-it-happen-again-20210518-p57syw.htm.

Yusoff, K. 2012. "Aesthetics of Loss: Biodiversity, Banal Violence and Biotic Subjects." *Transactions of the Institute of British Geographers* 37 (4): 578–92. http://www.jstor.org/stable/41678656.

Zhang, Y. 2013. "Examining Scientific and Technical Writing Strategies in the 11th Century Chinese Science Book *Brush Talks from Dream Brook*." *Journal of Technical Writing and Communication* 43 (4): 365–80. https://doi.org/10.2190/TW.43.4.b.

Zoetewey, M. W., and J. Staggers. 2004. "Teaching the Air Midwest Case: A Stakeholder Approach to Deliberative Technical Rhetoric." *IEEE Transactions on Professional Communication* 47 (4): 233–43. https://ieeexplore.ieee.org/document/1364072.

Zografos, C. 2022. "The Contradictions of Green New Deals: Green Sacrifice and Colonialism." *Soundings: A Journal of Politics and Culture* 80: 37–50. https://www.muse.jhu.edu/article/856495.

Zwagerman, S. 2019. "How Not to Stop a Pipeline: A Critique of Activism in the Burnaby Mountain Protests." In *The Rhetoric of Oil in the Twenty-First Century*, edited by H. Graves and D. E. Beard, 271–94. Routledge.

Index